Proactive Child Protection and Social Work

LIZ DAVIES AND NORA DUCKETT

Series editors: Jonathan Parker and Greta Bradley

LearningMatters

In memory of Aliyah and Eloise

First published in 2008 by Learning Matters Ltd
Reprinted in 2009

British Library Cataloguing in Publication Data
A CIP record for this book is available from the British Library.

ISBN 978 1 84445 131 9

Cover and text design by Code 5 Design Associates
Project management by Deer Park Productions, Tavistock
Typeset by Pantek Arts Ltd, Maidstone, Kent
Printed and bound in Great Britain by Bell & Bain, Glasgow

Learning Matters Ltd
33 Southernhay East
Exeter EX1 1NX
Tel: 01392 215560
info@learningmatters.co.uk
www.learningmatters.co.uk

Proactive Child Protection and Social Work

Contents

Acknowledgements

We thank Stephen Fox, Academic Leader, who has shown continual support and interest and the social work writing group at London Metropolitan University for their encouragement and comments on draft chapters. Particular appreciation goes to Michael MacKay and Brian Douieb, both children's services managers, who scrutinised diagrams of child protection processes to make sure these were consistent with current practice. We acknowledge the contribution of both Dr Sarah Nelson whose research enabled us to learn from the views of child victims of sexual abuse and Dr Ximena Poblete whose clinical work with children emotionally abused informed our analysis. We also acknowledge the contribution of the many survivors including the Jersey Care Leavers from whom we continue to learn so much. We remember the children and families in the London Boroughs of Islington and Westminster and where we worked together in the London Borough of Harrow, whose lives we recalled over and over again in writing this book. Primarily the book has been written for social work students, however, much of the content reflects what students at London Metropolitan University have also taught us.

Introduction: Legal safeguards and protective processes

Protecting children from significant harm, being proactive in keeping them safe from abuse and the crimes perpetrated against them, is a key role for all social workers. Hearing and responding to children's voices is an essential component of the professional response to abused children. Child abuse is abuse of power and to deny children's voices and fail to protect them constitutes discrimination against children and is an example of how adults misuse their power. *Childism* is the oppression of children. Anti-oppressive practice is integrated throughout this book as it is central to social work. An awareness of and ability to proactively confront and challenge childism, as with racism and other forms of oppression, must be demonstrated throughout all social work practice in protecting children. The United Nations Convention on the Rights of the Child is the framework for children's rights in the UK although in some respects the UK is non-compliant with this legislation (United Nations, 1989).

The Children Act (CA 1989) (s1) states unequivocally that the welfare of the child must be the paramount consideration. This is sometimes referred to as the paramountcy principle. The welfare of the child refers to children in need, including those in need of protection. It is difficult at the current time to achieve the complex task of child protection because the Every Child Matters (ECM) political agenda is to provide all children with universal services as children in need rather than to identify those at risk of significant harm and provide them with a specialist response. ECM sets out five outcomes for children, one of which is *staying safe* (DfES, 2003). This is quite different from a children's rights perspective that governments *should make sure that children and young people are protected from abuse, neglect and being harmed by the people looking after them* (United Nations, 1989, Article 19). Outcomes do not give children legal rights to protection but rather place expectations upon them to be good citizens (CRAE, 2006). Since 2003, children have received more government attention as potential criminals than as victims of abuse requiring protection. The police role outlined in ECM is within the Youth Offending Team rather than the Child Abuse Investigation Team (CAIT) and probation, the key agency in assisting risk assessment of perpetrators, was omitted altogether from the hub of agencies included in the child's protective network. The ECM agenda focuses on socially disadvantaged children in need and their families as part of a policy of social inclusion. Child abuse does not simply correlate with social and economic deprivation but takes place within every strata of society and there is a risk that policies which focus on safeguarding the socially disadvantaged will miss protecting children in more affluent families. Poor children are of course easily visible to the authorities, the systems assessing their wellbeing and research, all of which will primarily locate child abuse in that sector.

This shift away from policies focused on protecting children has resulted in a change of professional language (Munro and Calder, 2005). Policy refers to assessment, need, concern and safeguarding instead of investigation, risk, abuse and protection. Parton comments that the concept of *safeguarding* is that of minimisation of harm and promotion of wellbeing rather than protection from significant harm (2005, p7). The *Working Together* definition of safeguarding includes child protection as only a part of the concept:

> *Protecting children from maltreatment*
> *Preventing impairment of children's health or development*
> *Ensuring that children are growing up in circumstances consistent with the provision of safe and effective care and undertaking that role so as to enable those children to have optimum life chances and to enter adulthood successfully.*
> *Child protection is a part of safeguarding and promoting welfare. This refers to the activity that is undertaken to protect specific children who are suffering or are at risk of suffering significant harm.*
>
> (DfES, 2006,1.18)

In this book, safeguarding is defined in the dictionary sense *of protection, security, safe-keeping, security from danger, being protected against hurt or injury (Oxford Dictionary* cited in Parton, 2005). A central theme of this book is the implementation of section 47 (CA 1989) investigation and an exploration of child protection from the perspectives of both the safety of the child and the targeting of the perpetrators. Section 47 (CA 1989) states that it is the:

> *local authority duty to investigate when they have reasonable cause to suspect that a child in their area is suffering or is likely to suffer significant harm. Harm is defined as ill treatment or the impairment of health or development, including for example impairment suffered from seeing or hearing the ill-treatment of another. Development means physical, intellectual, emotional, social or behavioural development and health means physical or mental health. Ill treatment includes sexual abuse and forms of ill-treatment which are non-physical.*
>
> (DfES, 2006, 1.25)

It is a matter for professional judgement as to whether these criteria apply in a particular case, making comparison with what could reasonably be expected of a similar child. This book provides opportunities for the reader to practise making judgements about what constitutes significant harm. Practitioners reach agreement about the threshold for protective intervention through debate and analysis at multi-agency statutory child protection forums such as child protection conferences and strategy meetings.

A vast knowledge base exists about the protection of children derived from the hundreds of conclusions and recommendations of serious case reviews following the death or serious injury of children. It has been commonly reported in these reviews that there was professional non-compliance with section 47 (CA 1989) procedures. The vulnerable child was generally referred to children's services and defined as a child in need (s17 CA 1989 – which is to promote the welfare of the child and provide relevant services) rather than a child in need of protection and consequently no multi-agency protection plan was in place. In this book current difficulties in achieving compliance with child protection procedures are examined and some of the confusion caused by recent policy developments explored. For instance, *Working Together* states that the core assessment is the means by which a section 47 (CA 1989) inquiry is carried out (DfES, 2006, 5.60). This is inaccurate. Assessment informs the section 47 (CA 1989) investigation but as a single process will not provide a child with protection from abuse. In this book, a critique is presented of current assessment protocols and there is opportunity for the reader to evaluate the limited application of these protocols to the protection of children.

In April 2008, the Child Protection Register was abolished on the basis of no research findings at all (Dhanda, 2007). This was the cornerstone of statutory forums and was effective, tried and tested. If Victoria Climbié's name had been on the register she would have had a child protection plan to keep her safe, hospitals and police would have been alerted to the risks, professionals would have followed her care from borough to borough and the case would have been analysed in a multi-agency setting. Yet surprisingly, Lord Laming recommended the abolition of the register (Laming, 2003, 17.110). This register provided a confidential alert system to hospitals and police facilitating the identification of particularly vulnerable children and enabling swift intervention to protect them. Studies of serious case reviews demonstrated that few children who died had been on the Child Protection Register (Reder, et al., 1993; Reder and Duncan, 1999).

There is no replacement for the register although there is now provision for a child to be designated as the subject of a child protection plan. A children's database for every child in the country now named ContactPoint and systems such as the Common Assessment Framework, Initial and Core assessments and Integrated Children's Systems (ICS), dovetail into the same computer formats based on the assessment triangle (Department of Health, 2000a) and represent an unprecedented and unwarranted invasion of children's and families' privacy. Professionals overwhelmed with meeting performance targets, responding to low-level concerns, preoccupied with data entry, and under pressure to close cases within predefined timescales for assessments, find it difficult to focus their attention on children at risk of harm. Research by the University of York confirmed that social workers found the ICS forms too prescriptive, repetitive and time-consuming and that the tick boxes were often irrelevant or too imprecise to be useful. The forms were unwieldy and not fit for use as court reports or reports for conferences. On average it took 8.5 hours to complete a core assessment and 2.5 hours for initial assessments (Bell, 2008).

Laming recommended that the police should focus on crime, which has raised the threshold of police work in child protection (Laming, 2003, 14.57). The police CAITs have reduced in numbers, some teams have combined and a referral sergeant filters calls. Social workers now complete assessments and the police investigate crime, leading to a minimisation of both jointly investigating significant harm and consequently there is risk of children remaining unprotected. This represents a significant change from the 1990s when some authorities had joint police and social work child protection investigation teams which had developed a high level of specialist skill. Social workers and police are now paralysed in their practice to work jointly to protect children as a result of recent policy shifts.

Protecting children is a complex and highly skilled task. Reder and Duncan (2004, p112), with reference to the Climbié case, expressed concern at the lack of child protection training for social workers in practice, commenting that, since *the findings of any next inquiry could reasonably be predicted before it has taken place, we would like to propose that no further public inquiries are commissioned before all training and resource deficiencies identified over the last 30 years have been remedied.* It is therefore particularly important to include a comprehensive knowledge base of this subject within social work academic programmes.

Book structure

This book is written primarily for undergraduate and postgraduate student social workers developing their skills and understanding of the requirements for practice and will inform their practice placements. Because every social worker must be fully aware of how to protect children, the book will be relevant both to qualified children's social workers and those working with adults. Other professionals from all the agencies represented on the Local Safeguarding Children's Boards and the Multi Agency Public Protection Arrangements, as well as those working in the voluntary sector, will also find this book an excellent source of information about the specialist social work role in working together to protect children from significant harm.

It is not possible or advisable to provide social workers seeking to protect children with a prescriptive checklist of what to do and when. Such an approach would deny the varied and skilled nature of the task. Reder and Duncan consider that *the key aims of training are to arm practitioners with knowledge, skills and the capacity to think* (2004, p109). Thinking means questioning and critically examining evidence which can be difficult and uncomfortable for those working to protect children and to challenge powerful child abusers – a task which can at times be overwhelming.

Munro suggests that child protection workers should be like detectives making a thorough search for the truth with an open mind that considers different possibilities and tests conclusions (2002, p170). Social workers need to combine analysis with intuition. Analysis is an intellectual process derived from a knowledge base, whereas intuition is an unconscious process which draws on experience, metaphor, imagination and feelings. Of course, intuitive reasoning can be guided by understanding of theories and knowledge of legislation, policies and practice guidance and analysis requires intuitive skills in collecting, selecting and organising information (Munro, 2002, p112). Making decisions to protect children involves making judgements about whether or not an action or inaction is abusive, considering how abusive an action is and assessing what level of response is needed to provide the child with safety. Social workers may conclude *false positives* by thinking everything will be OK when it is not; or *false negatives* by thinking everything will not be OK when actually it is. To guard against these possibilities of error, social workers should always scrutinise their decisions from the opposite perspective and learn to rigorously examine their judgements. For instance, if a decision has been made to remove a child from a neglectful home the social worker should ask the question *what are the risks of harm to the child by leaving the child with the family?* Conversely, if the social worker has decided to support the family in caring for the child, the question must be asked: *what are the risks to the child of not removing them from this abusive situation?* It is equally important to consider what information may be missing from the analysis which would hinder the possibility of achieving a sound judgement.

Social workers tend to act on vivid, recent and easily available information whereas inquiries inform us that much highly relevant information is hidden and less obvious. It can be useful to always ask: *what is the Factor X in this situation – what can I not see, what have I not been told, what information have I not acquired?* Evidence would then need to be sought to prove or disprove the hypothesis formed.

Children only gain effective protection when professionals work together. The task will not be achieved by one agency or worker acting in isolation. Each professional holds prime responsibility for the protection of the child and must follow guidance in working with other professionals, challenging them where necessary and making sure conflict is addressed and resolved. The lawyer for Mr and Mrs Climbié in her summing up to the inquiry stated that:

> *Victoria's parents have noted that social workers blame doctors, front line staff blame management, managers blame the council, the councils blame the Government for lack of funding. Typical responses to failings have been 'I am poorly managed', 'we did not have the resources' or 'it was not my job'. Victoria's parents have been left with the strong impression that when giving evidence the primary objective of certain witnesses was to avoid acknowledging their personal responsibility at all costs.*
>
> (Laming, 2003, evidence 19 February 2002, p97)

The concept of *respectful uncertainty* was raised during the inquiry to describe how professionals need to show mutual respect and at the same time confidently challenge each other's practice with the child firmly at the centre of all decisions.

This book has been written to support the development of critical skills in analysing information and to encourage the use of intuitive abilities. Each chapter has an evidence-informed analysis including definitions, facts, indicators and types of abuse relating to each of the four categories of child abuse: emotional, sexual, neglect and physical, as outlined in *Working together to safeguard children* (DfES, 2006,1.30–3). A range of practice issues can be found in each chapter, which are applicable to every form of abuse. These include professional dangerousness, assessing parental responses and adults' ability to protect, as well as practice tools such as a chronology which can provide the basis of case analysis.

A case study from a child abuse inquiry is included in each chapter. In the first chapter the emotional abuse Victoria Climbié suffered is presented, a perspective rarely acknowledged in this case (O'Hagan, 2006). In Chapter 2, an inquiry about a case of organised sexual abuse of children involving a number of adult perpetrators in the Western Isles of Scotland identified a lack of focus on the child victims (SWIA, 2005). In the case of Paul, who died from neglect, outlined in Chapter 3, many professionals responded to the adults' needs and lost sight of the child (Bridge Child Care Development Service, 1995). Sukina Hammond, who died as a result of violent physical assaults, is discussed in Chapter 4, drawing attention to the fact that serious physical violence escalated following physical punishment which gained no professional protective response (Bridge Child Care Consultancy, 1991).

Learning from serious case reviews of the deaths of children from abuse is relevant to all child protection work. Most of the children who have died or have been seriously harmed as a result of child abuse did not obtain protection through the implementation of statutory child protection procedures. No child protection investigation was carried out, for instance, in the Victoria Climbié case because, as Reder and Duncan comment, *a referral received by social services which indicated the likelihood of non-accidental injuries to Victoria was labelled from the outset as 'child in need'* (s17, CA 1989) (2004, p104).

Children's voices, with particular reference to disabled children, are included in each chapter to model good practice so that the child is heard at every stage from the initial contact, throughout an investigation and during proactive action. Autobiographical accounts by survivors inform our understanding of this subject because it is from their experience of professional responses to child abuse that there is the most to learn.

A critique of current *Every Child Matters* (DfES, 2003) policy directives will enable the social worker to move away from a prescriptive approach and to engage with and respond meaningfully to each child's protection needs with sensitivity and creativity. Four protocols are included as follows:

Chapter 1: Common Assessment Framework;

Chapter 2: Assessment and Progress Record for Looked After Children;

Chapter 3: Core Assessment;

Chapter 4: Initial Assessment.

Responding early to protect children is examined from the perspective of a child's need to be safe from harm and includes the importance of targeting perpetrators. Each chapter includes an in-depth analysis to examine making judgements, encourage careful thinking and acting to protect, in relation to one example of significant harm:

Chapter 1: a child emotionally abused whose main carer has mental health problems;

Chapter 2: a child who is sexually exploited through prostitution;

Chapter 3: a child left home alone;

Chapter 4: a child subjected to physical punishment.

Learning features

The book is interactive. You are encouraged to work through the book as an active participant, taking responsibility for your learning in order to increase your knowledge, understanding and ability to apply this learning to practice.

You should have an overview of the law relating to children, particularly the Children Acts 1989 and 2004. It is important to recognise the distinction between criminal law, which targets the perpetrators of crime and where evidence is tested *beyond all reasonable doubt*, and civil law, where children may gain protection on the lower *balance of probabilities* level of proof. In child protection it is difficult to achieve the prosecution of abusers; however, if there is no criminal prosecution, social workers must still protect the child using civil proceedings and consider application for criminal injuries compensation.

You should become familiar with the main articles relating to child protection in the United Nations Convention on the Rights of the Child (United Nations, 1989) which are referred to throughout the book and include the following key articles relating to children under the age of 18 years.

- Article 3. In all actions concerning children, whether undertaken by public or private social welfare institutions, courts of law, administrative authorities or legislative bodies the best interests of the child shall be the primary consideration:

- Article 19. States parties shall take all appropriate legislative, administrative, social and educational measures to protect the child from all forms of physical or mental violence, injury or abuse, neglect or negligent treatment, maltreatment or exploitation, including sexual abuse while in the care of parents, legal guardians or any other person who has the care of the child. Such protective measures should include effective procedures for social programmes to provide support for the child and for those who have care of the child, as well as for other forms of prevention and identification, reporting, referral, investigation, treatment and follow-up of instances of child maltreatment and as appropriate for judicial involvement.

You should access your Local Safeguarding Children Board child protection procedures and Chapter 5 of *Working together* (2006), which are essential reading to support activities in this book. This statutory guidance states:

> *For those children who are suffering or at risk of suffering significant harm joint working is essential to safeguarding and promoting the welfare of the child and where necessary to help to bring to justice the perpetrators of crimes against children. All agencies and professionals should:*
>
> - *be alert to the potential indicators of abuse;*
>
> - *be alert to the risks that individual abusers or potential abusers cause to children;*
>
> - *share and help to analyse information so that an assessment can be made of the child's needs and circumstances;*
>
> - *contribute to whether actions are needed to safeguard and promote the welfare of the child;*
>
> - *take part in regularly reviewing the outcomes for the child against specific plans;*
>
> - *work cooperatively with parents unless this is inconsistent with ensuring the child's safety.*

(DfES, 2006, 1.16)

You will need a basic understanding of the roles and responsibilities of the two key organisations, the Local Safeguarding Children Board (LSCB) and the Multi Agency Public Protection Arrangements (MAPPA), established to protect children.

The Children Act 2004 requires each local authority to establish an LSCB which is the key statutory mechanism for agreeing how relevant agencies and organisations in each local area will co-operate to safeguard and promote the welfare of children. The LSCB must be effective by providing training, conducting serious case reviews, resolving conflict and scrutinising service delivery, policies and procedures (DfES, 2006, 3.1–80). It should promote its activities and be accessible to professionals and the public. Each agency has specialist child protection advisors, such as the named safeguarding nurse, doctor and midwife and the named teacher for child protection, acting as consultants both within and outside their own agencies.

A MAPPA is in place in each area for the assessment and management of risk posed by serious and violent offenders including those considered to pose a risk or potential risk of harm to children. Police and probation services have statutory duties to protect the public through these arrangements and to manage the Sex Offender Register. The panel is managed by a senior police officer with officers in the Public Protection Unit and has senior representatives from key local agencies enabling multi-agency planning. Social workers have a responsibility to refer to the panel any suspected or known child abusers and to implement risk strategies (DfES, 2006, 12.12–21).

The flowchart below provides a guide to child protection procedures from referral, to section 47 (CA 1989) investigation, strategy meeting, child protection conference and action to protect. It includes details of the main child protection procedures which are also referred to throughout the book. You will need to be particularly well informed about the two main statutory meetings to protect children: the strategy meeting and the child protection conference. Social workers need to be absolutely clear that these two meetings have a foundation in law with accountability for all professionals involved and must never be replaced by processes such as network or professionals meetings as these are not statutory instruments and are simply the wrong tools for the job. Such meetings may be additional forums for professionals, families and children but are not alternatives to the meetings designated within statutory child protection guidance.

The strategy meeting

(DfES, 2006, 5.54–57)

This meeting must be chaired by a children's services manager to share information, plan section 47 (CA 1989) enquiries and agree whether single or joint agency investigation and any immediate action to protect, including legal action are needed. Importantly it is a professionals only meeting and parents or carers must only be informed about it if this does not place the child at risk. The police, usually from the CAIT, must attend as well as any professionals with relevant involvement, particularly from health, education, probation and a paediatrician for specific medical consultation. Consideration must be given to including specialist advisors at the meeting to inform on issues such as disability, ethnicity and specific cultural practices. Careful consideration must also be given to the child's safety and best interests throughout the process of investigation and professionals must agree how the child's wishes and feelings will be taken into account within the process.

Decisions must be made about if and how information is to be shared; who should interview whom for what purpose, where and when; the need for visually recorded interviews; the need for paediatric assessments (in consultation with the paediatrician); how to obtain and secure forensic evidence; whether to convene a child protection conference; and make arrangements for review strategy meeting/s. The social worker must follow police advice about the requirements of any criminal investigation including forensic evidence. Professionals at the meeting must consider the needs of other children who may have been abused and plan the core assessment in parallel with the section 47 (CA 1989) investigation. If a decision to convene a child protection conference is reversed this must be approved by a senior manager in children's services.

The investigators must collaborate with the MAPPA if the alleged or known perpetrator is thought to pose a risk to others in the community. If the allegation is against a member of staff, following immediate protective action, any disciplinary action must await the outcome of the child protection investigation and any criminal proceedings. In complex abuse situations the named officer for safeguarding within children's services should be informed. Non-abusive parents or adults with parental responsibility must be informed of the investigation as long as this does not place the child at risk or compromise any criminal investigation.

Child protection conference

(DfES, 2006, 5.80–143)

This conference must be held within 15 days of a strategy meeting decision to convene one or in response to notification from another authority about a child in the area who is already the subject of a child protection plan. The conference is chaired by a senior social worker independent of the allocated social worker's line management and is attended by professionals involved in conducting the section 47 (CA 1989) investigation as well as those working with the child and family. Specialist advisors may also need to be included. The child and/or family can attend with or be represented by an advocate. By agreement with the chairperson, the child may attend for all or part of the conference or may meet with the chairperson on their own beforehand and may be supported to present their views, for instance, by letter, drawing, audio or visual recording. Children who attend should not be exposed to parental conflict, adult language or content and professionals must be sensitive to the impact on the child of any contribution. A conference can be interrupted at any time to ensure that the child's rights are respected.

The purpose of the conference is to share and analyse information, particularly the outcome of the section 47 (CA 1989) investigation, make professional judgements about the likelihood of a child suffering significant harm and decide whether the child is at continuing risk of significant harm based on evidence or research findings. The social worker must provide a detailed report of the single or joint agency investigation and information from a core assessment. Any concern about presenting sensitive information must be discussed with the chairperson prior to the conference. Each agency presents background information about the child and family who (if present) contribute and are invited to comment throughout. Following discussion, a decision is reached about whether or not the child, and any other children in the family or children identified as a result of the investigation, needs to be the subject of a child protection plan and the relevant category/ies of child abuse (emotional, sexual, neglect, physical) are identified. The chairperson reaches a decision taking into account the views of other professionals but is not bound by them and any dissent must be recorded. A conference must be convened prior to the birth of a child when there is concern that an unborn child may be at future risk of significant harm.

Parents and carers are central to processes for keeping children safe and the vast majority of children who are subject to investigation remain with their families. Social workers must do everything possible to bring parents and carers on board to contribute to the conference unless to do so would place the child at risk or interfere with and undermine the protection process. Parents may be excluded if there is risk of violence or if to include them might compromise a police investigation. During the conference parents and carers and/or children should not be surprised by sudden disclosure of sensitive and personal information and there must be recognition of their relative powerlessness. The following quotes illustrate some parents' experiences of conferences.

> *Things were brought up about my husband's past which I didn't know. I think he should have been notified that this would be done so that he had the chance to tell me first.*
>
> *I could feel they had power and I had none.*
>
> *It was difficult to keep track of what was happening. I felt that everything was pushing in on me.*
>
> *We had to introduce ourselves and I was asked to go first. I messed up. I couldn't say my name and who I was. That finished it. I didn't come in with much confidence but after that I felt really stupid.*
>
> *When we got there and went into the room, I was amazed at the size of the table. I thought I hope they don't fill all these chairs. They did.*
>
> (Peake, 1997, pp32–3)

When working with parents it is very important to understand the legal definition of the concept of parental responsibility which applies throughout the case studies in this book. As a legal term, *parental responsibility* attempts to focus on the parent's duties towards their child rather than the parent's rights over their child and is defined as: *all the rights, duties, powers, responsibilities and authority which by law a parent of a child has in relation to the child and his property* (CA 1989, s3.1). It is awarded automatically to mothers and to a child's father according to marriage status at the birth of a child or by registering as the father on the child's birth certificate.

People other than parents can acquire shared parental responsibility. The local authority acquires shared parental responsibility if a Care Order or Emergency Protection Order is made and they may limit the extent to which parental responsibility can be exercised by a parent. If a Residence Order (s8, CA 1989) is made determining where a child must live, shared parental responsibility is awarded to the person looking after the child. Parents can delegate responsibility to someone else without losing it themselves.

Social workers need to be aware of the following range of legal safeguards and protective processes which are outlined further in the flowchart, are referred to throughout the book and feature in the diagrams at the end of each chapter.

Immediate protection (DfES, 2006, 5.49)

Police powers of protection (s46, CA 1989)

Emergency Protection Order (s44, CA 1989)

Supervision Order (s31, CA 1989)

Exclusion Order (with or without power of arrest) (s52 Family Law Act 1996)

Strategy discussion and/or meeting (DfES, 2006, s54–60)

Investigative interview (CJS, 2007)

Paediatric assessment (LSCB, 7.9.1–29)

Child protection conference (DfES, 2006, 5.80–140)

Care Order (s31, CA 1989)

Provision of accommodation (s20, CA 1989)

Prohibitive Steps Order (s8, CA 1989)

Specific Issues Order (s8, CA 1989)

In all court proceedings the *welfare checklist* will be applied (s1(3), CA 1989).

The welfare checklist includes:

- the wishes and feelings of the child, as far as the court can find these out;

- the physical, emotional, and educational needs of the child;

- the likely effects on the child of any changes in his or her circumstances;

- the age, sex, background and any other characteristics of the child that the court considers to be relevant;

- any harm which the child has suffered, or is at risk of suffering;

- how capable each parent or other relevant person is of meeting the child's needs;

- the range of powers available to the court.

The court will not make any order unless to do so would be better for the child than making no order at all. This is often referred to as the *no order principle*. Social workers need to be mindful that when presenting to court, their planning must be in place prior to proceedings. The Ministry of Justice has published the Public Law Outline (2008) which sets out the requirements for the pre-proceedings checklist. This must include a social work chronology, a record of the strategy meeting and any single or joint agency materials as well as a care plan.

The referral
An allegation or evidence of child abuse

Gathering information
The social worker must gather information from the referrer, from existing records for the child, children and other relevant adults, and from all other agencies, to establish important details that will inform decision-making. Information gathering must never delay taking urgent action to protect a child from harm. Seeking the consent of parents, carers and children for this process is not required if to do so would place the child at risk. Social workers should always consult children's legal services for advice about legal safeguards.

Immediate action
If there is a risk to the life of a child or possibility of immediate significant harm, the social worker must act to protect. This may be achieved through a protective parent or carer removing the abuser, removing the child or children to a safe place or the abuser agreeing to leave the household. For children needing urgent medical attention this must be arranged through hospital admission, liaison with the child protection paediatrician or forensic medical examiner (via the police). It may be necessary to use statutory powers. The police may remove the abuser from the world of the child using additional criminal justice measures. These actions would usually follow a strategy discussion/meeting.

Emergency Protection Order
The SW must obtain from a magistrate an Emergency Protection Order (EPO) s44 (CA 1989) which gives the applicant shared parental responsibility. The grounds are that the child is likely to suffer significant harm if not removed or if the child does not remain in a place they are accommodated or s47 (CA 1989) inquiries are being frustrated for example where the SW is denied access to the child. This is effective for no more than eight days and can be extended for a further seven days. Conditions may be attached for medical or psychiatric examination, investigative interviews, to exclude somebody from the household or area, to gain powers of entry or regarding contact with parents and carers. Any person can apply. An interim care order (ICO) may he applied for to extend the EPO.

A Recovery Order
For children who run away, are missing or who have been unlawfully taken away, a Recovery Order s50 (CA 1989) can be sought. This enables the police to search and recover a child who is subject to an EPO, a Care Order or Police Powers of Protection.

Police powers of protection
The police may be requested to use police powers of protection to secure the immediate safety of the child by removing the child to suitable accommodation or preventing the removal from a safe place such as a hospital. This lasts for up to 72 hours s46 (1) (CA 1989) and does not require a court order.

Single agency investigation – police or children's services. Emotional abuse and less serious neglect: children's services. Historic abuse: police unless abuse of children is indicated.

Joint agency investigation – police and children's services. Allegations or evidence of physical abuse, sexual abuse, serious neglect/cruelty – actual or likely significant harm. Crimes against or involving children.

The child must be safe while the investigation is ongoing. This may be with agreement from adults with parental responsibility (s20, CA 1989) or through obtaining an Emergency Protection Order or other legal safeguard. A number of strategy discussions and/or meetings may be required as the investigation progresses to evaluate the evidence and risk to the child.

Strategy discussion
An immediate and formal discussion between the social worker, police and a senior medical professional if relevant, (usually) by telephone to facilitate urgent action to protect a child or to agree the need for a strategy meeting and s47 inquiries. This may take place following a referral or at any other time. A record of the decisions, responsibility for actions and timescales should be circulated within one working day. This must not take the place of a strategy meeting and it is not appropriate to rely on the discussion as a child protection decision-making forum. In addition it must never be a mechanism for saving time or resources.

Strategy meeting
A professionals-only meeting chaired by children service manager held at a mutually convenient location e.g. surgery or hospital. This includes police, education, health and other professionals with relevant knowledge about the child, family or alleged perpetrator. A non-professional referrer may attend to provide information and respond to questions but must not be included in the discussion and decision making of the main meeting. A record of decisions, responsibility for actions and timescales to be made immediately for all participants.

Achieving best evidence interview (CJS, 2007)
This is a formal interview primarily for criminal proceedings but also used in civil hearings. Conducted in a child interview suite and visually recorded. Interview planned and conducted jointly by police officer and social worker trained for this task. The child must consent and consent of a non-abusive adult with parental responsibility unless this compromises the child's safety, must be sought.

A paediatric assessment
This may be required to provide the child with necessary treatment, secure forensic evidence, obtain medical documentation, reassure the child/parent and plan follow-up. Only a doctor can physically examine a child. The social worker must be sensitive to the child's need for privacy during any examination. Following the decision at the strategy discussion/meeting, the named child protection doctor will decide, in consultation with the police if necessary, which medical specialist is the most appropriate to conduct the examination. The child must consent to any medical examination and if reluctant may be offered an initial consultation. Even a very young child may express very clearly that they do not consent to an examination. Seek consent of a non-abusive adult with parental responsibility unless this comprises the child's safety.

A child protection conference
This should be convened within 15 days of the strategy meeting decision to have one or in response to notification from another authority about a child already subject to a child protection plan. It is chaired by a social worker who is independent of the social work line management. It is attended by the professionals involved with the investigation, professionals who have knowledge of the child and other children in the family and the parents, carers and sometimes the children themselves. The purpose is to reach a decision about whether or not the child and any other children in the family or children identified as a result of the investigation need to be the subject of a child protection plan and the relevant category/ies of child abuse are identified.

Child Protection Plan
A key social worker from children's services must be appointed to co-ordinate the plan. A core group of professionals and family members must be identified to develop, implement and review the plan including any legal safeguards. The plan needs to include who has responsibility for the agreed actions within timescales and how implementation will be monitored. There must be contingency planning in place should the child/ren not be protected. The first review can take place at any time but is usually after three months with subsequent reviews at six-monthly intervals until the plan is discontinued when the child/ren are no longer at continuing risk of significant harm, have left the area or have reached the age of 18 years.

Public Law Outline (Ministry of Justice, 2008)
This must be completed prior to proceedings and must include a record of the strategy discussion, record of the single agency or joint agency materials, a social work chronology, a care plan and pre-existing care plans.

Interim/Care Order, Interim/Supervision Order, section 8 Order
These can be obtained by the local authority, which acquires parental responsibility for the child. The grounds are that the child is suffering or likely to suffer significant harm, such harm is attributable to the care given to the child not being what it would be reasonable to expect a parent to provide or likely to be given if the order were made or if the child is beyond parental control. Conditions may be attached as with an EPO. It may mean an abuser is removed from the household or the child's environment. A Prohibitive Steps Order (s8, CA 1989) may be used to prevent a person with parental responsibility taking actions with regard to the child, such as removing them from the country. A Specific Issues Order (s8, CA 1989) can help determine any specific question about the way a child is brought up. It might be about schooling, health, or religion.

Case studies in this book will help you to examine models for social work practice. The activities require you to reflect on experiences, situations and events and help you to review and summarise learning undertaken. In this way your knowledge will become deeply embedded as part of your development. When you begin to work in an agency reflection undertaken here will help you to improve and hone your skills and knowledge. You will have an opportunity to consider five options (as stated below) as part of a proactive social work response to a child protection referral and to reflect on how you made judgements in each case.

A A child is not thought to be at any risk of child abuse.

B There is concern about the abuse of a child.

C There is suspicion of likely or actual significant harm to a child (s47 enquiry, CA 1989).

D A section 47 (CA 1989) investigation of a child is indicated.

E Immediate action to protect. Evidence of actual significant harm and/or criminal offence.

Diagrams illustrating the five stages of professional response to child protection allegations in relation to the in-depth analysis are included towards the end of each chapter. The case studies are mainly non-specific so as to enable some flexibility in applying and evaluating the impact of factors of ethnicity, religion, socio-economic status and other issues relating to oppression, powerlessness and social inequity. To facilitate learning, the case studies are presented in a chronological order although in practice social work interventions will rarely progress in a predictable way. For instance, although checks will be made prior to an urgent strategy discussion, further information often emerges as the investigation develops. Similarly, action to protect a child from a dangerous situation may take place immediately prior to a strategy meeting or child protection conference.

The case studies are framed around both the single agency and joint police/social work investigation required by section 47 (CA 1989). Assessment protocols (Department of Health, 2000a) will be implemented in parallel to child protection investigation and planning, each a distinct process informing the other. A Common Assessment (CAF) or initial assessment (7 days) must never be a reason for delay in providing a child with protection and a core assessment (35 days) must not distract from implementing the decisions of a strategy discussion/meeting or child protection conference. A strategy discussion/meeting should take place within three working days of a referral being received by children's services unless there is a need for immediate action to protect the child, there is a need to preserve forensic evidence or the allegations indicate serious risk of harm. In these cases the strategy discussion should take place on the same day as receipt of referral. A child protection conference must take place within 15 working days of the decision to convene one made at a strategy meeting. However, a joint investigation cannot be restricted by timescales. Gaining an abused child's trust and a non-abusing parent or carer's co-operation, collating evidence about an alleged abuser and having multi-agency debate and analysis of the risk of harm to a child or children, may take days, weeks, months or even years.

While an assessment is of the child' and family's needs, an investigation also requires a focus on the alleged or known abuser, which is not addressed in the assessment framework (Department of Health, 2000a). Whereas social workers conduct assessments and police investigate crimes, these case studies focus on the process of joint police and social work decision making and investigation of actual or likely significant harm and decision-making through statutory multi-agency meetings and procedures. Focusing solely on assessment of the child and family, without this being firmly within the context of an agreed multi-agency investigation process, may, in some cases, interfere with the ability to protect the child effectively. This is most evident where a child may have alleged sexual abuse and assessment might alert the alleged perpetrator, leaving the child at risk of further harm and of threats or pressure to retract. Assessment protocols require consent to be gained from parents and carers for checks to be made. Interviews and medical examinations of children require parental consent in the context of working in partnership during an assessment, unless Gillick competence applies and the child is of an age and understanding to give informed consent themselves (House of Lords, 1985). However, within a section 47 (CA 1989) investigation, the protection of the child is the paramount consideration and consent must be gained only where this is in the best interests of the child and when it does not interfere with any criminal investigation by the police. For instance, conducting an initial assessment might interfere with police interviews of the parents/carers as suspects or witnesses and the interview of the child might be inappropriate if a visually recorded interview is indicated in compliance with statutory guidance (CJS, 2007). Decisions about consent to information sharing and interventions are complex within child protection investigations and must be made at a strategy discussion/meeting and based on local procedures and professional judgement in each case.

The case studies are designed to aid a questioning approach to the process of protecting children and to promote social workers' confidence to act swiftly to protect when necessary. The case studies usually progress from referral to investigation and action to protect. When reading the case studies, structure your thinking and questioning around the following points but do not be limited by this list. Some suggested questions are listed below but continue to add your own questions and to consider the implications of these in each case. When protecting children it is always important to reflect on the blocks that might interfere with good practice. In child protection work professionals may unwittingly collude with, or maintain the dangerous dynamics of abuse – these pitfalls in practice are known as *professional dangerousness*. You may want to think about what systems need to be in place to support the social worker in safe practice in these cases.

Referral

What was the nature of the referral and reason for making it?

What might be the immediate/short-term/long-term risk to the child/ren of actual or likely significant harm?

What has been said to whom, by whom and in what context?

What has been observed?

Was the information provided fact and/or opinion?

How are these differentiated?

Has the referral been made in time to meet the protection needs of the child and/or other children?

Have the needs of disabled children been addressed?

Has the childrens' and families age, ethnicity, culture, religion and language been addressed?

Have any crimes been reported?

Who else has knowledge of the referral?

What child protection procedures have been followed in making the referral to the named person or agency?

What key information has been reported about the child/ren, parents and carers, extended family and alleged abuser/s?

Investigation

Has the child been kept safe?

Has the investigation ensured that the child's best interests were paramount?

Have the needs of disabled children been addressed throughout?

Have checks been made with all the relevant agencies/organisations and individuals been contacted for information gathering?

Were the needs of the children in relation to their gender, ethnicity, culture, religion and language addressed?

What were the consent issues in relation to the checks being obtained?

Has a decision been made to begin child protection procedures?

Was this a single agency (police or children's services) or a joint investigation?

Did a strategy discussion take place at the right time for the child to gain protection?

Was there a strategy meeting and arrangements to review the decisions made?

Were the appropriate professionals present at the strategy meeting to ensure the full sharing of relevant information?

Has the child been interviewed?

Was the child interviewed in a suitable environment and in a child-centred way?

In the decision about who interviewed the child, was account taken of gender, ethnicity and other relevant factors i.e. any resemblance to the abuser?

Did a visually recorded interview take place?

Was the interview conducted in accordance with the *Achieving best evidence* guidance? (CJS, 2007)?

Have the child's wishes and feelings been taken into account?

Was there a paediatric assessment or medical examination?

What were the consent issues in relation to the interviews and medical examinations?

Was there a home visit? Were the children's bedrooms, kitchen and other areas seen?

Was there a need for forensic evidence and was this obtained in line with police protocols?

What other interviews took place?

Was the parental/carer response evaluated?

Was the alleged abuser arrested?

Has there been a risk assessment of the non-abusive parent/carer's capacity to be protective?

Were all the decisions of the strategy meeting carried out as agreed?

Child protection intervention and planning

What measures are in place to protect the child?

What civil legal proceedings are in place to protect the child?

Has a child protection conference taken place?

What agencies are contributing to the protection plan?

Are the arrangements to review the child protection planning in line with local and national procedures?

Have any crimes been committed?

Has the abuser been arrested/charged/prosecuted?

Has an application for criminal injuries compensation been made?

Has anything prevented the plan from being carried out?

FURTHER READING

Bell, M (2008) Research finds disquiet with ICS. *Community Care*, 5 June 2008.
This article reports concerns about the design and use of the Integrated Children's System and questions its fitness for purpose.

Calder, M and Hackett, S (eds) (2003) *Assessment in child care*. Lyme Regis: Russell House.
This excellent book provides the reader with an overview and critical analysis of current practice and policy initiatives, enabling a more thoughtful and informed approach to assessment in child care.

Davies, L (2006) *Protecting Children*. Gloucester: Akamas.
A book and course reader that clearly and accessibly sets out the practice of protecting children and how this is informed by law, policy, research and survivors' voices.

Davies, L (2008a) In the shadow of a tragedy.
www.guardian.co.uk/society/2008/jan/28/climbie.childprotection.

This article critiques Lord Laming's inquiry following the death of Victoria Climbié in terms of its reccommendations and the limitations of subsequent policy objectives.

Davies, L (2008b) Reclaiming the language of child protection. In Calder, M (2008) *Contemporary risk assessment in safeguarding children*. Lyme Regis: Russell House.
This book chapter provides a critical account of changes in language and implications for social work practice in assessing risk and protecting children from harm.

Munro, E and Calder, M (2005) Where has child protection gone? *The Political Quarterly*, 76 (3), 439–45.
A journal article arguing that the prevention agenda associated with Every Child Matters has drawn attention away from child protection systems.

Reder, P and Duncan, S (2004) Making the most of the Victoria Climbié inquiry report. *Child Abuse Review*, 13, 95–114.
This article highlights how the skills, experience and qualities needed to effectively protect children are being undermined by an emphasis on more technical, tick-box approaches encouraged by current policy guidance. It argues for social workers to develop a healthy scepticism in terms of their abilities to reason and integrate subjective and intuitive approaches with objectivity.

WEBSITES

www.arch-ed.org
Action for the Rights of Children is a website committed to ensuring that children's voices are heard and acted upon. ARCH conducts research, publishes information and promotes the recognition by policy-makers of their obligations to children under existing human rights legislation.
For three videos about the children's databases and abolition of the Child Protection Register see: www.youtube.com/user/Archrights.

www.childrenslegalcentre.com
The Children's Legal Centre is an independent UK-based charity, staffed by lawyers and professionals with experience in child law and provides legal advice and representation to children, their carers and professionals.

www.crae.org.uk
Children's Rights Alliance for England is a coalition of over 380 organisations committed to the full implementation of the United Nations Convention on the Rights of the Child.

www.dcsf.gov.uk
The Department for Children, Schools and Families is the government department responsible for developing policy and practice to improve outcomes for children.

www.everychildmatters.gov.uk
The Every Child Matters website provides links to Children Act 2004 guidance and other statutory guidance and to the forms and protocols referred to in this book.

www.frg.org.uk
The Family Rights Group campaigns to improve services and provide legal and professional advice and resources to increase the voice of children and their families in the services they use.

www.nspcc.org.uk/Inform
The NSPCC Inform website is a free child protection resource providing research, statistics, news and information.

Chapter 1
Emotional abuse

ACHIEVING A SOCIAL WORK DEGREE

This chapter will help you to meet the following National Occupational Standards (see the Skills for Care website, www.skillsforcare.org.uk).

Key Role 1: Prepare for, and work with individuals, families, carers, groups and communities to assess their needs and circumstances.
- Assess needs and options to recommend a course of action.

Key Role 2: Plan, carry out, review and evaluate social work practice, with individuals, families, carers, groups and communities and other professionals.
- Respond to crisis situations.
- Address behaviour which presents a risk to individuals, families, carers, groups and communities.

Key Role 3: Support individuals to represent their needs, views and circumstances.
- Prepare for, and participate in decision-making forums.

Key Role 4: Manage risk to individuals, families, carers, groups, communities, self and colleagues.

Key Role 5: Manage and be accountable, with supervision and support, for your own social work practice within your organisation.
- Manage, present and share records and reports.
- Work within multi-disciplinary and multi-organisational teams, networks and systems.

Key Role 6: Demonstrate professional competence in social work practice.
- Research, analyse, evaluate and use current knowledge of best social work practice.
- Manage complex ethical issues, dilemmas and conflicts.

It will also introduce you to the following academic standards as set out in the social work subject benchmark statements. See
www.qaa.ac.uk/academicinfrastructure/benchmark/honours/socialpolicy.asp#1

5.1.2 The service delivery context
- The significance of legislative and legal frameworks and service delivery standards.

5.1.4 Social work theory
- Research-based concepts and critical explanations from social work theory and other disciplines that contribute to the knowledge base of social work.

5.5 Problem-solving skills

5.5.2 Gathering information.

5.5.3 Analysis and synthesis.

5.5.4 Intervention and evaluation.

5.6 Communication skills
- listen actively to others, engage appropriately with the life experiences of service users, understand accurately their viewpoint and overcome personal prejudices to respond appropriately to a range of complex personal and interpersonal situations;
- follow and develop an argument and evaluate the viewpoints of, and evidence presented by, others.

5.7 Skills in working with others
- consult actively with others, including service users and carers, who hold relevant information or expertise.
- act with others to increase social justice by identifying and responding to prejudice, institutional discrimination and structural inequality.
- challenge others when necessary, in ways that are most likely to produce positive outcomes.

7.3 Knowledge and understanding
- an ability to use research and enquiry techniques to collect, analyse and interpret relevant information;
- a developed capacity for critical evaluation of knowledge and evidence from a range of sources.

Introduction

I've been bad for years and years.
Written on the wall of a cellar of Haut de la Garenne children's home in Jersey
(Batty, 2008)

I shall remember forever and will never forget.
Monday: my money was taken.
Tuesday: names called.
Wednesday: my uniform torn.
Thursday: my body pouring with blood.
Friday: it's ended.
Saturday: freedom.

The final diary pages of 13-year-old Vijay Singh. He was found hanging from the banister rail at his home (Marr and Field, 2001).

I was full of anger and resentment, that bullying bastard saying I was mental...The physical pain of the beatings I could take, although it did hurt a great deal. Worse was the mental anguish which they brought. I felt trapped and totally helpless and defenseless. The staff had all the power and they undoubtedly abused that power: they controlled the amount of food we had, the amount of sleep we had and the amount of money we had. They were in an awesomely powerful position and the beating reinforced this. They are adults. I was the child. And they left me with psychological scars that may never fully heal.

(Fever, 1994, p157)

This chapter focuses on protection of children from emotional abuse. It begins by looking at definitions and moves on to consider the knowledge required to make professional judgements. The complexities of this form of abuse will be examined to support an informed approach to children's circumstances. Research into children's views and survivor perspectives provides a basis for sound decision-making. Five case studies provide opportunity for further application of knowledge to practice. The chapter concludes with case examples of emotional abuse involving children whose parent or carer has mental health problems which will take the reader through an investigative process escalated through five levels of social work intervention to support in-depth analysis.

Definition of emotional abuse

The persistent emotional maltreatment of a child such as to cause severe and persistent adverse effects on the child's emotional development.

- *It may involve conveying to children that they are worthless or unloved, inadequate, or valued only insofar as they meet the needs of another person.*

- *It may feature age or developmentally inappropriate expectations being imposed on children. These may include interactions that are beyond the child's developmental capability, as well as overprotection and limitation of exploration and learning, or preventing the child participating in normal social interaction.*

- *It may involve seeing or hearing the ill-treatment of another.*

- *It may involve serious bullying, causing children frequently to feel frightened or in danger, or the exploitation or corruption of children.*

- *Some level of emotional abuse is involved in all types of maltreatment of a child, though it may occur alone.*

(DfES, 2006, 1.31)

Underlying emotional abuse may be as important if not more so than other more visible forms of abuse in terms of its impact on the child.

(DfES, 2006, 9.7)

Learning about emotional abuse

ACTIVITY **1.1**

A number of commentators suggest that emotional abuse is only harmful when it is persistent. Do you think that emotional abuse must be persistent to significantly harm a child?

Comment

Beckett maintains that any kind of neglect, physical abuse or sexual abuse, in fact conveys to a child a negative message about their worth and this is why emotional abuse is present in all forms of child abuse and is therefore the primary form of abuse (Beckett, 2007, p70). The abuse may be by acts of commission such as acts of verbal abuse, or omission such as by ignoring a child's achievements.

The inclusion of *persistent* in the definition is significant. It recognises that potentially emotionally abusive behaviours can feature in children's lives from time to time. For example, where an adult may be overtired or stressed by an experience or event such as a loss or bereavement that may result in them being unable temporarily to prioritise the child's emotional needs. While survivor accounts convey that even a single act can be harmful, for example witnessing a violent act on television, the persistent nature of emotional abuse is a key characteristic.

3

Defining a child as in need of a child protection plan under the category of emotional abuse only takes place if it is the sole or main category. Glaser and Prior (1997) consider that this factor may lead to some delay in providing emotionally abused children with protection. Wilding and Thoburn (1995) noted that in cases of emotional abuse there was often no further action taken after section 47 (CA 1989) enquiries and no assessment of the need for services.

O'Hagan usefully describes his difficulty as a practitioner in protecting a child from emotional harm:

> *I have a vivid memory of the first time I attempted to initiate care proceedings in respect of a child whom I believed was being emotionally abused. I recall a tortuous discussion with the local authority children's solicitor, in which I was trying to persuade him about such abuse. I shared with him my observations over many months, my discussions with parents, teachers and health visitor and my conversations with the child himself. The solicitor listened intently; he frequently nodded courteously and unconvincingly; then he proceeded to interrogate me on 'what injuries the child had sustained recently'.*

(O'Hagan, 2006, p18)

O'Hagan states that current definitions are *flawed and culturally biased* and should refer to *context, duration and consequence* (2006, p39) because definitions often involve lists of abusive behaviours; for example, parents or carers being critical, undermining and/or verbally abusive, and these can be experienced by almost every child at some point without a child necessarily being emotionally or psychologically abused. O'Hagan also suggests that social workers should distinguish between emotional (i.e. what we feel) and psychological (i.e. what we think) abuse, while other commentators see *cognition* and *emotion* as mutually dependent (Glaser and Prior, 2002, p698).

Some facts about emotional abuse

- The number of children made the subject of a child protection plan because of emotional abuse increased from 6000 in 2006 to 7,100 in 2007 (DCSF, 2007).

- An emotionally well child or young person demonstrates empathy, self-awareness, an ability to manage their feelings, motivation and good social skills. A child or young person who has good emotional wellbeing is one who works well, plays well, loves well and expects well (NCH, 2007).

- An NSPCC survey of 1,795 adults found that 17% of the children were regularly shouted or screamed at, 6% were regularly really afraid of their father, mother or carer, 5% were regularly called stupid, lazy or worthless, 5% were regularly humiliated or made to feel embarrassed and 4% were regularly hurt or upset on purpose or made to feel disliked (NSPCC, 2006a).

- The NSPCC estimated there could be 1.4 million children today who feel unloved. A study showed how the devastating impact of missing out on a parent's love can last well into adulthood. A quarter said it had damaged their confidence, adult relationships and job prospects, many reported feeling angry and resentful and said that it was always preying on their mind (NSPCC, 2006a).

- In another study, 8% of young adults said they had never been praised for doing well at school during their childhood, and 5% said that they had never been congratulated. 11% of young adults said that they had not been made to feel special by anyone during their childhood (Cawson, et al., 2000, p68).

- More than 100 children were moved from long-term placements when more than 65 children's homes and 14 schools for children with complex needs were closed because one company went into liquidation (Meghji, 2007, p1).

- In a study of children whose names were on the child protection register, 17% in the category of emotional abuse had eating disorders, 21% were not attending school and in 14% of cases, threats of suicide and self-harm were evident (Doyle, 2003, p252).

- Employment, occupation and class are not clear indicators of emotional abuse, as 17% of a sample of children registered under the category emotional abuse were from social classes 1 and 2 (Doyle, 2003, p256).

- One million children are estimated to be living in families with problem drinking – four times more than those affected by problem drug misuse (Tunnard, 2002, p7).

CASE STUDY

Victoria Climbié

Victoria Climbié died in 2000 aged 8 years. The much publicised diagram showed 128 physical injuries on Victoria's body, many of which were unexplained. Kouao, the so-called aunt, and Manning her boyfriend, were convicted of her murder. There is no doubt that Victoria suffered physical abuse, neglect and possibly sexual abuse, yet the Inquiry report made little mention of emotional abuse (Laming, 2003). O'Hagan refers to this as a lost opportunity: *No person reading the lengthy section devoted to Victoria herself could fail to realise that as well as being tortured and battered to death, she endured an emotional and psychological hell.* O'Hagan points out that the *emotional and psychological abuse of Victoria began long before she arrived in England* (2006, p10).

Little is known about why Kouao approached Victoria's parents in the Ivory Coast, but what is known is that Kouao did not provide Victoria with an education or a social life. Victoria spent five months in France where there were concerns for her welfare. Testimonies from people who knew Kouao suggested that she had exploited Victoria to promote her own interests. Kouao changed Victoria's name to Anna and gave her a false passport. This was a denial of Victoria's identity. In England, Victoria's appearance was noted to be unkempt in contrast to that of Kouao. Victoria would have witnessed Kouao lying about the causes of some of her injuries, and been unable to reveal what was happening, because English was her third language.

Victoria was one of seven children but her parents seemed to show little interest in her after she left the home with Kouao, who was her father's aunt. Victoria had no contact with her siblings from that time. Laming said that Victoria's parents' reasons for allowing her to travel to Europe with Kouao were *not a matter I will be dealing with* (Laming, 2003: 3.5). Victoria's parents attended the Inquiry but there was no explanation for their lack of contact with Victoria. Laming speculated that it was common for African parents to send their children to Europe for educational reasons, yet there was no evidence that this applied to Victoria's situation.

A childminder noticed how Victoria stared at the floor when in Kouao's presence, rubbed her hands together vigorously, which may be a sign of anxiety and fear, and remained silent when called a *wicked girl*. The hospital staff saw Victoria wet herself and jump to attention in Kouao's presence. At a later time, Kouao regarded Victoria as her *little Satan* and possessed with evil spirits. Manning spoke of beating Victoria and that she did not cry. During a home visit, Victoria accused the social worker of not respecting her or her mother (Kouao) and not finding them a home. The children's services managers thought that Kouao and Manning were using Victoria to obtain housing. It was thought that a sexual abuse allegation was for the same purpose because Victoria provided an account that appeared coached by the adults. It was emotionally abusive for Kouao and Manning to use Victoria to obtain their own ends.

Adjo was Victoria's African name yet the Inquiry chose to use the name Victoria. This added another dimension to her loss of identity even after her death. The Inquiry viewed Victoria as a child abused and murdered in the UK by her carers (Garrett, 2006). This was a limited approach which denied a perspective of her as an African child who spoke an African language and who was removed suddenly from her large extended family in the Ivory Coast (Chand, 2008).

Disabled children and emotional abuse

Disabled children are 3.9 times more likely to be emotionally abused than non-disabled children (Sullivan and Knutson, 2000a, p1257).

Why do you think disabled children are particularly likely to experience emotional abuse?

Comment
One of the biggest barriers faced by disabled children is that they are commonly seen as their impairment. Their age, gender, ethnicity, religion and culture that make up their unique individuality are subsumed into this one dimensional labelling (NSPCC, 2003, p58). Negative attitudes towards disability mean that disabled children are more vulnerable to bullying and to abuse by peers and the internalisation of oppression can result in compliant victims who may see themselves as deserving of harmful or neglectful treatment.

Despite knowledge about the need for children to have secure attachments, disabled children often receive service provision which involves them sleeping in several different places during the course of a week and the greater the impairment, the greater the likelihood that they will live away from home (NSPCC, 2003, p59). Doyle commented that there appeared to be no type of child more particularly vulnerable to emotional abuse in terms of age, gender, position in the family and health except for disabled children and their siblings because isolation and discrimination compound the abuse (Doyle, 1997, p335).

RESEARCH SUMMARY

Increasing criminalisation of young disabled children constitutes emotional abuse.

A survey of youth offending teams by the British Institute for Brain Injured Children revealed that over a third of under-17s issued with an anti-social behaviour order have a diagnosed mental health disorder or learning difficulty, including conditions such as autism and depression (Community Care, 2007).

Emotional abuse of children at different ages

ACTIVITY *1.3*

Social workers sometimes think that children are more vulnerable to abuse at particular ages. At what age do you think children are more likely to experience emotional abuse?

Comment

There is some evidence derived from analysis of serious case reviews which indicates that emotional abuse may begin pre-birth (Reder, et al., 1993, p40). A parent may not want to develop an emotional connection with the baby if they have had ambivalent attitudes to being pregnant, became pregnant as a means of leaving home or through unplanned sexual contact, or as a result of rape. A disinterest in the forthcoming baby may manifest as lack of access to antenatal care, wanting the baby adopted and the parent changing their mind at the last minute, making no material preparations for the baby, expressing a view that they only want a child of a specific gender and referring to the unborn child in negative terms. Sometimes a termination of pregnancy was desired but did not go ahead.

A level of awareness of typical child development for individual children is essential when assessing the impact of emotional abuse. It is interesting to note that many of the influential social work educational texts which look at child development (for example Bee, 1992; Sheridan, 1992) pay very little attention (if any, in the case of Sheridan) to emotional development (O'Hagan, 2006, p29). Knowledge of how children's physiological development is affected by the quality of their care is increasing. For example, it is known that children's brains are shaped by affection, that this can happen before the birth of the baby (Cairns, 2002; Gerhardt, 2004) and their brain development is altered as a result of abuse. Some research shows that this abuse can lead to children becoming perpetrators of violent behaviour themselves (Sroufe, 1996; Smith 2007). This knowledge should help protective, therapeutic and healing interventions but should not be used as predictive of future behaviours as survivors responses to abusive experiences are individual and unique.

Attachment theory provides a framework of ideas about how babies and their care givers bond together to ensure the baby's survival. Bowlby describes attachment as a *lasting psychological connectedness between human beings* (Bowlby, 1969, p194). Where this attachment relationship is deficient and the parent does not or is unable to respond appropriately to the child's attachment-generating behaviours such as eye contact, smiling, crying and reaching out, the child is left feeling emotionally insecure and anxious. The child conveys this through any series of identifiable behaviours such as withdrawal, avoidance of contact, ambivalence, frustration, anger or suppression of anger, overvigilance, overcompliance and frozen watchfulness (Ainsworth and Bell, 1970).

It is sometimes assumed that older children are more resilient to the impact of emotional abuse. However, an analysis of serious case reviews of children who died or were seriously harmed through child abuse emphasised a focus on the needs of older children as 25 of the sample of 161 children were over the age of 11 years and 9% over the age of 16 years. Nearly all the reviews of those over 16 years were because a young person had died as a result of suicide:

> *It was clear that most of the teenaged children had grown up in climates of significant adversity. The deaths of older adolescents show the consequences of the failure to address trauma. A trauma perspective would acknowledge the cumulative stresses to which these older young people had been exposed through their lives. When trauma is not addressed there are risks for school failure, anxiety, depression, substance misuse and engaging in violence.*
>
> (Brandon, et al., 2008, p109).

A study by the Children's Society which gathered information from over 13,000 young people across the UK concluded that a significant number, aged 7 and over, had experienced scapegoating in the family, were regularly maligned by their parents and treated differently from their siblings. Some said they felt unloved and unwanted and carried the blame for parental conflict and others spoke of the pressure to achieve becoming unbearable and said they were not listened to or trusted in the family. Conflict with siblings unaddressed by parents was also a factor as well as being rejected following criminal behaviour or taking drugs. A fifth of the young people who had run away overnight had been forced to leave by their parents (Safe on the Streets Research Team, 2005).

Thinking about types of emotional abuse

Emotional abuse of children by their carers

In thinking about types of emotional abuse or psychological maltreatment, it may be useful to think in terms of dimensions as opposed to categories because emotional abuse is essentially repetitive and sustained. Hart and Brassard (1991) have identified five dimensions, which are: spurning, terrorising, isolating, exploiting, and denying emotional responsiveness.

Glaser and Prior provide headings which usefully describe aspects of emotional abuse (2002, p59). Survivors' accounts have been added to illustrate these categories.

Emotional unavailability, unresponsiveness and neglect
The adults are preoccupied with their own problems such as mental health problems, substance misuse or overwhelming work commitments.

> *There was no bonding in relationships at home and I got no kissing or cuddling whatsoever as a child – none. Even if I fell down or had an accident. I think they generally regarded me as a nuisance and did not want to spend money or time on me.*
>
> (Fyfe, 2007, p162)

Negative attributions and misattributions to the child

The adults perceive the child negatively and as deserving of maltreatment. The child internalises their hostility. This may include humiliation, threats of abandonment or singling out one child for inferior treatment.

> *'I've been telling you for such a long time now that you're ugly. How long has it been? Years ... Have you listened to me? No ... Instead you bring your ugly pictures home ... Tell me Clare do you think I should pay for these?'...*
>
> *I looked at it. I was actually very ugly. My head was too big, my lips were too large, I was covered in spots and my nose was too wide. I was not smiling...*
>
> *'I don't think you should pay for the photographs.'*
>
> *'Why not?', my mother asked*
>
> *'Because I don't want you to waste your money.'*
>
> *'And?', she said*
>
> *'And because I'm ugly'.*
>
> *At school I told the teacher; Mum says the photos are too dark and they don't bring out my best features.*
>
> (Briscoe, 2006, pp52–3)

Developmentally inappropriate or inconsistent interactions with the child

The adult expects more than the child is developmentally able to achieve. They may be overprotective and this may include the child being pressurised to achieve educationally. The child is exposed inappropriately to emotionally harmful events such as domestic violence and self-harm. Interactions with the children are often misguided and unintentional, often based on their own childhood experiences, leading to a chaotic and unpredictable environment for the child.

> *Living at home was like living under a lightning storm, you never knew when you might get struck. There were no firm boundaries and I never knew where I stood. I would behave in a crazy or bizarre way or be very naughty as a cry for help to get attention and no one cared or listened. So therefore I would hide in my room but then get punished for being lazy ... To maintain control over me insults were screamed at me.*
>
> *When I was nine or ten, I wouldn't come home until very late at night or I wouldn't come home at all and no one would bat an eyelid. But when I broke a plate insult after insult was screamed at me. If I apologised I'd be told off for saying sorry. They'd tell me that if I was really sorry then I wouldn't have been evil in the first place. No matter what I did within the walls of that house, whether it was good or bad, nothing made any difference.*
>
> (Fyfe, 2007, p196)

Following the death of Aaron Gilbert, age 13 months, a neighbour reported to the court that she had seen the mother's partner hold Aaron by the ankles and spin him in circles as he screamed and cried. The partner was alleged to have told the neighbour *this will toughen him up. I want him to be hard* (BBC, 2006b).

Two children aged 2 and 3 years were forced to hit, punch and kick each other and this was filmed by their mother and grandmother. The mother said, *I didn't see any harm in toughening them up*. When the children resisted or tried to escape they were ignored and called names such as *wimp* and *faggot* (BBC, 2007d).

Failure to recognise or acknowledge the child's individuality and psychological boundary

The child is used for the fulfilment of the adult's psychological needs such as when used as a pawn in relationship conflict or as a means of gaining attention for the adult by fabricated illness. The adult does not distinguish between their own distorted sense of reality and that of the child.

> *Mum loathed everything about me. Her derision would start with something really small. For example, that I hadn't put our toys away, and it would build up into a storm of bellowing. Sometimes it didn't even make sense. I remember her shrieking at me one day that my favourite colours were 'pink, red and green' ... I would only have been about six years old at the time ... I just remember the constant rage and screaming. I was very very good so that I could be as sure as possible of not doing anything wrong.*
> *I also tried to keep still and quiet – again so that I wouldn't do anything worth the blame. I was equally afraid of tongue lashing and physical violence. I was just afraid all the time.*
>
> (Fyfe, 2007, p138)

> *My father had this strange habit of never using my name. I found this odd but could never work it out. Once at my grandmother's house my father said, ask him what he wants to eat ... He'd never say ask John what he wants to eat. He always called me you or him.*
>
> (Fyfe, 2007, p162)

Failing to promote the child's social adaptation

This may involve corruption of the child, such as by involvement in criminal acts. This can include grooming behaviour, allowing the child access to adult activities such as illegal substances, sexual activity or encouraging the child to lie, such as in the case of Victoria Climbié. The adult may harm or threaten to harm something that is treasured by the child such as their pet or a toy. The adult may not encourage the child's cognitive development and experiential learning and the child may be isolated within the family or from the community.

> *I didn't like any of it to start with, but over time I grew used to it. They were giving me money and buying me clothes. I had lots of free time going to pubs and clubs. I regret what I did now but at the time I felt needed and wanted. It seemed better than the children's home.*
>
> (D'Arcy and Gosling, 1998, p200)

> *I did try hard at school at the beginning. I would have a go at things, but there was always this suppressed feeling inside me. Even though I tried I got so frustrated. Much of this was because I never received praise for anything I did achieve. Eventually it didn't seem worth the effort. I grew disheartened, nobody was going to appreciate anything I did. We had sports days and things like that, but Dad never came and Mum turned up only very occasionally .*
>
> (West, 1995, p 110)

When I went to stroke the head of the older girl she jerked her head away. Don't do that she snapped at me. My mamma said I mustn't let you touch me. She said that you're sick and have diseases and that you're dirty. I'll tell on you ... Now even the children were treating me like an animal. Worse than an animal as even dogs were patted and stroked.

(Nazer and Lewis, 2004, p141)

ACTIVITY **1.4**

Making reference to the above descriptions of emotional abuse, consider the following examples and think about whether or not the children are being harmed.

- *Child witnesses a parent shouting racist abuse at a bus driver and is encouraged to join in.*

- *A grandparent tells a child about his war experiences which distresses the child.*

- *A mother does not tell a child that the child is adopted.*

- *Parents insist that a child sees the body of a dead relative before the funeral.*

- *A child using the internet unsupervised is groomed by a child sex abuser and persuaded to meet.*

- *A child is not allowed to speak to anyone about her mother who committed suicide.*

- *Parents take a child to religious services where the child is frightened by sermons about hell.*

- *A foster carer tells a child that their birth father is a wicked man.*

Comment

All these examples involve emotionally abusive behaviour towards children although the professional response to such examples will vary.

Children caring for their parent

Aldridge and Becker (2003, p15) state that 3 million children in the UK under the age of 16 years live in households where a member has chronic physical or mental health problems, illness or disability. An NSPCC survey cited by Aldridge and Becker (2003) found that 4% of 18–24 year olds reported having regularly cared for a sick or disabled family member throughout their childhood, a third of the adults had mental health problems or drug and alcohol misuse. The children reported performing many tasks, including personal care, paperwork, giving medicines, providing company, practical chores, taking their parent out, caring for siblings, role reversal, i.e. bringing themselves up, and being responsible for the parent's emotional wellbeing. Sometimes the label *young carer* is perceived as a stigma. The child's role, wishes and feelings must be respected as long as the situation is not abusive.

The children reported often hiding the extent of their caring role for fear of professional interference or because they did not recognise what they do as unusual and may fear a punitive approach to their non-school attendance or educational underachievement. They said they wanted ongoing support including information about the illness and prognosis, recognition of their role in the family, practical and domestic help, a contact person in the event of a crisis and someone to talk to. Howe (2005, p194) considers that caring may come at a developmental price as child carers are not always able to recognise their own needs.

> *My mother was depressed, I was unable to be with my friends. I looked after her all the time. If I was out I worried about her and I would come rushing back.*
>
> (Falkov, 1998, p125)

Bullying based on perceived difference

Bullying is defined as any hostile or offensive action against people because of their perceived difference. For example, racial and homophobic bullying is of particular concern to young people.

Emotional bullying can include:

- insulting or degrading comments, name calling, gestures, taunts, insults or jokes;
- offensive graffiti;
- humiliating, excluding, tormenting, ridiculing or threatening;
- making fun of customs, music, accent or dress.

Children have legal rights to be protected from bullying. The Race Relations Act 1976 (amended in 2000) states that schools and governing bodies have a duty to ensure that students do not face any form of racial discrimination, including attacks and harassment. The *Sex and relationship education guidance* states that schools have to provide for the needs of young gay men and lesbians and deal with homophobic bullying (DfEE, 2000,1.32). The Equality Act (2006) makes it illegal to discriminate on the grounds of religion or belief or the lack of religion or belief in the provision of goods, facilities and services. As faith schools are exempt from this requirement, children in these schools may be more isolated and vulnerable to abuse.

RESEARCH SUMMARY

Racist bullying

A London report found that black, Asian and refugee children were three times more likely to be attacked in the street than white children. Of those questioned, 10% had been physically attacked, 80% had been racially abused or threatened and more than a third had direct experience of crime in the past year (GLA, 2003).

Children of all ages from ethnic minorities, particularly those living in areas with few minority ethnic communities, are more likely than their white counterparts to experience bullying. The perpetrators are mainly young people who frequently use violence and racist name-calling and inconsistently may hold anti-racist beliefs whilst also being racist. Racism is recurrent and may be accepted by the young people as an inevitable part of life rather than as a deviant or pathological activity. Disabled minority ethnic children commonly experience both verbal and physical forms of racial abuse and harassment and dual heritage children can experience racial abuse, both verbal and physical, within their family settings, mostly by a white relative. Racism in middle class areas has not been examined in research (Barter, 1999).

A friend who was with Stephen Lawrence the night he was murdered, said he *was always walking around on his toes on the street just in case he needed to run as hard as he could.* He said he had always known racism … *if you were a black kid it was wise to be in your house if Millwall were playing at home (Brooks, 2006).*

Homophobic bullying

A survey of 1,145 young people found almost two-thirds of lesbian, gay and bisexual children in schools in the UK have suffered homophobic bullying. Almost all had experienced verbal bullying but 42% had been physically attacked, and 17% had received death threats (BBC, 2007a).

A study found around 40% of gay adults, bullied at school, said they had attempted suicide at least once and more than half had contemplated self-harm (BBC, 2000).

I did think about taking my own life when I was at school … but I didn't really have the bottle. It was just a build up of pressure from the constant name calling and harassment. They didn't know I was gay but they thought it might be [the case] because I was quite quiet. It happened every day more or less, getting called names and pushed around in the corridors. It did affect my school work because I had to have all my focus on just surviving rather than the lessons.

(Taylor, 2005)

On my way to class people kept tripping me up and calling me faggot … one of them punched me in the face and knocked me down. Then they all started kicking me. I reported it at school and the boy who punched me was suspended, but I didn't say what it was about … for the next two weeks I was beaten regularly. I didn't tell my parents.

(Valios, 2003, p33)

Domestic violence

Children experience emotional abuse through witnessing violence, which can occur in a number of ways beyond direct observation. Many children may be in close proximity and hear the abuse rather than see it directly and others may notice the injuries after the event. The impact of witnessing domestic violence is similar to post-traumatic stress disorder, and may include: numbness and detachment, disturbed sleep, nightmares, flashbacks, impaired concentration and memory and hyper vigilance, which may be short- or long-term. Children who see the effects of abuse of power in close relationships may find it difficult to develop reciprocal relationships with peers. In recognition of this impact, the Adoption and Children Act (2002) extended the definition of harm to include impairment suffered from seeing or hearing the ill treatment of others. Knowledge of family violence will indicate the need for a pre-birth child protection conference to ensure a protection plan is in place for the child at birth. The risk of violence can increase during pregnancy and childbirth.

Children exposed to domestic violence show higher rates of psychological problems compared to other children. They also experience disruption to their lives of having to leave their family, school and friendship networks. For black and minority ethnic children they may have to leave communities that protect them against racism and for disabled children there may disruption of their care packages (Humphreys, 2000, p3).

Children will develop strategies to survive the trauma experienced. They may show a range of emotional responses, including fear, helplessness, feeling responsible, anxiety, anger, confusion, shame, guilt, upset and sadness, as the following quotations illustrate.

I used to feel I was bleeding inside.

There was a lot of arguing but I didn't understand what was happening.

It was the worst part of my life constantly being shouted at, frightened, living in fear. You will never know what it is like thinking every day will be your last day.

I used to think it was my fault because I was in the middle of it a couple of times.

If I was brave enough I would have gone and told him to stop.

(Mullender, et al., 2003, pp6–43)

I used to try and protect the little ones. Sometimes I'd try and hide them. I'd lock us in a room. To this day I panic if I am in a small room or if I get locked in anywhere.

I had to leave my house, my school, my dad. Now I live in a room with my mum and hate it. Some days I just want to die.

(Barnardo's, 2002, pp6–19)

Parental alcohol and substance misuse

Living with two alcoholic parents for the amount of time I did was the most hellish experience that you could ever imagine.

(Bancroft, et al., 2004, p7)

I'm scared. I'm always scared in case he's sick in his sleep or something. So I'm always turning him over and all that.

(Bancroft, et al., 2004, p9)

Forrester and Harwin (2006) reported that parental substance misuse accounted for 62% of all children subject to care proceedings and 40% of those defined as needing protection. Cleaver, et al. (1999) suggest parental drug and alcohol misuse featured in about 20% of child protection referrals although for the majority their parenting responsibilities were met. Tunnard found that increasingly women are using drugs, many of whom, particularly in the case of heroin users, are parents and commonly use more than one substance (Tunnard, 2002, p7). Problematic alcohol misuse most significantly leads to a parent being emotionally unavailable, inconsistent and unpredictable. Bancroft noted that children slowly realise that their childhood is not 'normal' sometimes through hearing relatives talking about it, and experience the problem constantly throughout their lives (Bancroft, et al., 2004, p5).

Pre-birth it is important to follow *Working together* guidance and convene a child protection conference to examine the risk of harm to the baby (DfES, 2006, 5.140). The impact on the newborn baby of opiate withdrawal may lead to the baby being removed from their mother for medical attention over several weeks and this can interrupt the process by which the mother and the infant become attached. Medical advice not to breast feed can also hinder this process (Tunnard, 2002, p23). The baby will be needy and demanding of a parent. The baby may display symptoms such as irritability, hyperactivity, abnormal sensitivity to touch, shivering, fever, diarrhoea, vomiting and even convulsions. A vicious cycle may set in whereby the parent, finding it hard to cope, may resort to further substance misuse.

Both drugs and alcohol are mind-altering substances. The parent's behaviour may appear confusing and frightening to the child and the parent is not available to respond to the child's emotional reactions, leading the child to feel unsafe. In addition, for some parents the substance misuse is a response to childhood trauma and their own history of emotional abuse may impact on their parenting.

The parent's lifestyle may be chaotic and centred around their own needs and there may be numerous lengthy separations while the parent is in prison, hospital or residential treatment. Children may also witness frightening events such as police raids in their home and feel acute embarrassment and shame. *Stigma was a major concern. Children were left feeling worthless, ignored by parents whose main preoccupation was the pursuit of drugs or told to keep home life secret* (Tunnard, 2002, p31). Bancroft, et al., found that children of drug-misusing parents are often under pressure to keep the abuse secret because of the illegal nature of the activity. Some parents become emotionally reliant on their children and speak to them inappropriately about adult issues and others make threats such as of suicide or self-harm (2004, p12).

Institutional abuse

In 1991 the Pindown Report about abuse of children in residential care (Staffordshire ,1991) showed that some residential staff used solitary confinement and sensory deprivation to control children's behaviour. Children were kept in indoor clothing, given tedious tasks to complete and made to stay silent, amounting to a regime of sensory deprivation and torture which Latham, the manager of the homes, said was justified as a means of *re-establishing control of the young people* (Wolmar, 2000, p27). The regime was used on 132 children as young as 9 years, often for long periods of time. No prosecutions followed.

Survivors' accounts of their experience of Beck, manager of the Beeches children's home in Leicestershire, emphasise the emotional abuse used as part of an oppressive regime of institutional abuse:

> *He was a very snidey kind of person, he had a way of trying to slide into your personal fears ... he operated on a personal level, arm on shoulder, very touchy feely. He had a way of twisting words. He knew how to play with your emotions and your mind – a very sleazy kind of guy.*

> *Beck shouted at the children, reminded them of their worst experiences of their young lives. One girl in Beck's care, for instance was told, while being held on a child care worker's knee, that her mother had never wanted her. 'It must be something about you, she did not want you back,' the worker said.*

(D'Arcy and Gosling, 1998, pp47 and 83)

More recently, the social worker Simon Bellwood whistleblew on an oppressive regime in a Jersey secure unit where children as young as 11 years were routinely locked up in solitary confinement. The system, known as *Grand Prix,* was used on admission to the unit as well as subsequently as a form of control. One young man reported being in solitary for nine months (Syvret, 2008)

There is some concern that joint investigation by police and social workers of institutional abuse has substantially reduced in recent years and between 1997 and 2000 the Crown Prosecution Service rejected 79% of cases of institutional abuse referred by police (Utting, 2005, p141).

Grooming – emotional abuse of a child prior to sexual abuse

Child sex abusers will engage in an emotionally abusive process known as grooming. Sexual crime may not take place until the abuser is quite sure the child is completely entrapped and less likely to tell about the abuse. The grooming process will involve preying on already vulnerable children and slowly gaining their trust. They will use bribery and deceit, often steadily undermining the child's family, school and peer relationships and substituting activities within the abuser's network. The abuser will use distorted thinking to define abusive behaviour as pleasurable and acceptable, so that the child actually believes they are enjoying the activity or are responsible for it. Many victims report a sense of guilt and this is increased if they enjoyed the physical response and increased attention, were given financial rewards or introduced other children to the abuse. Children may mistakenly believe they could have stopped the abuse. The knowledge gained from the grooming process in sexual exploitation needs to be extended to child victims of gangs who are exploited for organised crime.

> *Being involved in a ring gives a sense of identity and belonging and there may be intense loyalty to the group and a fear of loss of what is perceived as emotional support. Because of the secrecy induced out of threats or fear there may be intense isolation from siblings, peer group and family. If the young person has turned to the abuser because of their own sense of privation, being victimised ... may lead to difficulties trusting.*

(Bentovim, in Bibby, 1996, p61)

A child sex abuser described to Wyre (1996) how he made *straight* kids *bent* and groomed a boy prior to committing sexual crimes. This starts with identifying a boy as a likely victim, finding out about the boy's school, home, hobbies, extent of parental influence and whether he is a loner.

> *The abuser will then decide when to make the first approach such as at the sweet shop and will casually offer to pay for some sweets. He meets the boy again and finds out how much pocket money the boy gets and undermines the parents. He finds out more about the boy's interests and what the parents do not let him do. He hopes he will be*

introduced to the parents and he may use a false name. He will begin to take the boy out and at some stage tells the boy he is a photographer and offers to take pictures of him. He leaves abusive images of children around for the boy to think this is acceptable and then offers money for a natural pose. The boy is trapped and another boy is introduced and mutual masturbation takes place followed by other sexual crime. The boy's name and address are circulated and the boy may be sexually exploited by many abusers.

(Wyre, in Bibby, 1996, p103)

RESEARCH SUMMARY

Some emotional effects of organised abuse are described by a group of boys who were friends attending the same school.

- *It changes your whole life and scars your brain.*
- *It has made it hard to go to sleep at night and I have nightmares.*
- *It makes us scared when we walk on our own.*
- *I think about it every day.*
- *Sometimes I worry about AIDS.*
- *We think about sex more.*
- *Not being able to trust anyone anymore.*
- *I imagine I see Mr B in the dark.*
- *Running about because I don't want to hear about it.*
- *I think I'm gay.*
- *I think I'm dirty.*
- *I would be afraid of telling a girlfriend what happened to me.*
- *I want to go to court.*
- *My brother doesn't want to sleep with me, he thinks I'm a pervert.*
- *I get reminded of him when I see fat men.*
- *I don't wear white pants because it reminds me of him.*
- *I just keep drinking out of people's glasses at parties and getting legless.*
- *He has taken my sex life away.*

(Peake, in Bibby, 1996, p136)

The social work role and emotional abuse

ACTIVITY 1.5

How do you think a social worker might emotionally abuse a child?

Comment

A study of serious case reviews concluded that high workloads, lack of supervision, poor inter-agency co-operation and wrangles about thresholds for intervention led to professional delays in response to children experiencing significant harm (Brandon et al., 2008, p87)

One serious form of emotional harm by social workers is when they do not listen to a child's disclosure about abuse. In her book *Trust no one*, Cooper writes about her attempts to inform social workers that she was experiencing a violent, abusive drug regime of control in the children's home and kept in isolation. Teresa realised that she was being repeatedly raped while drugged and almost unconscious. The social workers seemed to accept the abusive regime as normal and told her the psychiatrist was a wise person. Teresa was not heard or believed (Cooper, 2007).

Some children have expressed their views about social workers as follows:

> *The social workers I've had never tried to get to know me for who I am, never take their eyes off their paperwork and question how I'm doing. I've done what he wanted me to. I've listened to the meaningless terms and signed the documents.*

> *I hate it when social workers change often especially when there is one you like. I think I once had a social worker I'd never met!*

> *My social worker's six-weekly visits have turned into a 6-monthly phone discussion. He comes late but I'm grateful he has even shown up.*

> (Michael and Fernando, 2007, pp20–21)

Social workers may emotionally abuse children through their own actions or inactions by:

- labelling, stigmatising and pathologising children and mechanistic form-filling, therefore not hearing their views;
- not challenging social work systems which are not child-centred;
- exposing a child to information inappropriately at a conference or review such as details of sexual crime or parental criminal convictions;
- exposing a child to parental or professional conflict during a social work meeting;
- interviewing children about abuse allegations with the abusive parent present rendering them silent about what has happened. Rushton and Dance (2005) found that children were only spoken to alone in 13 out of 31 cases;
- making false promises to the child which cannot be met;
- breaching a child's right to privacy although sometimes information must be shared against the child's wishes in order to protect them;
- attending medical examinations of the child instead of waiting outside for the doctor to report back;
- making children wait to be seen or being late for appointments;
- not accurately recording information such as about the child's life and identity;
- not implementing procedures to protect the child or to respond to their needs;

- failing to communicate effectively with disabled children, which increases their vulnerability to abuse;

- using some practices designed to protect disabled children which in fact do the opposite such as forms of restraint or reduced physical contact.

Considering the significance of physical and behavioural indicators of emotional abuse

Social workers need to recognise signs which may indicate emotional abuse. Although some indicators will be definitive, most will need evaluation through child protection processes and multi-agency debate. On their own or grouped together they may be indicative.

Behavioural and psychological indicators

Sleep disturbance.

Physical symptoms without obvious cause.

Global developmental delay.

Behaviour extremes: overactive or withdrawn.

Lacking in confidence and self-worth.

Constantly trying to please adults.

Unusually fearful of criticism – may lead to lying.

Attempted suicide or self-harm.

Compulsive behaviours.

Eating disorders.

Limited attention span.

Socially isolated.

Over or underachieving.

Reluctance to go home.

Showing fear in presence of carer.

Shame and/or guilt.

School non-attendance.

Running away.

> *When we see children who are failing to thrive – and who are sometimes obese – and there is no medical cause, we find that there are often subtle, and sometimes not so subtle, interactions that take place between the carers and the child. When the parent calls the child 'greedy' or says he is 'like a pig' or steals food then our hearts sink because this tells us about how the child is viewed. The child who is emotionally starved will not grow and develop normally.*
>
> (Hobbs, in Vevers, 2008, pp16–17)

RESEARCH SUMMARY

Seven to fourteen per cent of adolescents will self-harm at some time in their life, and 20 to 45% of older adolescents report having had suicidal thoughts. About 30,000 children attend hospital each year as a result of overdosing, and prevalence is likely to be far more common, with four times the number of girls to boys and with Asian girls under-reporting. A study including 6,020 school children between 15 and 16 years found the most common forms were self-cutting and self-poisoning. Self-harm in boys and girls is associated with low self-esteem, pressure of school work, difficulties in peer relationships, sexual abuse, bullying, sexual orientation and having a friend who recently self-harmed; also anxiety and depression were more significant for girls. Motives included to cope with distress, get relief from a terrible state of mind, to find out whether someone loved them and to frighten someone. This study omitted children in pupil referral units, boarding schools or residential schools including those for disabled children (Hawton, et al., 2006).

(Usually it doesn't hurt) but I remember once I felt it hurt, but the physical pain sort of took over the emotional hurt, so I suppose it sort of counteracted it out.

(Spandler, 1996)

Responding to children's need for protection from emotional abuse at an early stage

Emotional abuse, like any other form of abuse, is damaging. Children will not realise what is happening to them emotionally and psychologically, and therefore may be unable to describe the abuse they are experiencing. It is the responsibility of adults to protect children, but personal safety training can give children enough information and understanding to be able to respond safely to an abusive or uncomfortable situation before it becomes serious. Emotionally abused children may internalise the abuse making it more difficult to disclose.

I was told every day that I was evil. I did not want anyone near me. I felt so disgusting and dirty. I didn't want to exist. It did not matter how much people said they hated me – I hated myself much much more. I absorbed the words and the voices around me all the time and held onto their every word ... I look back now and wish that I had told someone and maybe would have been fostered, anything would have been better than the nightmare at home.

(Fyfe, 2007, p212)

RESEARCH SUMMARY

Survivors have assisted understanding of children's experience of emotional abuse. Kent and Waller (1998) interviewed over 200 women to evaluate whether they felt ridiculed, insulted or disliked by their parents, if they were often the target of their parents' anger, if their parents shouted at them particularly when they least expected it, and whether they felt unfairly blamed. They found that high scores in these responses were linked with levels of anxiety and depression in adulthood.

Every Child Matters protocol (DfES, 2003) – an analysis

The Common Assessment Framework (CAF and e-CAF)

This protocol has been developed to assist the early reporting of concerns about children's wellbeing. The threshold for completing this is lower than that of abuse, with the aim of supporting early intervention. However, the process involved may lead to confusion about defining and reporting abuse in an effective way to protect a child.

The *Leaflet for children and young people* (DCSF, 2008c) states that the CAF involves *listening to you to find out what help you need, and what is working well in your life*. Practitioners in a wide range of agencies referring to children's services will be required to complete a Common Assessment Framework form, which is available from the Every Child Matters website. It is a generic assessment to address child concerns such as about their health and welfare, behaviour, progress in learning or any other aspect of their wellbeing. A CAF is designed to help to identify needs and to obtain services to meet these needs.

It is very important that the completion of this document does not delay referral of a child protection matter and the protocol must not replace a telephone call to a children's social worker, the police child abuse investigation team, or a named safeguarding doctor, nurse or teacher, in order to seek advice. The form requires comment on the child's development, the parents and carers and the family and environmental factors. Some practitioners will not feel sufficiently competent or trained to make an assessment of some of the complex issues included in the form, such as the child's fine and gross motor skills, parental mental health, disability or abusive behaviour. Each professional has a specialist area of expertise which might be within health services, education, police or social work. It is dangerous to make an assessment on an area of practice that is not your specialism. However, the form does not divide into particular specialist contributions. For instance, not every practitioner is trained to interview a child. Think about the validity of a housing or immigration officer assessing a child's sexual behaviour or criminality or a police officer assessing a child's disability or performance in class.

ACTIVITY 1.6

As a social worker referring a case of emotional abuse to children's services, or a children's worker receiving the referral, how would you define some of the following areas for assessment as outlined in the CAF? Think about your approach to the factor as either a child concern or an indictor of child protection.

Negative friendships

Sense of belonging

Anti-social behaviour in area

Effects of hardship

Sleeping arrangements

Absent parents

Abusive behaviour

Stimulating family environment

Engagement with services

Safe and healthy environment

Level of adult interest in education

Experiences of discrimination

Comment

Each of these statements is open to wide interpretation and judgement. For example, *Negative friendships* might mean a child having a friend who smokes cigarettes or a child being groomed for abuse. *Abusive behaviour* might mean a child calling another child names or a child witnessing domestic violence. *Sleeping arrangements* might mean the family are too poor to buy a new cot for a baby or a family where an abusive mother sleeps with an adolescent boy. *Absent parents* might mean a caring father who works abroad or a parent who is emotionally absent through substance misuse.

To complete a CAF effectively, social workers would need to obtain specialist opinion from teachers and educational staff, health professionals (general practitioner, health visitor, school nurse, dentist, optician, hospital staff, etc.), police (domestic violence teams, police child abuse investigation teams, the Multi Agency Public Protection arrangements, etc.), youth offending teams, mental health teams, probation services, housing, environmental health and other relevant sources. Not to do so would risk making serious errors of fact. Other staff completing the CAF may only be able to complete a small part of the form from their particular viewpoint.

The social work response

ACTIVITY 1.7

Deciding to what extent a child is at risk is based on professional judgement and the application of knowledge to individual cases. Here are four cases to which the authors have had to provide a protective social work response. Make a decision about which of the categories of response apply to these cases.

A The child is not thought to be at any risk of child abuse.

B There is concern about emotional abuse of a child.

C There is suspicion of likely or actual significant harm to a child (s47 enquiry, CA 1989).

D A section 47 (CA 1989) investigation of child abuse is indicated.

E Immediate action to protect. Evidence of actual significant harm and/or criminal offence.

1. *Three children regularly witness their father's violence towards their mother. One child is beginning to be violent towards other children in his school.*

2. *One child aged 7 years, of a sibling group of four sisters, is picked on by her mother, called stupid, fat and dirty and wets herself during the day at school and during the night.*

3. *A child in foster care is regularly disappointed because his parents promise to visit him but do not arrive at the agreed times.*

4. *A girl is the main carer for a parent with multiple sclerosis and is regularly absent from school.*

ACTIVITY 1.7 *continued*

In relation to these cases:

- *Think about what criteria you would use in making judgements about emotional abuse.*

- *Think about what may influence your selection of these criteria.*

- *How do you differentiate between situations that include risk but do not reach a threshold of actual dangerousness?*

- *At what stage is professional intervention indicated?*

- *What level of intervention is appropriate?*

- *When does emotional abuse of a child become a crime?*

- *When is immediate action needed to protect the child from harm?*

- *Are there other children who may be being abused?*

Comment

Perhaps you based your decision-making on your:

- experience as a child, as a parent or from your observation of and interaction with children;

- professional experience of a particular case;

- cultural or religious perspective of family life;

- knowledge of the law and child protection policy and practice guidance;

- knowledge of lessons learnt from child abuse inquiries and serious case reviews;

- understanding of the concept of emotional abuse;

- your knowledge base of the subject from research findings;

- media reporting.

Each of the above cases did require a proactive social work intervention ranging from family support to section 47 (CA 1989) enquiries and investigation to legal safeguards. The detailed analysis below will assist your later reflection on your decisions in the above scenarios.

Making judgements when a child is emotionally abused whose main carer has mental health problems

About one in four adults will experience a mental health problem during their lifetime, in which time at least a quarter will be parents. Considering moderate to severe mental health problems, this amounts to 1.7 million adults and 2.5 million children in the UK (Tunnard, 2004, p10). However, not all children whose parents have mental health problems will inevitably experience difficulties.

> *Some people experience problems with their mental functioning to a degree that this impacts upon, or threatens to impact upon, their ability to protect and care for their children. Sometimes these problems are the result of symptoms which are generally recognised and defined by a particular psychiatric label such as 'depression', 'schizophrenia' or 'personality disorder'.*
>
> (Beckett, 2007, p132)

However, Reder, et al. (1993) point out that the parental behaviour is more important to assess than the diagnosis or psychiatric label. In *Lost innocents,* out of 35 perpetrators of fatal child abuse, 40% had been currently suffering an active mental health problem and in about half of these cases there was also substance misuse. Sometimes there was no clear psychiatric diagnosis despite a history of violent threats to others and irrational behaviour and in such cases the threat to the child was missed by professionals.

In 2007, Vivian Gamor killed both her son and daughter while thinking she was the daughter of God and that her children were not really hers. After she was discharged from psychiatric hospital, children's services had allowed her to have unsupervised contact with the children (Brody, 2007). Falkov found, in a survey of 100 child deaths, that 32 contained clear evidence of parental mental ill health and the most common method of killing was asphyxia followed by use of implements and poisoning (Falkov, 1995, p8). There is no doubt that some children will be at serious risk of harm if the parent has mental health problems and the assessment of risk by professionals in both children's and mental health services is critical in such cases. Deaths from child abuse typically occur when the parent is in an acute phase of an illness and children are most vulnerable when mental ill health, abuse of drugs or alcohol coexist with domestic violence (Cleaver, et al., 1999).

In some cases the parent is fabricating illness in the child in order to gain attention for themselves. Children may not be aware that they are victims of abuse and parents can be very skilled in teaching their children to present *a rosy picture to the external world whilst they were being subjected to extensive physical and emotional abuse at home* (DCFS, 2008a, p11). Children become confused about their state of health and may express suicidal thoughts as a result of their despair. Children may feel anger at their betrayal by their parents and lack trust in anyone caring for them, especially medical professionals. Many child victims suffer long-term impairment of their physical, psychological and emotional development (DCFS, 2008a, p10).

The extent of abuse of children when a parent or carer has mental health problems

- Between 20% and 50% of adults known to mental health services have children although very little is known about the extent and nature of children's needs, including their need for safety and protection (Falkov, 1998, p11).

- A quarter of all adults referred for in-patient hospital treatment are likely to have dependent children (Tunnard, 2004, p9).

- Mental illness of a parent was recorded in 13% of families referred to local authority with child protection concerns (Bell, et al., 1995).

- Among children on the child protection register, 31% included children whose parents had mental health problems (Glaser and Prior, 1997).

- About one-third of children referred to child and adult mental health services (CAMHS) had parents with a significant mental health problem (Dover, et al., 1994).

- Between 6,000 and 17,000 children in the UK care for a parent who has mental ill health (Green, 2002).

- About a third of children living with a parent with mental health problems will themselves develop significant psychological problems, and a further third will develop less severe emotional difficulties (Falkov, 1998, p28).

- Women with very young children are at particular risk of developing depression (Falkov, 1998, p35).

- The prevalence of non-psychotic major depressive disorders in mothers during the early weeks after childbirth is 10–15%, with an estimated 50% of these going undetected. Episodes last usually two to six months with some depressive symptoms common up to a year after delivery. The risk is increased if there is conflict in the parental relationship and when there is an absence of support. A history of depression is a risk factor (Falkov, 1998, p43).

- Parents with mental health problems are at high risk of living in poverty and have low employment rates. The isolation of living with a mental health problem is compounded by the fear and experiences of racial discrimination and stigma (Tunnard, 2004, p17).

The law

Government should make sure that children and young people are protected from abuse, neglect and being harmed by the people looking after them (United Nations, 1989, Article 19). The Children Acts 1989 and 2004 state that significant harm includes emotional harm, including for example impairment suffered from seeing or hearing the ill-treatment of another. Development includes emotional development and health, which includes mental health. Ill-treatment includes sexual abuse and forms of ill-treatment which are non-physical (DfES, 2006, 1.25).

Where workers have concerns that children may be being emotionally abused, this should prompt a child protection plan that includes assessing the nature of the abuse, introducing time-limited and specific interventions, assessing the family's response to the process and its outcome. This determines intervention, the need for statutory involvement and at the same time provides a basis for any legal action (Glaser and Prior, 2002). The threshold for recognition of forms of abuse such as emotional abuse is often overly high compared with other forms of abuse such as physical and sexual. *I have encountered situations where a multitude of support services have been provided but where these serve to mask the absence of a viable parent–child relationship with a result that children are left for long periods in harmful emotional environments* (Beckett, 2007, p139). Because emotional harm is not readily visible, it is important not to deny children protection through legal safeguards although evidencing emotional harm may take time and detailed collation of evidence and expert opinion.

The jigsaw of information – working together to protect children

ACTIVITY 1.8

Think about the indicators of emotional abuse which apply in the following account of Jason, Ben and Lucy, which is based on an actual case, and evaluate the mother's ability to be a proactive protector of the children. Consider the difference early intervention might have made in the life of this family and possible interventions that might have led to a different outcome. A snapshot of a detailed chronology based on the children's services case file is included as an example of good practice and to illustrate the value of this form of analysis particularly where there are clusters of indicators requiring professional judgements over time.

CASE STUDY

Jason

Jason is born. He has a sister Lucy aged 7 years and brother Ben aged 6 years. The mother is a survivor of child abuse and domestic violence. Both children had a child protection plan in place because of neglect, which was concluded when the abusive father left the household, four months prior to Jason's birth. Subsequently the family were defined as needing family support under section 17 (CA 1989). The family are white, UK.

Jason is 10 months. He has reached his developmental milestones. The social worker is concerned about neglect of both Ben and Lucy because the mother is depressed and relies on Lucy to care for Jason and Ben. Lucy has to do household chores and make meals. Lucy is rude to the social worker and tells her to go away. The school inform the social worker that Lucy cannot concentrate in class and is often late or absent. She told the teacher that she is tired because Jason keeps her up at night and she is worried about leaving him during the day. The social worker is concerned that all three children are emotionally and physically neglected and that Lucy has inappropriate caring responsibilities.

Jason is 17 months. Jason becomes distraught when he cannot get his own way. He hits his mother, Lucy and Ben. The mother is loving to the children but does not provide adequate supervision as she spends much time isolated in her bedroom. Jason and Ben are made the subject of a child protection plan because of neglect. Lucy is made the subject of a child protection plan for emotional abuse because she has not been learning at school, has been running away and coming home late. She refuses to follow school rules by being late for class, not doing class work, hiding in the toilets and constantly challenging the school staff. The mother asks her doctor for help with her parenting and a referral is made to CAMHS. The child protection plan includes a parenting assessment by CAMHS, social work contact with the children and the GP to respond to the mother's mental health needs. All professionals have responsibilities to monitor the children's safety and wellbeing.

Jason is 20 months. He presents to hospital with burns from touching an unguarded electric fire, caused when unsupervised while in Lucy's care. Ben witnessed the incident. Jason is removed from the family and placed in foster care under section 20 (CA 1989), i.e. accommodated with the mother's agreement. The mother is taking medication for depression which makes her drowsy. Lucy misses Jason and wants him to come back home. She blames herself for the accident and starts to cut her arms. The CAMHS report that Lucy has told the play therapist that she wants to die. Ben is withdrawn and has limited interaction with the teachers, finds it hard to make friends and reacts anxiously to any suggestions of change. A review conference is held, which confirms the decision to place Jason in foster care and for Lucy and Ben to remain the subject of child protection plans.

Jason is 21 months. He is reaching his developmental milestones. The foster carer reports that he is a happy child who has settled well into the placement. He is no longer the subject of a child protection plan. The family receive support from CAMHS. Lucy runs away, misses her CAMHS appointment. She is excluded from school because of carrying a small knife. Ben is compliant at school but is noticed to be avoiding contact with his sister. He is often found crying.

Jason is 26 months. He is accident-prone and very active. He has no interest in play and a referral is made to a nursery and to CAMHS. The foster carer finds him difficult to care for as he fights with her own children and will not settle at night. There are ongoing concerns with the mother's parenting as CAMHS report that she is not learning from the parenting programme and seems more depressed. Lucy and Ben remain subject to the child protection plan and have regular contact with Jason. Lucy has one-to-one support in school and Ben seems to avoid attention.

Jason is 36 months. Jason is overly demanding of attention. He kicks and bites. He has sleeping difficulties and problems settling into nursery. He has no awareness of danger and ran into the road. The foster carer asks for Jason to be moved to a different placement. Lucy is diagnosed with attention deficit hyperactivity disorder (ADHD) and has additional learning support. Ben also has learning support, particularly around social skills and self-esteem. The mother continues to co-operate with children's services but has not progressed in her parenting skills.

Jason is 38 months. In his new placement, where he is the only child, the foster carer says that he bites himself, bangs his head, is hyperactive, unable to understand boundaries, refuses to eat, finds it difficult to play with other children, and has no awareness of strangers.

Chronology – children's service file Jason 20-21 months

Date time	Source	Key events	Other information	Health issues	Carer's view	Child's view	Professional comment
12 May	Paediatric report	Admission to hospital	The mother brought Jason to Accident and Emergency Unit with siblings Ben and Lucy at 9 pm on 11 May. Lucy told the paediatrician that it was her fault for not watching Jason properly because she was watching TV. Ben sat quietly with a computer game. Children are the subject of a child protection plan for neglect.	Accidental burn to the palm of his right hand caused by touching the electric fire. The injury was consistent with the accounts given by mother, Jason and Lucy. Jason was in his pyjamas, and seemed well nourished but needed a bath before settling for the night on the ward.	*I asked Lucy to watch Jason as I was having a short sleep. He's always getting into trouble, touches everything – he's hyper.*	Jason said *Lucy went away and I hurt myself. Mummy put my hand under the cold water and it hurt a lot.*	Paediatrician concerned at Jason's attitude in turning to Lucy for comfort rather than his mother, who appeared unresponsive to his emotional needs.
12 May	T/C to health visitor		Health visitor has received report from health visitor liaison officer at the hospital. She knows the family well. Will attend hospital today.	Jason has reached his developmental milestones. Mother is depressed and the GP has prescribed some medication. She tries very hard with the children and accepts the health visitor's help and advice.	Mother thinks Jason is over active and difficult to control.		The health visitor thinks that the child protection plan needs to be reviewed in the light of this accidental injury. The mother is a caring woman who has had a difficult life.
12 May	Discussion with police Child abuse investigation team	Strategy (s47, CA 1989) discussion	Police agree single investigation as paediatrician has confirmed the account given of the injury. Checks show no recent police involvement.				Police agree to attend the child protection strategy meeting to take place tomorrow.
12 May	T/C to Lucy's and Ben's school named safeguarding teacher		Teacher reports concern at Lucy's repeated absences and lateness. Her behaviour is challenging. Ben in contrast is a withdrawn, quiet and isolated child.	School nurse noticed Lucy had small abrasions on her arms and had referred this to the GP.		Lucy told the school nurse that she hurts herself.	

Date time	Source	Key events	Other information	Health issues	Carer's view	Child's view	Professional comment
			The head teacher has sent the mother a letter asking her to come in to talk things over.				
12 May	Interview with mother		Mother agrees for social worker to interview Lucy on her own tomorrow and is informed about the strategy meeting. Jason to remain in hospital until outcome of strategy meeting. Mother agrees for paediatrician to see Lucy and Ben.	Mother takes anti-depressants prescribed by the GP. She says they make her drowsy.	Mother says she finds it difficult to cope with Jason's behaviour. She says Lucy is a big help. Since her partner left, she feels very alone and has no one to talk to. She has no family support and feels isolated. She does talk to the health visitor.		
13 May 9.00 am		Strategy (s47, CA 1989) meeting held at the hospital	Attended by: health visitor, social worker, school nurse, teacher, social work team manager (chair), paediatrician, ward nurse, police officer. All professionals share their information and concerns about the care and safety of all three children with regard to neglect and emotional abuse. Health visitor contributes GP information. Referral by GP to CAMHS to be progressed swiftly. Referral to community mental health team for mental health assessment to include an assessment of mother's ability to parent.	Jason's development is progressing well as he is meeting all his developmental milestones and there are no health concerns. Jason will be discharged home today as hand is healing. Ward nurse says Jason settled well on the ward and the family have visited and brought him his toys. He has told the nurse that Lucy is his 'Mum'. He showed no distress on separation from his family.	Social worker feeds back from interview of mother.	School nurse reports Lucy's views and paediatrician reports Jason's account of the injury.	

1

Date time	Source	Key events	Other information	Health issues	Carer's view	Child's view	Professional comment
			Social worker to interview Lucy, Ben and Jason today. Paediatrician to see Lucy and Ben today. Decision about whether it is safe for Jason to return home to be made following interviews and paediatric assessments. Hospital staff anxious to discharge him quickly. Lucy needs, as a young carer, to be assessed. Review strategy meeting to be held at 4 p.m. A review child protection conference has already been organised for a week's time.				

Comment

The indicators you might have considered include the following:

Jason: hyperactive, head-banging, biting, hitting, eating disorder, lacks boundaries, no sense of danger, no concept of strangers, sleeping difficulties, poor social skills, accident-prone, no ability to play, when separated from family he showed no sign of distress, separation from the family, lack of family and community network of support, no positive relationship with father.

Lucy: running away, poor attention span at school, self-harm, inappropriate caring responsibilities for siblings and mother, separated from Jason, lack of family and community network of support, no positive relationship with father.

Ben: withdrawn, isolated, lack of emotional response in the crisis, separated from Jason, lack of family and community network of support, no positive relationship with father.

Mother: depressed and self-preoccupied, lacks parenting skills, unrealistic expectations of all children but especially Lucy, false compliance with professionals, history of domestic violence, unresolved issue relating to history of childhood abuse, unsafe home environment, lack of boundaries for children, isolated from family and community networks.

Father: absent from the children's lives, history of violence.

> ### Other relevant questions
> *Why was it only when Jason became physically harmed that action was taken to protect him?*
> *On what basis was the decision made not to accommodate Ben and Lucy as well?*
> *What action might have been taken earlier to protect the children from emotional abuse?*
> *What are the implications for each family member of removing Jason from the household?*
> *What might adult psychiatric services have contributed to the protection of the children?*

Consider how the children's emotional needs were defined and what might the implications be of such labelling.

When Jason was born, children's planning for the family was defined under section 17 (CA 1989) which involved providing support. The children required services as children in need. The abusive father had left the household. However, when Jason reached 10 months the concerns about the care of his siblings were escalating. At this point section 47 enquiries (CA 1989) should have begun. These enquiries in relation to emotional abuse allegations will commonly be agreed by the police to be carried out by children's services as a single agency. It is still very important to feed back the outcome to the police child abuse investigation team and to convene a strategy meeting to allow for full professional debate. This strategy meeting would be attended by the social worker, health and education professionals as well as the police. There would have been debate about the level of risk of significant harm posed to the children as a result of the mother's depression. All information, past and current, would have been collated and this would have included a mental health assessment of the mother's ability to parent. Collating information systematically over time is especially relevant to emotional abuse.

The child protection conference, the key forum for multi-agency risk assessment, was attended by the mother and provided an evaluation of the outcome of the section 47 (CA 1989) enquiries as well as writing the child protection plan for each child. As Lucy is a young carer she has a right to an assessment. The Carers Recognition and Services Act 1995 covers children and young people who provide or intend to provide a substantial amount of care on a regular basis. The Carers and Disabled Children Act 2000 extended assessment and services for young people with care responsibilities at home.

While some laws apply to the protection and wellbeing of the children, the mother would be assessed using the Care Programme Approach, which was introduced in 1991 and updated in 1999. This procedure provides a structure of assessment, review and key working for those with mental health problems. The parallel processes in adult and children's services must be well co-ordinated to ensure that the needs of both the mother and the children are met. This is best achieved by the adult workers attending the children's strategy meetings and child protection conferences and the children's workers attending the Care Programme Approach meetings. There must be multi-agency paths of communication through key workers in both sectors and clear allocation of tasks.

It is professionally dangerous if either sector becomes defensive about their practice; for instance if an adult mental health worker considers their service user to be unfairly treated if their ability to care for a child is called into question. Any conflict between the agencies must be resolved at managerial level with issues taken to the Local Safeguarding Children Board for resolution.

The structural division of adult and children's services can be a block to good practice. In his study of serious case reviews where a parent had mental ill health, Falkov (1995) found that the professional focus was usually on the needs of the adult rather than the vulnerability of the child and that mental health professionals were generally unaware of the needs of their client's dependent children. Children's workers may have been informed of a mental health diagnosis but have little understanding of the meaning of this for the safety of children. Falkov recommended that adult mental health professionals should assess the effect of the parental mental health problems on children and inform children's workers as to the level of risk. It is only through multi-agency working that the risk of harm can be fully evaluated. Assessment processes with a tick-box approach are particularly unhelpful because of the wide range of difference in parenting ability from case to case and changing abilities over time and depending on a range of complex factors.

The child's view

Children describe feelings of anxiety, guilt, fear and uncertainty, embarrassment, concern about their own mental health, confusion, anger, isolation, worry, depression and frustration (Falkov, 1998, p123).

> *People cuss us for having a mad mother all the time.*
>
> (Falkov, 1998, p125)

> *When someone is ill it can be scary. When it is someone you love it can be very, very upsetting and maybe you feel very sad inside. If it's the person who looks after you most you may feel angry with them. You may feel so cross that you want to shout or stamp or break something. If it is your Mummy or Daddy or another special person in your life you may even think they don't love you any more. You may even think it's all your fault.*
>
> (Falkov, 1998, p183)

Speaking about the impact of their illness on their child, mothers said:

> *They have seen the effects of me cutting. How I have harmed myself – left mental scars. Mainly on the oldest one. He doesn't talk about it. Even when he was in care he used to come home from school to see how I was. Felt responsible for me. He grew up too soon.*
>
> *At first it was scaring my kids – they didn't know what I would say next.*
>
> (Stanley, et al., 2003, p64)

Social workers should ask the following questions when assessing the risk to a child of a parent with mental health problems:

How much does the child know about their parent's illness? What do they think caused the illness?

How does the child conceptualise the illness? Does the child see the illness as e.g. the parent being difficult, that they have something wrong with their brain or as a response to stress?

How does the child feel about their situation? Is the child confused, worried or frightened?

How does the child perceive their relationship and their parent's feelings about them? Has the relationship changed because of the illness? Has the parental illness affected the child's other relationships such as with friends and extended family?

What are the consequences of the illness? Who cares for the child when the parent is ill? Is the child exposed to the parent during acute phases of the mental illness? Does the parent's illness affect the child's role within the home, school or with regard to social activities?

What, if any, are the responsibilities of the child when their parent is mentally ill? Is the role the same as when the parent is well? Is the child a carer?

How does the child think about the future? Does the child see the parent getting better or worse? Does the child worry about getting ill themselves? Does the child worry about who will look after her/him?

(Falkov, 1998, pp156–7)

Is the parent proactively protective?

Howe (2005, p191) states that when a parent is emotionally unavailable it can be devastating for children who rely on their carers for encouragement, feedback and comfort. The effect of symptoms may lead to poor concentration and poor parental care exposing the child to danger or extreme parental exhaustion and inability to perform the usual responsibilities such as taking a child to school or preparing meals. A parent with depression may provide unpredictable responses to a child who does not understand what to expect from their parent. A parent may be emotionally unavailable through delusional ideas, obsessions or irrational anxieties or even from the effects of psychiatric medication (Beckett, 2007, p133). A parent's delusions may not affect parenting but could be terrifying for a child if for example the parent thinks their food is poisoned, or the child is evil or hates them.

The impact on the child will vary according to the severity and duration of the mental health problem. A child whose parent is repeatedly hospitalised and who is exposed to traumatic emergency situations will be affected not only through the absence of the parent but also through the chaotic and unpredictable home environment. This may also lead to changes of roles within the family, separation and exposure to parental relationship difficulties. *Some children's concerns were linked to interrupted routines – they worried about having no-one to look after them and about where they would live* (Tunnard, 2004, p21). Few children could visit their parent in hospital because the setting was often thought to be unsuitable or there were no family facilities. Even if the mental health problem is episodic, the impact on the child's emotional wellbeing may be serious because the child struggles with uncertainty and fear about the future and even in remission a parent may not be able to fully respond to the child's needs.

Evaluating the safeguards in place for the child with a parent who has mental health problems

Support must be in place for the parent and the child. Professionals who took part in a survey by Stanley, et al. (2003) identified that where abuse is suspected, parents with mental health problems most needed support with child care, practical and financial help, development of parenting skills, emotional support and help for their mental health problems, particularly talking therapies. They want professionals to be respectful of them. Strengthening informal friendships was of particular assistance as were home visits which assisted parenting skills. For children subject to a child protection plan, evaluation will take place through the child protection review conferences and the work of the core group of key professionals. If a case is not defined as section 47 (CA 1989) then the professional network must liaise closely across adult and children's services and reach agreement about what would need to happen to trigger the implementation of child protection procedures. An adult may be identified within the child's world such as a teacher or nursery worker who the child knows they can talk to about problems as they arise. This is to provide effective monitoring of the child's safety and to ensure swift reporting of any changes in parental behaviour or attitude to the child.

Investigating allegations about a child emotionally abused whose main carer has mental health problems – deciding the threshold for intervention

ACTIVITY *1.9*

The following case studies are designed to aid a questioning approach to the process of protecting children. They usually progress from referral to investigation and action to protect. When reading the case studies, structure your thinking and questioning around the points listed in Chapter 1 but do not be limited by this list. Continue to add your own questions and to consider the implications of these in each case.

CASE STUDY

• A mother tells a midwife she does not feel affection for her newly born child, thinks she cannot be a parent, feels depressed, has a sense of failure and did not expect to feel this way.

• Both parents had wanted and prepared for the baby. The mother is a child psychotherapist.

• There are no concerns about the baby's physical health.

• The father, an IT consultant, is supportive and anxious, and is willing to seek professional advice.

• Maternal grandparents move in with the family. Paternal grandparents also assist in the baby's and mother's care and reassure the midwife that they can cope as a family.

• Midwife refers to the Community Mental Health Team (CMHT).

• Mother has no history of depression, has good family support and two weeks after childbirth, is reluctantly continuing to breastfeed and is not caring for herself. She feels guilty about her lack of affection for the baby.

• CMHT social worker (SW) makes a referral to children's services and realises that the mother has very high expectations of herself as a new parent.

• In the first six weeks after childbirth the mother attends an outpatient appointment. The psychiatrist diagnoses postnatal depression and because of breastfeeding no medication is prescribed.

Child emotionally abused and not thought to be at risk of abuse

• Children's services SW closes the case.

• Family continue to gain support from the health visitor and GP.

• Health visitor confirms she has observed the mother being more attentive to the baby.

• Mother continues to attend the support group and the NCT meetings.

• Review meeting is held in one month.

• Maternal grandparents have returned to their home but continue to visit each weekend.

• Father has taken extended leave to be the prime carer.

• Mother slowly improves, engages more with the baby, attends outpatient appointments with the CMHT and a local support group and finds the NCT visitor very helpful.

• Children's services SW completes an initial assessment and with mother's agreement checks with the midwife, general practitioner (GP) and CMHT. The SW convenes a professionals' meeting to assess the risk of emotional harm to the baby, which is attended by the midwife, health visitor, GP, adult psychiatrist and mental health SW.

• Given the family support network, mother's willingness to work with professionals and her lack of a history of depression, the assessment concludes that this is a child in need, s17 (CA 1989) case.

• Decisions are made to review in one month; refer the family to a local support group and the National Childbirth Trust (NCT); complete a core assessment and CMHT continue to monitor.

35

CASE STUDY

• The girl continues to be monitored at school and through child- in-need review meetings.

• Her parents take advice not to enter her for the independent school examination which is in line with the girl's wishes to go to the local secondary school and remain in her friendship group. She no longer attends the eating disorder clinic but continues to see the psychotherapist at CAMHS.

• The family attend family therapy.

• A 10-year-old girl, preparing for secondary school entrance examinations, is noticed by her teacher to have lost weight and appears anxious. The girl tells the teacher that if she is successful her parents will buy her a horse.

• Her parents want her to go to an independent school. They tell the teacher their daughter is not very intelligent and needs extra homework and that she has private tuition most evenings.

• The teacher discusses her concerns with the named safeguarding teacher.

• The safeguarding teacher has also had reports from another teacher regarding how thin the girl has become and had seen her throw away a packed lunch.

• The form tutor speaks with the girl about nutrition and she denies there is a problem, saying she just wants to lose weight to look like a well known celebrity. The teacher explains her worries to the girl and the school decide to speak with the parents.

• The family attend CAMHS and begin to work towards more realistic expectations of their daughter and begin to respond to their daughter's individual needs and to accept the difference between her and their sons.

• Her weight is regularly monitored and she maintains, but does not increase, her body weight.

• The mother accesses adult psychiatric services for help in managing her symptoms (OCD) and to understand the impact of her behaviour on the daughter.

Concern about a child emotionally abused

• The parents attend a meeting at the school, agree their daughter has lost weight and say this is because she has had a sudden growth spurt. They say she eats a balanced diet at home, is naturally slim and is working very hard for her examinations. They describe her as a worrier and that she finds school work difficult.

• The teacher expresses her concerns and tells the parents she will refer to children's services.

• The parents are very upset about this.

• Children's services SW arranges a home visit with the parents, and sees the girl separately. The SW obtains permission for checks to be made and completes an initial assessment.

• Checks confirm no known concerns about two older brothers who board at a public school. The SW notes that the parents have very high expectations of their daughter. The girl tells the SW she is anxious about failing her exams and disappointing her family and that her mother is constantly cleaning and preoccupied with hygiene. The girl is worried that if she fails her exams her mother will become ill. The SW refers the family to the child and adolescent mental health services (CAMHS). The GP confirms that the mother has accessed help in the past for an obsessive compulsive disorder (OCD) from adult psychiatry. The SW contacts adult psychiatry who agree to liaise with CAMHS. Children's services define the case as child in need, s17 (CA 1989).

• The family accept services and although the girl has experienced emotional abuse she responds to the services offered. A strategy meeting s47 (CA 1989) will be convened if she continues to lose weight. A core assessment will be completed.

• The school nurse contacts the general practitioner (GP) after seeing the girl at school fall asleep in the classroom and because of the concerns about weight loss.

• The GP invites the parents to the surgery. The mother and daughter attend. The father is working away from home. The girl tells the GP that she has stopped eating. The GP is concerned about emotional abuse and makes a referral to children's services and to the eating disorder clinic.

• A careful decision must be made at a further stage as to whether or when to confront the mother with the medical facts while ensuring the child's safety.

• A 7-year-old boy, after arriving at a new school, tells his teacher he has haemophilia and wears a bracelet to alert others to this.

• The teacher is surprised not to have been informed about this before and discusses it with the school nurse.

• School nurse contacts the boy's mother who confirms he has haemophilia and provides emergency contact details.

• The mother gives permission to check any records, tells the nurse she is a single parent, that the boy is her only child and that he is not in contact with his father.

• The boy tells the school nurse he might bleed to death if he falls over in the playground or during sports activities.

• A follow up strategy meeting, at the hospital, agrees ongoing s47 (CA 1989) enquiries, with very clear timescales, to ensure the child protection plan is carried out.

• A SW is allocated and is to set up meetings with the mother. The strategy meeting is to be reviewed in one month. The SW, school and paediatrician agree to develop a supportive relationship with the boy and the mother. Agreement is not to proceed to a child protection conference as it is important not to alert the mother at this stage. The child is discharged home.

Suspicion of actual or likely significant harm to a child emotionally abused. S47 enquiry

• After a fall in the playground, where the boy sustains a leg injury, the school calls an ambulance which takes the boy to the local hospital accident and emergency department. The mother attends after being informed by the school and confirms that the boy has haemophilia.

• The doctor carries out blood tests which show no evidence of haemophilia and subsequently contacts the child protection paediatrician.

• The boy tells the doctor he is frightened he is going to die.

• The wound is dressed, the boy is admitted to the children's ward for further tests and a second medical opinion is sought.

• The paediatrician is concerned about fabricated illness, makes a referral to children's services but does not inform the boy's mother that this is happening because doing so may increase risk of harm to the child.

• Children's services convene a strategy meeting for the following day, at the hospital, attended by the police CAIT, child protection paediatrician, GP, school nurse, children's services solicitor, social worker (SW) and team manager.

• Further tests confirm that there are no clinical signs of haemophilia, the wound is healing well, the mother has visited regularly and appears very caring in her interactions with the boy.

• The meeting agree there is evidence of emotional abuse, that the boy needs to be reassured about his health and this must be balanced with the need to work with the mother. The paediatrician explains that the child is not at risk of physical harm apart from through unnecessary medical interventions.

• Paediatrician and SW to speak to the mother together to explore why she believes the child has haemophilia but without alerting the mother, at this stage, to their knowledge that this is not the case as this may increase risk of harm to the child. SW to make checks with previous schools, GPs and hospitals. The child to remain in hospital while checks are made to gain a clear understanding of the mother's beliefs.

• A strategy discussion takes place between children's services and the police Child Abuse Investigation Team (CAIT) who agree a single agency response as part of s47 (CA 1989) enquiries.

CASE STUDY

• At the six-month review the children are no longer thought to be in need of a child protection plan, their mother is an effective protector and the agencies continue to work together, monitoring the father's mental health and the impact on the family.

• The case is now defined as s17 (CA 1989) as children in need rather than in need of protection.

• A mother tells a children's services duty social worker (SW) that her two children can't sleep as their father is up all night making noise, disturbing the family, cooking food and leaving the gas on.

• The SW arranges to speak with the children and with the mother's agreement makes checks.

• Checks show a police 78 report (a child coming to police attention) was received by children's services two months ago as the father threatened to set fire to the shed. The police had calmed the family and took no further action.

• Housing reported the family had recently been burgled because the father had left the front door open; neighbours were also complaining about noise at night.

• The GP is concerned about the father who is known to adult psychiatry due to a diagnosis of bipolar affective disorder (a mood disturbance with episodes of mania and depression). He often refuses to take medication and will not meet with the community psychiatric nurse (CPN).

• The school report both children aged 6 and 8 years are often exhausted, unable to concentrate and recently they have been late for school and absent a few times without explanation.

• A review conference takes place after three months and both children are reported to be more settled at school and no longer tired. Their attendance has improved although they miss occasional days through visiting their father.

• The child protection plan remains in place to be reviewed in six months to ensure that the protection of the children is sustained and to have a clear structure for multi-agency planning and co-ordination.

S47 investigation of a child emotionally abused

• The SW interviews both children at school individually. They speak of continual noise through the night, their father plays loud music, sings whilst he cooks and expects them to join in. They are very embarrassed because the neighbours are also disturbed by the noise. The children are worried about their mother who tries to care for him as he is mentally ill and she has to stay up to watch him all night. They want him to be a nice dad again and get help.

• The SW makes referral to the police CAIT, conducts a s47 (CA 1989) strategy discussion, agrees a strategy meeting and informs the mother of this.

• Following discharge from hospital, the CPN visits the father in his new home and he attends out-patient appointments regularly.

• The CMHT liaise with children's services to monitor and agree the nature and frequency of contact between the father and the children. This is ongoing as the father's mental health is unpredictable.

• The mother and children are no longer exposed to this distress but when he is well they maintain contact.

• A child protection, conference is convened. The core assessment is completed. Child protection plans for both children include a referral to CAMHS for therapy and a core group is agreed including the children's SW, mother, mental health SW, GP and teacher.

• The Multi Agency Public Protection panel (MAPPA) monitor the risk posed by the father to his family and within the community.

• The housing representative on the MAPPA agrees to seek to rehouse the father within the locality, in line with the mother and children's wishes to continue to have contact with him.

• The SW team manager chairs the strategy meeting which is attended by the police CAIT, school housing, GP and community mental health team (CMHT) SW.

• They agree the children are experiencing emotional abuse as a result of their father's mental ill health. An urgent mental health assessment is planned and a core assessment.

• With treatment, the father's mental health improves and the children enjoy positive contact visits with him.

• The children's SW attends Care Programme Approach (CPA) meetings and the mental health SW attends the core group to implement the decisions of the child protection conference. With good liaison between these services the children's safety is assured.

• The mother is recognised to be a proactive protector of the children.

• The mental health assesment confirms the mother and children's account of father's behaviour. He is not taking medication and is compulsorily admitted to a psychiatric unit under Section 2 of the Mental Health Act 1983.

• The mother tells the SW she wishes to leave her husband. For the first time in months the mother and children have a good night's sleep.

CASE STUDY

• After an assessment of the parental uncle and aunt the boy is placed in their care.

• The boy continues to have periods of depression but is no longer suicidal. He has begun to engage more in school work and activities. He begins to enjoy childhood games and activities that he had not previously experienced.

• Contact with his mother continues to be well managed by his carers.

• Children's services receive a referral from a family therapist in CAMHS about a boy of 14 years who is threatening to commit suicide.

• The therapist asks for a meeting because of concerns about emotional abuse and that the boy will carry out the threat as he has thought carefully about it, and planned how he will carry it out by jumping off the top of the multi-storey car park.

• The therapist arranges a mental health assessment with a psychiatrist and admission to an adolescent psychiatric unit.

• The boy is in foster care under s20 (CA 1989) because his mother is an in-patient in a psychiatric hospital as she experiences paranoia and delusions. She has attempted suicide in the past. The boy's father died four years ago from a heroin overdose.

• The conference takes place and agrees a child proection plan. A Care Order (s31 CA 1989) is to be applied for and a permanent placement sought either with the boy's foster carer or paternal uncle and aunt.

• All contact with his mother is now well managed and supervised.

• CAMHS provide psychotherapeutic support for the boy to help him understand the impact on his childhood of his mother's delusional beliefs, as well as to talk about the death of his father.

• The school provide one-to-one learning support and a strategy to assist the boy's sense of self-esteem and increase his confidence in his abilities.

Immediate action to protect a child emotionally abused

• Following a strategy discussion and agreement with the police CAIT to proceed single agency children's services arrange a professionals' meeting with the adolescent mental health key worker, children's services SW, CAMHS and school.

• The foster carer has been concerned for some time about the boy as he is very quiet and stays in his room for long periods of time. He makes regular visits to his mother at the hospital and to his home and his mother sometimes arrives to see him unannounced as she is worried he is smoking cannabis and taking heroin. The foster carer does not think this is true, as there is no evidence.

• The boy is extremely anxious about his mother, who has a difficult and long history of repeated hospital admissions and chaotic patterns of caring for him leading to repeated emergency foster care placements.

• The school is worried about the deterioration of his school work.

• CAMHS say he is preoccupied with his father's death, believing his mother will also die and sees no point in living.

• The SW makes checks with the police who report they have had several nuisance calls from the boy's mother saying he is using heroin.

• The SW identifies a paternal uncle and aunt who are willing to consider caring for the boy on a permanent basis and applying for a residence order (CA 1989).

• The hospital report that the boy is still very depressed and self-harming.

• Safe and supervised contact arrangements with his mother are facilitated by the SW and co-ordinated with adult psychiatric services.

• Contact with the boy's paternal uncle and aunt is also facilitated. Children's services attend Care Programme Approach (CPA) meetings for the boy's mother.

• A child protection conference is convened to take place in 15 days.

Now return to the four cases in Activity 1.7 and try constructing some diagrams for these. What factors might make these children more or less safe?

C H A P T E R   S U M M A R Y

A range of types of emotional abuse, including in the context of institutional abuse and the grooming process of child abusers, are examined in this chapter, demonstrating that intervention to protect children from emotional harm may be more difficult to evidence than other forms of child abuse. Survivors' accounts provide essential knowledge about the experience and impact of this form of child abuse and their inclusion informs anti-oppressive practice. A case study about a child who is removed from his family and placed in foster care is presented. A chronology, as a systematic collation of information, is included. This is a tool for use in practice and to further analytical skills. The CAF as an ECM protocol is explored in the context of early intervention. A detailed study of social work intervention responding to the protection needs of a child who lives with a parent with mental health problems concludes the chapter.

FURTHER READING

Brandon, M, Belderson, P, Warren, C, Howe, D, Gardner, R, Dodsworth, J and Black, J (2008) *Analysing child deaths and serious injury through abuse and neglect: what can we learn? A biennial analysis of serious case reviews 2003–5.* London: DCSF.
This important and critical report provides an overview analysis of serious case reviews (cases of child death or serious injury through abuse) and draws out themes and trends to inform both policy and practice.

Doyle, C (2003) A framework for assessing emotional abuse. In Calder, M and Hackett, S (eds) *Assessment in child care.* Lyme Regis: Russell House.
This chapter provides a framework for assessing emotional abuse.

Fyfe, M (ed.) (2007) *Survivors' stories.* Hitchin: 11th Commandment Publishing.
This book provides examples of physical, emotional and sexual abuse and neglect from the perspectives of six survivors.

O'Hagan, K (2006) *Identifying emotional and psychological abuse: a guide for childcare professionals.* Buckingham: Open University Press.
This book provides an understanding of concepts and practice in order for social workers and other professionals to identify and respond to emotional and psychological child abuse.

WEBSITES

www.careleavers.com
Care Leavers Association is a non-profit-making organisation run by and for care leavers. It provides support and advice for care leavers and conducts research.

www.edauk.com
Eating Disorders Association/Beat is a charity providing advice and information to people with eating disorders and their families.

www.newpin.org.uk
Newpin is a charity which helps parents under stress. It has a network of local centres offering a range of services for parents and children.

www.parentlineplus.org.uk
Parentline plus provides information, advice and training and a free and confidential helpline for parents and carers.

www.selfharm.org.uk
A resource for young people who self-harm and those working with them.

www.victoria-climbie-inquiry.org.uk
The Victoria Climbié inquiry report and transcripts of evidence and seminars.

www.youngcarers.net
A website providing online support and advice for young carers.

www.youngminds.org.uk
Promotes child and adolescent mental health and mental health services. It is also involved in consultancy work, training, and producing information leaflets.

Chapter 2
Sexual abuse

ACHIEVING A SOCIAL WORK DEGREE

This chapter will help you to meet the following National Occupational Standards (see the Skills for Care website, www.skillsforcare.org.uk).

Key Role 1: Prepare for, and work with individuals, families, carers, groups and communities to assess their needs and circumstances.
- Assess needs and options to recommend a course of action.

Key Role 2: Plan, carry out, review and evaluate social work practice, with individuals, families, carers, groups and communities and other professionals.
- Respond to crisis situations.
- Address behaviour which presents a risk to individuals, families, carers, groups and communities.

Key Role 3: Support individuals to represent their needs, views and circumstances.
- Prepare for, and participate in decision-making forums.

Key Role 4: Manage risk to individuals, families, carers, groups, communities, self and colleagues.

Key Role 5: Manage and be accountable, with supervision and support, for your own social work practice within your organisation.
- Manage, present and share records and reports.
- Work within multi-disciplinary and multi-organisational teams, networks and systems.

Key Role 6: Demonstrate professional competence in social work practice.
- Research, analyse, evaluate and use current knowledge of best social work practice.
- Manage complex ethical issues, dilemmas and conflicts.

It will also introduce you to the following academic standards as set out in the social work subject benchmark statements See
www.qaa.ac.uk/academicinfrastructure/benchmark/honours/socialpolicy.asp#1

5.1.2 The service delivery context
- The significance of legislative and legal frameworks and service delivery standards.

5.1.4 Social work theory
- Research-based concepts and critical explanations from social work theory and other disciplines that contribute to the knowledge base of social work.

5.5 Problem-solving skills

5.5.2 Gathering information.

5.5.3 Analysis and synthesis.

5.5.4 Intervention and evaluation.

5.6 Communication skills
- listen actively to others, engage appropriately with the life experiences of service users, understand accurately their viewpoint and overcome personal prejudices to respond appropriately to a range of complex personal and interpersonal situations;
- follow and develop an argument and evaluate the viewpoints of, and evidence presented by, others.

5.7 Skills in working with others
- consult actively with others, including service users, who hold relevant information or expertise;
- act with others to increase social justice by identifying and responding to prejudice, institutional discrimination and structural inequality;
- challenge others when necessary, in ways that are most likely to produce positive outcomes.

7.3 Knowledge and understanding
- an ability to use research and enquiry techniques, to collect, analyse and interpret relevant information;
- a developed capacity for critical evaluation of knowledge and evidence from a range of sources.

Introduction

Q: How did the abuse make you feel?

A: I was never a child, always grown up. I always felt an outsider.

(Nelson, 2008, p2)

She remembered being made to sit in the living room and that there was a man on the bed with her mother. 'What I remember, this man's penis is all white, that's what I remember, really white and when he … er … you know, stuff comes, I just couldn't understand it, where it came from, you know, or what it was.' She moved her nose as if she was smelling something nasty. 'There was this smell, horrible, nasty like … But it was horrible, and then I was on the bed, and then … they turned on me … I was so frightened because before it, or later she says if I ever told anything I would be taken away and locked up. You know I told you about the sentry box on the Tyne Bridge? That's where she said I would go. And she said nobody would believe me. And anyway, I think I must have thought it was my fault. I had done wrong and was being punished. I … I …' She cried and cried. 'I felt so … so dirty.'

(Sereny, 1999, p335)

This chapter focuses on the protection of children from sexual abuse. It begins by looking at definitions and moves on to consider the knowledge required to make professional judgements. The complexities of this form of abuse will be examined to support an informed approach to individual children's circumstances. Research into children's views and survivor perspectives provides a basis for sound decision-making. Four case studies provide opportunity for further application of knowledge to practice. The chapter concludes with case examples of child sexual abuse involving child sexual exploitation, which will take the reader through an investigative process escalated through five levels of social work intervention to support in-depth analysis.

Definitions of sexual abuse

Sexual abuse *involves forcing or enticing a child or young person to take part in sexual activities, including prostitution, whether or not the child is aware of what is happening. The activities may involve physical contact, including penetrative (e.g. rape, buggery or oral sex) or non-penetrative acts. They may include non-contact activities, such as involving children in looking at, or in the production of, sexual online images, watching sexual activities, or encouraging children to behave in sexually inappropriate ways.*

(DfES, 2006, 1.32)

Commercial sexual exploitation *includes the prostitution of children and young people, the production, sale and marketing and possession of pornographic material involving children, the distribution of pornographic pictures of children over the internet, trafficking in children and sex tourism involving children. All commercial sexual exploitation of children is utterly unacceptable, exposes children to great danger and takes away their childhood.*

(Department of Health, 2001, 1.5)

Organised abuse *involves one or more abusers and a number of children. The abusers concerned may be acting in concert to abuse children, sometimes acting in isolation, or may be using an institutional framework or position of authority to recruit children for abuse.*

(DfES, 2006, 6.7)

Trafficking *involves the exploitation of children through force, coercion, threat and the use of deception and human rights abuses such as debt bondage and deprivation of liberty. Exploitation includes prostitution and other types of sexual exploitation. It includes the movement of people across borders and within borders.*

(DfES, 2006, 11.76)

Learning about sexual abuse

ACTIVITY **2.1**

Child sexual abuse is essentially abuse of power. What do you think unequal power between a child and adult means in the context of child sexual abuse?

Comment

Children, boys and girls, are sexually abused at all ages and within all cultures and religions by adult men and women child sex abusers as well as by young people themselves. Children are abused by those who are supposed to protect and nurture them within their families and care systems as well as by strangers. Disabled children are particularly vulnerable, as are children with few protective adults in their lives such as those who are homeless, unaccompanied minors or refugees. Child sexual abuse does not occur only in low-income families. A *growing number of studies have reported weak or no association between measures of family socio-economic status and risks of child sexual abuse* (Fergusson and Mullen, 1999, pp37–8). Child sex abusers have no limits in the crimes they perpetrate on children for sexual gratification and/or financial gain. Children have become commodities in a global sexual industry, the scale of which remains largely unknown. Sexual crime against children is now recorded and distributed across the world and law enforcement systems struggle to protect child victims.

Sexual abuse includes a spectrum of abuse including contact and non-contact and varying levels of physical and psychological violence. A child may be exposed to sexual language, suggestions, abusive images or to seeing or hearing sexual acts. An adult may deliberately expose their genitalia to a child, make a child touch the adult's genitalia or touch a child's genitalia. Sexual crime may be described to a child as a game. The abuse might include an adult putting objects or body parts (e.g. fingers, tongue, penis) inside the vagina, mouth or anus of a child or inappropriately watching a child undress or use the toilet or bathroom and taking photographs or filming a child in sexual poses or acts. The adult might orally, vaginally or anally rape a child or exploit a child through prostitution. Sometimes sexual abuse is perpetrated with the use of animals or by groups of adults. Abusers may coerce children to abuse other children. The abuse may include *physical violence such as beatings, burning, scalding, torture with electrodes, use of weapons, tying of wrists or ankles, isolation, drugging and deprivation of sleep food or drink* (Nelson, 2008, p9).

Children are abused by people who call themselves paedophiles, which literally means 'lovers of children', some of whom justify their crimes asserting that it is a child's right to have sexual relations with adults. Child sex abusers will *suggest that the taboo against child sexual abuse is part of ageism* (Wyre, 1996, p91). It is therefore very important to use the term *child sex abuser* rather than the abuser's term of *paedophile* which, although in common usage, does not reflect the horror of the crimes committed.

Child sexual abuse may be opportunistic or highly planned. There are reports of children sexually abused by religious leaders, sports coaches, music tutors, teachers, social workers, youth workers, lawyers, judges and politicians. Much sexual abuse takes place within large institutions and organisations where the power of the abuser is amplified through control of the child isolated from their protective family and community network.

The sexual abuse of children is one of the most difficult forms of child abuse to contemplate. A referral to children's services may be based on a child or adult statement, observation of a child's behaviour, medical, forensic or photographic evidence, adult witness testimony, police or other professional intelligence or an abuser's admission. Whatever the route of referral, social workers must work jointly with police to make sense of the information and to proactively investigate further. The Cleveland Inquiry examined professional intervention in child sexual abuse cases (Butler-Sloss, 1988) and Campbell, in her critique, comments that *one of the things at stake in Cleveland was the status of the suspicions, worries, snippets of evidence and their different status within different professions* (1988, p207). Collating small clues and working together with other professionals to recognise and evaluate their significance is key to protecting children but also to identifying and bringing perpetrators to justice.

Unless the professional focus is also on detailed analysis of information about the known or alleged perpetrator, children will not gain protection. The likelihood is that there may be other child victims of an abuser and therefore protecting one child may well mean protecting many. Seeking justice by gaining the prosecution and conviction of the abuser is very important for a child's healing. In Nelson's study of female survivors of child sexual abuse, she said *the survivors felt strongly that they should have been protected at an early age and that the perpetrators should have faced justice many years before* (Nelson, 2001, p111).

Social workers must have knowledge about the vast extent of sexual abuse of children if they are to suspend disbelief, retain an open mind to the possibility of sexual harm to children and act to protect.

Some facts about sexual abuse

- In 2007 there were 2,500 children who were the subject of a child protection plan, under the category of sexual abuse. This was a reduction since 2000, when there were 5,100 (DCSF, 2007).

- Cawson, et al. (2000, p85) reported that, in their study, 18% of children had experienced sexual abuse; 1% by a parent or carer before the age of 16 years, 2% with another family member, 11% by people known but unrelated to them and 4% by an adult stranger or someone they had just met.

- ChildLine figures for 2004–5 revealed that 11% of calls about sexual abuse concerned abuse by female abusers. Sexual abuse by women was referred by 3% of over 6,000 girls (2% about their mothers) and 35% of over 2,000 boys (17% about their mothers) (Ford, 2006, p10).

- More than 8 out of 10 children know their abuser, who are mainly family, friends, neighbours and babysitters. About a third are from professional backgrounds (Cawson, et al., 2000, p86). A police report found that the majority of online child abusers are predominantly white males age 36 to 45 years. Almost all have no sexual abuse convictions and those recently caught include many professionals including many whose victims are their own children (Townsend, 2008).

- Over a quarter of all rapes recorded by police are committed against children under 16 years old (Harris and Grace, 1999, p7).

- According to one study, 80% of sexual assaults against children take place in the home of the child or the abuser (Grubin, 1998, p15).

- 1 in 9 young people are sexually assaulted when they run away from home (Biehal, et al., 2003, p32).

- About 29,000 individuals were registered as sex offenders in England and Wales in 2006. This figure includes offences against both adults and children. The Sex Offender Register came into force in 1997 but those convicted before 1997 are not required to register (Batty, 2006).

- As much as 95% of sexual crime against children goes unreported (National Criminal Intelligence Service, 2003).

- One in four child sex abusers who had abused children outside the family were reconvicted within six years (Hood, et al., 2002, p1).

- Some 43% of children thought it was easier to tell a friend about sexual abuse but often through fear or uncertainty children instruct their friends not to tell anyone else (Nelson, 2008, p26).

- Fewer than 1 in 50 sexual offences against children result in a criminal conviction (Stuart and Baines, 2004). In particular, children under five, disabled children and children for whom English is not their first language are often excluded from the legal processes, and *the most vulnerable children are almost totally failed by the criminal justice system* (Utting, 2005, p140, and 1997, 20.10).

The Western Isles (Eilean Siar)

During October 2003, 13 adults were arrested in Scotland and England in relation to alleged abuse of three girls in one family. Following statements by the mother and children, nine adults were subsequently charged with rape, indecent practices and making indecent computer images of children. However, there was no trial and there were no convictions. An inspection into the care and protection of the three children reported that over 100 professionals had been involved with the family and that there had been 29 conferences, 21 statutory reviews and 24 children's hearings about child maltreatment. The inspection concluded that the three children had experienced severe and prolonged physical, sexual and emotional abuse by their father and his friends. It stated that the social workers, managers and health professionals had failed to protect the children and should have acted sooner. The children had made repeated allegations and statements about sexual assaults by a number of adults There were no sexual boundaries in the home, a long history of health and behavioural indicators of sexual abuse and sexualised behaviour to children and adults, signs of emotional distress, conclusive medical evidence in one case and the mother, although co-operative with professionals, was not protective of her children.

The inspectors stated that professional interventions were flawed because the overwhelming emphasis of professional work was on helping the parents rather than protecting the needs and rights of the children, whose accounts, unlike those of the adults, went unheard. Professionals were often overoptimistic about the capacity of members of the family to overcome their abusive childhoods, manage their own mental and physical health problems, cope with poverty and poor housing and nurture and protect their children. The extent of the resources being provided and the willingness of parents to co-operate with workers did not in themselves indicate improved parenting and a family support model of social work took the place of protecting the children. The children were disadvantaged by the absence of debate among the professionals who conscientiously logged and shared concerns about incidents indicating sexual, physical, emotional abuse and neglect but did not make decisions to remove the children quickly enough (SWIA, 2005).

Disabled children and sexual abuse

Disabled children are 3.1 times more likely to be sexually abused than non-disabled children, although there are variations in the prevalence figures (Sullivan and Knutson, 2000a, p1257).

Welbourne, et al. (1983) interviewed 39 women visually impaired in childhood and found that more than 50% had been sexually abused. Chamberlain, et al. (1984) said that in their study, 25 of 87 young women with learning disabilities had been sexually abused. Sullivan, et al. (1987) found between 11% and 63% of the deaf students in residential and mainstream schools they interviewed had been sexually abused. Far more children were sexually abused when placed away from home in residential schools as opposed to those

RESEARCH SUMMARY *continued*

in mainstream education. Ammerman, et al. (1989) examined the medical, psychiatric, social work and nursing records of 148 children in the US who had multiple disabilities and found that 39% of the children had experienced all forms of abuse and of these 36% had been sexually abused. In the UK, Kennedy's (1989) survey of 156 teachers and social workers for deaf children found that, for 120 children sexual abuse was either confirmed or suspected and discovery of abuse was more likely to come from professionals noticing physical signs, behaviour or mood changes than from the child communicating explicitly about abuse.

ACTIVITY 2.2

Why do you think disabled children are particularly vulnerable to sexual abuse?

Comment

You might have considered the following.

- Multiple disabilities are considered to increase the risk of different types of abuse (Sobsey, 1994).

- It is commonly believed that sexual abuse of disabled children is less harmful than of a non-disabled child (NSPCC, 2003). Also, it is wrongly assumed that children who do not have an understanding of the abuse are less distressed by it (Marchant, 1991; Kennedy and Kelly, 1992).

- Signs and symptoms of sexual abuse, such as masturbation, are often wrongly attributed to the disability (Sobsey, 1994; Kennedy, 1996).

- Children with physical and learning disabilities are not regarded as credible witnesses in child sexual abuse cases, sometimes resulting in an unwillingness to pursue investigations or conduct visually recorded interviews (McCarthy, 1996).

- Abusers may think it is safer to abuse disabled children, particular those children who may be unable to escape or communicate their experiences easily (Kennedy, 1996). www.howitis.org.uk is a very useful website with a wealth of images to assist communication.

- As discrimination and unequal power relationships are an integral part of disabled children's experiences, sexual abuse and maltreatment are experienced more readily. Black disabled children experience multiple marginalisation. Professional responses to them are shaped by the negative stereotypes of disability, ethnicity and sexual abuse (Bernard, 1999). It is sometimes falsely assumed that child sex abusers will not be attracted to disabled children (Morris, 1993).

- It may be more difficult for disabled children to gain support and healing following sexual abuse, because of the isolation created by the disability (Cross, 1998).

- Much attention has been given to abuse of children by staff, but sexual abuse by fellow residents is also an important issue: the most severely disabled children, the children with the most complex needs and therefore greatest dependency on others for care have the greatest vulnerability (Paul and Cawson, 2002, p274).

Sexual abuse of children at different ages

Social workers sometimes think that children are more vulnerable to abuse at particular ages. At what age do you think children are more likely to experience sexual abuse?

Comment

There is no doubt that children may suffer sexual abuse at any age from birth to age 18 years. An NSPCC study found that in 67% of cases child sexual abuse began before the age of 11 years (NSPCC, 1997a). In 2006, the Internet Watch Foundation reported a fourfold increase in abusive images depicting the most severe forms of sexual abuse of children, with 91% of the children being under the age of 12 years (www.iwf.org.uk/media/news.196.htm). Of all rapes recorded by police, 27% were of children under 16 years, and children under the age of 12 were most likely to have reported rape by someone they knew well (Harris and Grace, 1999, p7). The age at which children are most likely to be subject to a child protection plan for child sexual abuse is between 10 and 15 years (Corby, 2006, p148).

There is an underestimation of sexual crime against young children because of reduced ability to report (Hewitt, 1998). An exception was during the Cleveland Inquiry when the average age of the 121 children in the paediatrician's caseload was between 6 and 7 years (Campbell, 1988, p207).

Although children as young as 3 years may be formally interviewed, one in three children who report sexual abuse are under 8 years and these cases rarely proceed to criminal proceedings and are therefore absent from crime statistics (Utting, 1997, p191). Because few cases reach court, little is known about the extent of abuse to younger children and also sexually abusive behaviour by them (Vizard, 2006, p2). Child sex abusers sometimes target children of specific ages and may also focus on those who are younger and less able to report. A police report found an increasing number of online images, many showing the rape of babies and children too young to disclose the abuse (Townsend, 2008).

Thinking about types of sexual abuse

Information and communication technology (ICT) based forms of abuse

A police report identified as many as 1 in 6 children as victims of online abuse (Townsend, 2008). It is known that over 100,000 websites contain abusive images of children (www.ceop.gov.uk). Every image found is a crime against a child and yet few of these child victims are ever identified or gain protection. In the UK, 7,200 men identified through Operation Ore, accessed a gateway to abusive images of children. Few of these led to section 47 (CA 1989) investigations and a total of 13,000 pictures of children only led to 25 having been identified in the UK (*Sunday Herald*, 2003). Another internet site called Wonderland contained 740,000 abusive images of children: 1,200 children were identified but only 18 were discovered, of whom three were in the UK (Downey, 2002).

Online abuse cannot be separated from offline abuse. Research shows that in the UK over 8 million children access the internet and about 1 in 12 of these have met someone offline who they initially had contact with online (LSCB, 2007, 5.23.15). The existence of a visual record, on a mobile phone or the internet, of the incident adds to the impact of the abuse.

An indecent image of a child is a visual record of the sexual abuse of a child by adults, other children or involving animals. Information about the law relating to the production, distribution and possession of abusive images of children can be accessed through the website www.iwf.org.uk/police/page.22.htm.

A referral may come to the attention of a social worker because:

- the images of a child being abused have been distributed on the internet or mobile phone;
- an adult (or child) may be using images to prepare the child to accept the abuse as if it was normal;
- an adult or child may be viewing and downloading sexual abuse images – children tend to be less inhibited while on the internet.

Following referral to the police, advice will be sought from the Child Exploitation and Online Protection Centre (CEOP) and it may be necessary to begin not just a section 47 (CA 1989) investigation but also organised abuse procedures (DfES, 2006, 6.7, and Home Office, and Department of Health, 2002). Checks must be made about any children to whom the person has access. CEOP provides a 24-hour online facility for reporting this crime. LSCBs have an important role in campaigning and raising awareness in the community about safe access to the internet and of the dangers and risks to children.

MySpace, a social networking website, located profiles of 29,000 known sex offenders and removed them from the site. However, the Home Office did not agree to disclose lists of child sex offenders to the website because the information is not public as it is in America (Richards, 2007). The Internet Watch Foundation states that it processes about 1,000 reports a month and about 80% of the images are of girls, but only 1% of abusive websites are now hosted in the UK (www.iwf.org.uk/media/news.179.htm). Renold, et al.,(2003) address patterns of production, distribution and consumption and the effect upon the child victims.

Forced marriage

A forced marriage is a marriage conducted, under duress, without the full consent of both parties, for which there can be no religious or cultural justification. It can involve emotional coercion, forced imprisonment, violence and in the extreme, murder. In 2008 the Home Office estimated that about 3,000 women every year are subjected to forced marriage in the UK and men can also be victims of this form of abuse (Khanum, 2008). In 2004, the government's definition of domestic violence was extended to include forced marriage and honour crimes perpetrated by extended family members as well as intimate partners. The NSPCC recommend a new criminal offence be introduced for forcing some-one into marriage (NSPCC, 2008).

Forced marriage may involve the child being taken out of the country for the ceremony, is likely to involve non-consensual and/or under-age sex and refusal to go through with the forced marriage is sometimes linked to honour killings. Forced marriages have involved children from South Asia, East Asia, the Middle East, Europe and Africa. Reasons given to justify forced marriage include the alleviation of poverty through strengthening family connections in order to ensure that property and wealth remain within the family. It may be to repay a debt, appease an aggrieved family member or as an attempt to control a woman or man's sexuality and sexual orientation. Disabled children are sometimes forced into marriage based on the assumption that they will not easily find a marriage partner and to remove the responsibility of caring from the family (LSCB, 2007, 5.15).

Intervention must be that of risk assessment using child protection procedures. The child's need for immediate protection must be considered, in which case the police child abuse investigation team must be involved in section 47 (CA 1989) procedures and protection planning and they may wish to pursue criminal proceedings. Mediation with the family in these cases may place the child at risk of harm and even of being murdered. Discreet means should be made of contacting the child and seeing them on their own in a secure and safe place and records must be kept confidentially and restricted to named staff. Members of the local community should not be used as interpreters and community leaders should not be used in mediation processes.

The young person may be advised to contact the Community Liaison Unit at the Foreign and Commonwealth Office for advice, and social workers should refer all cases to this government department and detailed practice guidance is available (Foreign and Commonwealth Office, 2004). Local Safeguarding Children Boards should promote awareness within the community about the illegality and abusiveness of forced marriage.

Children trafficked for sexual exploitation

Mende Nazer, a child slave in London until 2002, describes speaking with other girls who had also been abducted by traffickers from their families in Sudan. *Many of them had been raped, even some as young as nine or ten years old. They were in so much pain. But we were all too young to really understand what had happened.* The pain was also extreme because all the girls had experienced female genital mutilation (Nazer and Lewis, 2004).

RESEARCH SUMMARY

A report by CEOP urged Local Safeguarding Children Boards to respond to, record and analyse child trafficking cases in their localities. The study identified 330 children suspected or confirmed as trafficked in an 18-month period and of these 183 had gone missing from children's services care. Forty-four source countries were identified. In particular, 88% of Chinese children had gone missing. The top source countries were China, Nigeria, Vietnam, Afghanistan and Eritrea. Thirty-six African girls were known or suspected as being trafficked for sexual exploitation, the youngest being 12 years old. Fourteen girls from Eastern Europe and Russia were trafficked for sexual exploitation and reported being befriended by a 'boyfriend' before being trafficked. Nine main airports were also identified (CEOP, 2007).

51

The Sexual Offences Act 2003 introduced offences including trafficking into, out of or within the UK for any form of sexual offence. Intervention in trafficking cases requires joint investigation between social workers and police using section 47 (CA 1989) and organised abuse procedures (DfES, 2006, 11.76-80) and also following the Home Office guidance (2008).

Children abused through child sex tourism

Child sex tourists are largely male and usually travel from rich to less developed countries to commit sexual crimes against children. The majority of offenders do not have an exclusive sexual inclination for children but are opportunistic given the anonymity of being a tourist. The use of technology, cheaper air travel, the opening up of borders and visa-free travel all make it more difficult to monitor, prevent and prosecute those responsible (Bokhari, 2008, p22).

Since the Sexual Offences Act 2003, British citizens who commit offences against children overseas can now be prosecuted in the UK. All registered sex offenders have to notify police if they leave the UK for three or more days. This is a loophole in the law as the offenders can offend within the three-day period. Only five orders preventing child sex abusers foreign travel have been implemented between 2004 and 2007.

British child sex offenders travel mainly to Eastern Europe (particularly the Czech Republic and Rumania), South East Asia (particularly Thailand, Cambodia, the Phillipines and Vietnam), India (Goa), Brazil, Cuba, Spain and Greece, where there is often a lower legal age of consent. The organisation ECPAT has devised a Code of Conduct for the protection of children from sexual exploitation in travel and tourism available on the website **www.thecode.org**.

Historic abuse

Out of 2,000 child sexual abuse investigations in London each year, over 30% are historic. This means that adults disclose a history of being sexually abused as a child (Spindler and Fairhurst, 2005). This is not unusual as the majority of disclosures about child sexual abuse are by adults. Investigations are conducted by police officers in child abuse investigation teams because the abuser may still continue to abuse children and, with sufficient evidence, criminal prosecution may be possible. If the alleged abuser has been identified then a referral must be made to children's services. If the abuse relates to alleged abuse within an institution such as a children's residential home or a boarding school, then organised abuse procedures must be followed (DfES, 2006, 6.7; Home Office, 2002).

It is very traumatic for an adult to disclose child sexual abuse and social workers should provide access to counselling and survivors' groups. Social workers should inform the police at the earliest opportunity and alert their safeguarding manager. It may be necessary to co-ordinate the investigation beyond authority boundaries if other alleged victims and/or perpetrators are identified. Responsibility for the investigation is with the police team which covers the area where the alleged abuse is said to have taken place.

There have been many historic abuse investigations. The Waterhouse Report (2000) reported at least 651 children who had been abused in homes in North Wales by child sex abusers often acting within organised networks. At least 12 suicides of former residents were linked to the abuse they had suffered (Colton, et al., 2002, p543). One of the first investigations was at Castle Hill school in Shropshire where 57 victims made allegations against the manager of the home, Ralph Morris, who was jailed for 12 years (Brannan, et al., 1993). Wolmar says *no one has collected any statistics on the extent or timing of the scandals. There has been no attempt to standardise the investigation methods or to analyse the fundamental cause of the scandals* (2000, p18).

RESEARCH SUMMARY

Colton, et al. (2002) interviewed 22 male and two female survivors of institutional abuse who had been contacted by police and social workers as part of a proactive investigation and found that:

- *financial compensation was not the prime motivation leading to disclosure;*
- *long-term emotional pain caused by abuse left some with a strong desire to see the abusers brought to account in order to protect future victims;*
- *some had not reported the abuse because they thought they would not be believed;*
- *some had reported the abuse before but no action had resulted;*
- *some felt abuse carried a stigma and they spoke of feeling dirty and of personal shame and guilt;*
- *some feared loss of face with their families and friends and were concerned at the so-called cycle of abuse which resulted in victims/survivors being perceived as potential child abusers;*
- *if they hadn't been contacted, many might well not have come forward with evidence, and some felt very anxious and ambivalent about contact with the investigation;*
- *some continued because of a strong wish to protect future children and also to rid themselves of unresolved past trauma and they wished to seek justice;*
- *some spoke of the high price they had already paid for the abuse suffered, including loss of jobs, relationships, family breakdown, mental health problems, depression, self-harm, drug addiction and some in prison, as well as physical ailments;*
- *the fact that the perpetrator had been brought to justice was clearly a palliative for some but didn't automatically lead to a sense of justice;*
- *some felt that the investigation itself, driven by the requirements of the criminal justice system, was stressful and impacted on their relationships and psychiatric problems;*
- *some would have preferred an apology from the local authority even more than a prosecution or financial compensation;*
- *some later wanted to access their social service files to reflect and learn more about what had happened to them as children;*
- *support was difficult to access for those in prison;*
- *therapeutic support was seen to be valuable, as were survivors' groups.*

Ritual abuse

In 1994 the Metropolitan Police Ritual Abuse Investigation Team completed research into 40 cases of ritual child sexual abuse. A former superintendent in charge of the team stated that *it would be wrong to dismiss all allegations of ritual abuse as fantasy*. He suggested that in such cases professionals must listen, retain objectivity and examine each piece of evidence, patiently working towards a conclusion. *An investigator has to remember that at the heart of an allegation there may be acts that did take place but they may be rendered distorted or unbelievable by misinformation* (Hames, 2000, p184). Unfortunately, this important police research was not made public and there has never been an objective study by specialist police and social work investigators to examine evidence from historic and current cases.

Stobart (2006) investigated cases of child abuse linked to accusations of possession and witch-craft, which led to guidance on this area of work (HM Government, 2007). She found that a belief in possession is widespread and not confined to particular cultures, countries, religions or to recent migrants. The abuse of children mainly occurred when the child was exorcised and abuse included beating, burning, semi-strangulation, cutting, being tied up and starvation.

Considering the significance of physical and behavioural indicators of sexual abuse

I cried all the time when I was nine. You are just waiting for one person to ask that question

We cut and we didn't know why

I tried to kill myself at 4 and 10

Eating paper gave some sort of relief. Tore the covers off books and ate them

He (the abuser) encouraged me to antagonize other people. I became very angry ...

I was quiet anyway and became even quieter. I was trying so hard to hide it

I was not present mentally, I was falling asleep...

I went from being a cheeky, loud and popular girl to a quiet withdrawn very tearful girl ...

(Nelson, 2008, p18)

As with other forms of child abuse, social workers need to recognise specific signs which may indicate sexual abuse. Although some indicators will be definitive, most will need evaluation through the child protection processes and multi-agency debate. On their own or grouped together they may be indicative. It is always important to look beyond the behaviour and consider the possibility of abuse.

Physical indicators of child sexual abuse

Nelson compared physical disorders to accounts of child sexual abuse by adult survivors as well as making comparisons with the physical effects of torture and child marriage. She referred to violent repeated assaults on developing bodies untreated through lack of care or the desire to conceal evidence and drew attention to the impact on a child's back or pelvis of being crushed by a large adult, and throat rape leading to infections and diffi-culty in swallowing (2002, p52).

Possible physical signs of sexual abuse may include forensic findings such as semen present in the vagina, anus or mouth or on other parts of the body or items of clothing or bedding. Other physical signs are pregnancy, sexually transmitted infections, genital, anal or oral pain, bleeding, injury or soreness, vaginal or penile discharge, urine infections, bruising to inner thighs, breasts, or genital area, genital warts, bite marks or love bites, carpet burns to back, symmetrical marks from being restrained, constant unexplained sore throat, abdominal pain, difficulty walking or sitting and skin reaction to semen. Yet many sexually abused children show no physical signs because healing takes place rapidly and scarring is uncommon. With the exception of pregnancy or when there is forensic evidence, it is rare to find diagnostic signs of sexual abuse.

ACTIVITY **2.4**

Behavioural signs of child sexual abuse are also very important to identify. How would you recognise a child victim of sexual abuse? Consider the two examples below and write a list of anything that might be indicative of child sexual abuse.

A child in nursery school

We watch a little girl sitting with her nursery class around the dinner table. She can move, but she doesn't; she can eat but she doesn't – unless you put the spoon in her hand and move it to her mouth; she doesn't play; she doesn't appear to listen or to speak. It's as if she doesn't want to exist. She's one of the children who bring the staff close to tears. She arrives every day with a red, raw, vulva. Doctors have looked at it, worried about it, worried about her ... there are children who we are convinced are being sexually abused. It's not any one thing that makes us think it. You know children pretty well when you work with them every day and they can't always tell us in words, but they can tell you in pictures, in body posture, sometimes it's physical symptoms, sometimes they don't want you to touch them, sometimes they walk around wringing their hands, unable to tell what is wrong.

(Campbell, 1988, p196)

An adolescent

The foster carer says Natasha, aged 13 years, does not go to school, wets the bed, overeats, comes home drunk and excessively demands affection. Natasha tells the social worker that she sees herself as ugly and unlike other girls. She shouts at the social worker to leave her alone and does not comply with the child protection plan which states that she must not visit the home of her mother's partner, a known child sex offender.

Comment

In the above scenarios there are many potential indicators of sexual abuse but there may be abused children where none of these signs are obvious. Behavioural indicators may include a child avoiding home or school, fatigue, low self-esteem, sexual knowledge beyond age and developmental stage, obsessional behaviour such as constant cleaning or showering, enuresis (wetting), encopresis (soiling), reluctance to take part in sports or to remove clothing, fear of medical examinations, social isolation, substance misuse, eating disorders, sleep disturbance, angry outbursts, arson, running away, poor concentration, begging or stealing, self-harm, depression, anxiety and attention seeking (often misinterpreted negatively). It is important to recognise that over perfect behaviour can also be an indicator as the child does not dare to draw attention to themselves.

ACTIVITY 2.5

Think about Natasha, who is in a foster placement. She subsequently discloses to the social worker in some detail that her mother's partner made her touch his penis and he forced her to undress. She said she had told her mother, who had not listened. Natasha agreed to attend a visually recorded interview with the police. However, the next day at the interview suite she said nothing at all.

Why do you think Natasha would not speak to the police officer and social worker during the visually recorded interview?

What might have helped her to speak further about what had happened?

Refer to the quotation from Cries unheard *(Sereny, 1999) at the beginning of this chapter and make a list of all the reasons Mary Bell provides about why she could not tell about the abuse she was experiencing, and compare this list with your responses to why Natasha did not speak during the interview.*

Comment

> States parties shall assure to the child who is capable of forming his or her own views the right to express those views freely in all matters affecting the child or views of the child being given due weight in accordance with the age and maturity of the child.
>
> (United Nations, 1989, Article 12)

Children may not tell about sexual abuse for the following reasons.

- They feel they cannot trust anyone to tell.
  I thought all grown ups were the same anyway, didn't trust them and that they would hurt me.

- They are threatened by the abuser – the threats may be implicit given abuse of power.
  I was told people would die if I told. This was the threat.
  I feared for my life. I believed my abuser would know if I told. They had such power over me.
  I was made to see the psychologist but my mum told me not to speak.

- They think they are to blame and are afraid of punishment, particularly if they have been made to take a part in the abuse.
  I was so brainwashed into feeling I was bad.
  I felt I was responsible for not stopping the abuse.

- They fear loss of family, home or school.
  If you are different you are targeted – you tell one person and then the whole school finds out.

- They are emotionally and/or physically dependent on the abuser.
  You don't want to upset people.

- They have a low sense of self-esteem and think no one will believe them.
  My parents were respected. My father was a community man. Everyone admired him ... it seemed impossible to me to present people with a different image.

- They think the abuse is normal behaviour.
  You tell yourself it can't be that bad. 'I'm fine,' you say, 'it doesn't bother me.'

- They feel loyalty to the abuser.
  I was brought up to respect my elders (in the religious group) – to me I was doing what I was told because the abuser was my elder.

  I used to comfort my abuser who cried after abusing me.

  You feel sorry for them ... you actually protect them.

- They think that they will not obtain justice.
  We did the feeling Yes feeling No thing at school. I knew I was getting the no feeling but I believed it wouldn't matter what I said, it wouldn't make a difference.

- They lack the communication skills to be able to disclose abuse.
  First you don't know it's wrong; then when you find out you're stuck and trapped; then if I wanted to tell, physically my tongue would not move.
  I couldn't say the words but I began writing darker and darker poetry.

  (Nelson, 2008, pp11–14)

In a Swedish study of ten young adults sexually exploited as children through abusive images, none had told freely of the events in 28 years. This study showed that the children did not make false allegations: *during all the abuse the children have kept quiet about the events and kept it secret for many years thereafter.* The children feared the possible consequences of disclosure. *They do not want to remember and sometimes mentally exclude their earlier experiences ... Children are extremely reticent to talk about those acts that are associated with the strongest feelings of shame, unease or disgust* (Svedin and Bach, 1996, pp63–4).

Peter Saunders from the National Association of People Abused in Childhood (NAPAC) states that most survivors speak about the abuse for the first time when they contact the helpline as adults (www.napac.org.uk). An NSPCC study concluded that 72% of sexually abused children said they were too frightened to tell anyone at the time of the abuse and 31% still had not told anyone by early adulthood (Cawson, et al., 2000, p83). However, ChildLine, in a survey of calls concerning child sexual abuse, concluded that *on average children contact ChildLine much sooner after the abuse begins than they used to* (ChildLine, 2007, p1). A study of Bangladeshi young women showed that the issue of *izzat* (honour) keeps socially unacceptable behaviour such as sexual activity hidden, making it difficult for professionals to hear about allegations of sexual exploitation (Ward and Patel, 2006).

Over time children may develop a pattern of adjustment to abuse as a form of survival which in itself needs to be recognised as an indicator. The child abuse accommodation syndrome assists understanding of children's responses (Summit, 1983). Following disclosure the child is commonly met with adult denial and disbelief from their family, friends and local community. The child will be in crisis because of anxiety caused by the telling of the secret. They will be in fear of the response of the authorities and the impact on their lives and will carry responsibility for the possible destruction of the family unit by telling and so the child perpetuates the lie that nothing harmful has happened. The adults then suppress the allegation of abuse through covert and overt threats and in the absence of adequate family or other support, and fearing the offender, the child may retract, withdraw or minimise the disclosure. It is very common for children to retract their disclosure after the initial telling and retractions should always prompt questions about the reasons for the child changing their account.

The serious level of trauma experienced by child victims of sexual abuse may lead them to dissociate from the abuse and render them silent. This process of dissociation is described by Valerie Mason-John in her book *Borrowed body,* which explores the story of Pauline, a child in care. Pauline's survival mechanism is to go out of her body and enter a secret, protective world of spirit children and animals where her feelings find expression. The spirits occupy her body when she vacates it – at her most vulnerable and frightening times. *I feel like I am being sucked out of my body.* Pauline was sexually abused in care and describes how she squeezed herself out of her body and flew up to the ceiling during the abuse. She said that one of her spirit friends, *Sparky jumped all over the bed.* However, when others noticed her talking to herself Pauline had to send her spirit friends away (Mason-John, 2005, pp9,10 and 34).

Responding to child protection needs at an early stage

To protect children from sexual abuse there are three key strategies:

- to remove the abusers from the world of the child through professional intervention and prosecution;

- to provide children with strategies to protect themselves and knowledge as to how to gain protection;

- to ensure that the protectors in the community such as family, friends, neighbours, school and health services are knowledgeable about child abuse and how to report it.

(Davies, 2004)

Identifying child sex abusers

Convicted child sex abusers commonly have a previous history of abuse which did not lead to investigation or prosecution. Kelly (2004) examined 13 cases of sexually abusive incidents in the Huntley case and said, *even this is almost certainly not a complete list of the young women.* Huntley was convicted for the murder of Holly Wells and Jessica Chapman, both aged 10 years.

Knowledge gained from child sex abusers assists professional understanding of the enormity of the task of protecting children from sexual crime. Child sex abusers are often related or known to the child and may abuse many children. The abusers may be isolated individuals or through networking with others using international abuser organisations and websites.

It is very important to note that while many abusers have experienced some form of abuse, in the majority of cases, people who have survived child sexual abuse do not go on to become abusers (Grubin, 1998). One study found that 12% of male victims of child sexual abuse subsequently abused children themselves (Salter, et al., 2003). However, it is inaccurate and very insulting to survivors of abuse to suggest that experiencing abuse makes them more likely to become an abuser as they are often the most proactive protectors.

Young people who sexually abuse

Masson and Erooga (1999) estimated that between 25 and 33% of all alleged sexual abuse involves young, mainly adolescent perpetrators.

> *Evidence suggests that children who abuse others may have suffered considerable disruption in their lives, been exposed to violence within the family, may have witnessed or been subject to physical or sexual abuse, have problems in their educational development and may have committed other offences.*

(DfES, 2006, 11.32)

The young people who abuse are essentially children in need and some will be children in need of protection.

Other factors associated with such behaviour are:

- abnormal sexual environments – families where sexual boundaries were too rigid or too relaxed;
- sexualised models of compensation where sex is seen as a comfort in difficult times;
- a parental history of sexual or physical abuse;
- history of drug or alcohol misuse in the family;
- parental loss;
- social isolation, lack of confidence, lack of social skills and maladaptive coping skills.

(Calder, 1997, p51)

The quotation at the beginning of this chapter describes the abuse suffered by Mary Bell who was convicted for the murder of two children in 1968 at age 11 years. Mary Bell went to see an old man called Harry.

> *'I told you about dad's friend Harry Bury, the rag-and-bone man who lived upstairs? He was brilliant. He called me his lucky mascot. And one day I went to his room and he'd probably had a drink and was lying on his back. And I went up and fiddled with his trousers ... You know ... I opened his buttons or zip or whatever and took it out.'*

> *'You took his penis out? Why?'*

'I wanted to see whether he'd be like all the others. And he shot up and he was absolutely disgusted and said, "What the hell are you doing?" But then almost rightaway, he was like, "it's all right, it's all right. Let's go and have a cuppa tea and feed the cat". And after that I was OK, you know.'

(Sereny, 1998, p337)

Mary's experience of sexual exploitation had taught her no other way of behaving towards Harry. Harry was a protective adult and this incident might well have led to him referring to children's services. This is a good example of the importance of exploring the possibility of the child themselves being a victim of sexual abuse and of implementing child protection procedures.

RESEARCH SUMMARY

Not all children who sexually abuse are victims of abuse. For children who are themselves victims, the factors which affect the development of abusive behaviour are the age when abuse occurs, its duration, severity, the relationship between the victim and perpetrator and the use of physical force (Vizard, 2006, p4). Burton, et al. (1997, p157) found that 79% of a large sample of children age 12 years and under, who had sexually abused, were male and 72% of these were victims of sexual abuse. Johnson (1989) studied 13 female perpetrators age 4–12 years, who had mainly abused children within their family, and found that all had been sexually abused over long periods.

It is important when working with young people who sexually abuse to define the abuse as a pattern of behaviour which may be changed. *There is considerable confusion about what constitutes 'normal' sexual behaviour in children and adolescents, partly because of rapidly changing societal norms about children and sex and partly because of the ethical constraints in conducting research into childhood sexuality* (Vizard, 2006, p2). Professionals need to make judgements to distinguish between sexual experimentation between children and sexual abuse of one child by another.

The sexual activity will constitute significant harm if the relationship is coercive or involves other forms of abuse. The Sexual Offences Act 2003 defines children under 13 years as being unable to consent to sexual activity and therefore as victims of crime. Between 13 and 16 years sexual activity with a child is also an offence. For any child under 18 years it is an offence for a person to have a sexual relationship with them if the adult is in a position of trust or authority in relation to them. A strategy discussion provides the forum for debate and intervention to protect in each case, and in the majority of cases police will not pursue criminal action. The best interests of the child are paramount. Professionals will decide the need for child protection and child in need procedures as well as any criminal proceedings.

It is important not to criminalise all sexual activity among young people, to ensure that young people can freely access educational and health advice on sexual matters and obtain services. The Gillick judgement (House of Lords, 1985) stated that a child may be deemed competent to make decisions about health matters based on their age and understanding without parental consent. It is, however, important to balance the rights of the child with their need for protection and to recognise that they may be victims of sexual crime. If the child needs protection, the responsibility of professionals to promote the welfare of the child takes precedence and referral must be made to children's services. In order to determine whether a relationship presents a risk of harm to a child, factors such as the capacity of the child to consent to sexual activity, age differential and power imbalances in the relationship need to be considered. Power may derive from differences in size, age, material wealth, physical, social, sexual development, race, sexuality, disability and levels of sexual knowledge.

In institutional and organised abuse networks it is not uncommon for children to be used to procure other children for the adult abusers or to be abusive to other children. This is a form of control by the abusers and can make it difficult for children to disclose abuse as they feel guilty about the acts they have been forced to perpetrate on other children.

Female child sex abusers

There is much disbelief about child abuse by women yet self-report studies indicate higher levels of female perpetration than other research data (Ford, 2006, p16). Female abusers commit all types of sexual offences against children of all ages, groom their victims in the same way as male offenders, use distorted thinking to excuse the abuse and lack empathy for their victims (Ford, 2006, p33). An example of distorted thinking is when, instead of defining sexual activity as abusive, a women claims she is providing the child with sex education. Bunting (2005) found that there was a professional reluctance to accept that women may instigate abuse themselves and that it was often assumed that they are coerced by male partners.

There is some evidence that professionals tend to define abuse by women as less serious than that by men even though some abuse is violent. Women's sexually abusive behaviour is often defined as inappropriate affection rather than as sexual crime because women are socially constructed as carers of children (Saradjian, 1997, p2). Children abused by their mothers experience particularly strong feelings of betrayal and in cases of female perpetrators anger is not projected onto non-abusive fathers in the way that hostility is expressed towards non-abusing mothers (Saradjian, 1997, p9). Abuse by women may be less visible than that by men – for instance, it is less obvious when a women abducts a child.

ACTIVITY 2.6

Consider the following statements commonly made by child sex abusers to rationalise their abusive behaviour. Think about your possible responses to these distorted thought processes. How would you make sure that you do not in any way collude with the abuse? Think about when confronting an alleged or known abuser how important it is to keep the child's safety as the main focus.

- *I only touch her – nothing more.*
- *He likes being with me – we are close friends.*
- *I don't cause them any pain – I wouldn't do that.*
- *It didn't do me any harm.*
- *Children like sex.*
- *She doesn't notice, she's asleep.*
- *It's an illness that I can't stop.*
- *She is very mature for her age.*

ACTIVITY 2.7

Here are five descriptions of known child sex abusers. Think about each one and reflect on whether these accounts alter any stereotypical perceptions you may have about child sex abusers

- *Eight people, including a 75-year-old grandmother, on the Isle of Lewis in the Outer Hebrides were accused of raping and sexually abusing children in black magic rituals, of wife-swapping orgies in which they dressed in robes and masks, and of sacrificing cats and chickens and drinking their blood.*

  (Martin, 2005)

- *Claire, aged 29, a tennis coach, sexually abused a pupil. She was found guilty of four charges of unlawful sexual acts which began with holding the child's hand and kissing her, wearing her underclothes and adopting a similar appearance which were grooming behaviours prior to oral sex.*

  (Jenkins, 2007)

- *David, a senior nurse, was struck off the nurses' register for abuse of possibly over 100 teenagers while they were being treated for eating disorders. Some of them thought he was their boyfriend.*

  (Narain, 2007)

- *A former swimming coach age 79 years admitted sexually abusing boys and girls between 1942 and 2003. For more than 50 years he had preyed on young children, aged under 7 years.*

  (BBC News, 2007b).

- *Five child sex abusers who admitted a total of 77 offences including rape of a child, incitement to kidnap and distributing abusive images were all people you wouldn't glance at twice in the street said the police. One was an ex-army major and chair of governors at a college and an infant school.*

  (BBC News, 2007c).

Comment

The Multi Agency Public Protection Panel Arrangements (MAPPA) work to protect the public from child sex abusers. Officers visit known child sex offenders and review their cases regularly, constantly reassessing the level of risk to children. They hold multi-agency meetings to share information and agree interventions and also decide what information can be shared with the community. Some high-risk offenders are subject to surveillance, others access treatment programmes and some live in supervised accommodation where they can be watched, electronically tagged and put under curfew (Home Office, 2007, p8).

Raising awareness in the community and self-protection programmes for children

Prevention organisations work to raise awareness of child sexual abuse and to empower children to say no to the abuse and learn to keep themselves safe. This approach is valuable but must be used together with strategies to target perpetrators and implement child protection procedures. Children cannot be expected to solve the abuse themselves but do need age-appropriate knowledge of the risks posed by child sex abusers. There is evidence that a child's positive self-esteem can help to keep them safe. Child sex offenders have said that *children are most vulnerable to sexual abuse when they have family problems, are alone, lack confidence, and are indiscriminate in their trust of others* (Elliott, et al., 1995, p593).

Child Rescue Alert is a system available throughout the UK which works by interrupting television and radio programmes every 15 minutes with news flashes that a child has been abducted, alerting the public to the incident immediately – asking them to be vigilant and call 999 if they have crucial information. Organisations such as Stop it Now and Kidscape help to raise awareness of abuse and Thinkuknow is a website addressing online abuse. Local Safeguarding Children Boards have a responsibility to inform the public about child abuse and provide means of reporting.

The social work response

ACTIVITY **2.8**

Deciding to what extent a child is at risk is based on professional judgement and the application of knowledge to individual cases. Here are four cases to which the authors have had to provide a protective social work response. Make a decision about which of the categories of response apply to these cases:

A The child is not thought to be at any risk of child abuse.

B There is concern about the sexual abuse of a child.

C There is suspicion of likely or actual significant harm to a child (s47 enquiry, CA 1989).

D A section 47 (CA 1989) investigation of child abuse is indicated.

E Immediate action to protect. Evidence of actual significant harm and /or criminal offence.

1. Twin boys aged 5 years demonstrate differing but worrying behaviour in school. One is very withdrawn and the other is destructive of property. One boy, pointing to his penis, told the social worker that his mother tickled him and that his brother liked it as well. In a visually recorded interview, neither boy would speak about these events.

2. A 4-month-old baby girl is admitted to hospital with vaginal bleeding. The paediatrician confirms evidence of penetration, possibly by an object, as there is internal bruising and scarring. On the day of admission the baby had been cared for by both parents and maternal grandparents.

3. An 11-year-old boy living in residential care tells his teacher that a residential worker has offered to take him and his friend from the home to a local sauna. He feels uncomfortable about this because he knows that his friend, aged 13 years, has 'special' reading lessons from this worker and they read 'dirty' magazines like Boyz and Penthouse.

---

4. A youth worker reports that a 7-year-old girl writes a story in the after-school club about late-night parties where grown-ups wear funny masks and have sex with animals. She had drawn a picture of a dog showing an erect penis.

In relation to these cases:

- *Think about what criteria you would use in making judgements about sexual abuse.*
- *Think about what may influence your selection of these criteria.*
- *How do you differentiate between situations that include risk but do not reach a threshold of actual dangerousness?*
- *At what stage is professional intervention indicated?*
- *What level of intervention is appropriate?*
- *When is immediate action needed to protect the child from harm?*
- *Are there other children who may be also being abused?*

Comment

Perhaps you based your decision making on your:

- personal experiences;
- professional experience of a particular case;
- cultural or religious perspective of family life;
- knowledge of the law and child protection policy and practice guidance;
- knowledge of lessons learnt from child abuse inquiries and serious case reviews;
- your knowledge of sexual abuse from literature and research findings;
- media reporting.

Each of the above cases did require a proactive social work intervention ranging from family support to section 47 (CA 1989) enquiries, investigation and legal safeguards. The detailed analysis below will assist your later reflection on your decisions in the above scenarios.

Making judgements when a child is sexually exploited through prostitution

It cannot be assumed that sexually exploited children will seek help themselves as they do not always recognise themselves as victims. Professionals must be proactive in identification through raising community awareness and encouraging reporting of the abuse by young people, frontline agencies and the public (Davies, 2004; Nelson, 2004). Kane provides an example of a child who was protected by a responsible member of the local community and an effective professional response. Neither would have protected the child without the other being in place. A girl is seen by a woman getting into a car after a man had called out to her. The woman notes the number and calls the police. She approaches the child and offers to walk her home safely. As the car sped away the police identified the number as belonging to a known child sex abuser and proceeded to locate him for questioning (Kane, 1998, p128).

Children may present as having a relationship with an older person posing as and viewed by them as their friend. The child becomes emotionally and physically dependent on them, which may be reinforced by the use of drugs and alcohol. It is very important for the social worker to try to keep the child's world in place – family or placement, school, health services, drug/alcohol counselling, youth clubs/activities and religious/cultural groups. It will be difficult for the abusers to gain access to the child while there are strong protectors around them and while they are engaging with safe adults. Over time the abuser substitutes their world for the world of the child, which often alienates the child from accessing help as abusers try to separate the young person from protectors. The social worker may find their attention diverted from protecting the child as they themselves become under attack through various forms of intimidation. It is important to understand that these mechanisms are often used by abusers to gain increased access to the child. In order to maintain contact with the young person at risk, it is important to sustain the child's relationship with protective family members, school and health services. A network of children's safe accommodation and drop-in centres should be available across the UK for children to access in emergencies (Scott and Harper, 2006).

The extent of abuse of children through sexual exploitation

- *She had been walking this beat for three years now, ever since she was 11 years old. She reckoned she'd been earning about £800 a week for all those years and if she was charging say £20 to £40 for each punter, depending on what he wanted to do and where he wanted to do it, then she must have been doing about twenty five punters a week, so that meant by now, having reached the age of fourteen and a half she must have sold herself to something like three thousand different men. Could be more. She wasn't sure*

(Davies, 1998, p12)

- Up to 5,000 children at any one time are victims of child sexual exploitation (Melrose, et al., 1999, p5).

- Gallagher found that the criminal justice system is unable to deal with complex cases of organised abuse and only a minority of suspected perpetrators are convicted (Gallagher, 1998).

Sexually exploited children commonly have low self-esteem and have experiences which include the following.

- Going missing frequently from home or care, from a young age and away from their locality. Melrose, et al., found that 48% of their sample were involved before the age of 14 years (1999, p25).

- Bullying in and out of school. Melrose, et al., found 66% of their sample had a disrupted education (1999, p22).

- Previous and sometimes current sexual abuse, neglect, physical abuse and domestic violence within the family. The agency Streetwise Youth found that of sexually exploited boys, over 60% had experienced childhood sexual and physical abuse as well as emotional abuse and neglect (DoH, 2000b, p16).

- Family involvement in sexual exploitation, drugs or alcohol.

- Drug and alcohol misuse.

- Emotional symptoms including eating disorders, mood swings and self-harm (sometimes very extreme, e.g. genital cutting).

- Involvement in theft, shoplifting, deception often organised by the person exploiting them.

- A preoccupation with their mobile phone which indicates the child is being controlled (e.g. possession of multiple phones, extreme distress when one is lost or not working).

- Having limited freedom of movement.

- That they are unaccompanied minors.

- Showing signs of sexual behaviour/abuse, including sexually transmitted infections, terminations and pregnancy scares.

- Possession of money and goods not accounted for.

- Having an older 'boyfriend' – in some cases he drives them about.

  (LSCB, 2007, 5.40.7; Home Office, 2006, p27).

The law

Article 34 of the UNCRC states that *children have a right to protection from sexual abuse* and that all appropriate measures will be taken to prevent *the inducement or coercion of a child to engage in any unlawful sexual activity, the exploitative use of children in prostitution or other unlawful sexual practices, the exploitative use of children in pornographic performances and materials.* Article 35 states that *children have a right to protection from being abducted or sold* (United Nations, 1989).

The Sex Offences Act 1956 and the Street Offences Act 1959 still allow a criminal penalty to be applied against a child over the age of ten years who has been abused through prostitution. However, since the *Working together* supplementary guidance (DoH, 2000b) the numbers of cautions and prosecutions has dropped dramatically. The guidance states that criminal law should not be used to prosecute children exploited through prostitution and yet continues to recommend prosecution as a last resort when the young person returns *persistently and voluntarily* to a life of exploitation. By keeping loitering or soliciting as a criminal offence for children, it is claimed that the law underlines a message that such exploitation is unacceptable (Home Office, 2004, 7.24). However, children's rights groups consider that through this approach young people are criminalised and may be deterred from reporting the crime if they risk prosecution (www.ARCH-ed.org.uk).

The law has been tightened to protect young people from broader methods of sexual exploitation and more severe penalties have been introduced.

The Sexual Offences Act 2003

● The Act includes consensual and non-consensual offences against children and vulnerable adults. Offences include paying for the sexual services of a child which include vaginal, anal penetration or oral penile penetration.

● There is no defence of a belief that the young person was over the age of 18 years though such a belief may influence sentencing as a mitigating factor.

● A child under the age of 13 does not under any circumstances have the legal capacity to consent to any form of sexual activity.

● All penetrative sex (including penetration of the mouth) of a child under the age of 13 will be automatically classified as rape with a maximum penalty of life in prison.

● Sexual grooming is now an offence.

The Protection of Children Act 1999 states that it is an offence to take, make, permit to take, distribute, show, possess with intent to distribute or to advertise, indecent photographs of under 16s. This offence now applies to images of 16- and 17-year-olds.

The jigsaw of information – working together to protect children

In order to provide protection, social workers must not pathologise the child. Terms like *punter*, *pimp* and *prostitute* must be replaced by *abusing adult*, *child abuser* and *child victim* (Utting, quoting Barnardo's, 1997, 9.37). Children involved in prostitution and other forms of commercial sexual exploitation should be treated primarily as the victims of abuse, and their needs require careful assessment. They may include children who have been victims of human trafficking. The LSCB should actively enquire into the extent to which children are involved in prostitution in the local area. The emphasis must be to prevent the entry of children into prostitution and, where they are already involved, treat them as victims of abuse, apply protection procedures and provide exit strategies. Targeting abusers may involve prosecution for a range of offences. The police must be robust in seeking evidence to support charges such as grievous bodily harm, unlawful wounding, actual bodily harm, kidnapping, abduction, sexual crimes, false imprisonment as well as drugs offences and benefit or tax fraud (DoH, 2000b, 3.4; DfES, 2006, 6.2).

In 2006, the Home Office published a co-ordinated strategy and summary of responses to the consultation document *Paying the price* (Home Office, 2006, p5). This strategy focused on disrupting sex markets by preventing individuals, particularly children, from being drawn into prostitution. Pilot studies in Wolverhampton and Nottingham demonstrated the effectiveness of joint working to protect children sexually exploited: *a close working partnership between social services and the police was an essential pre-requisite to maximizing our joint efforts* (ACPO, 1998, p15). In both authorities a significant number of adults were proscuted for serious offences including unlawful sexual intercourse, kidnap and witness intimidation (ACPO, 1998).

Safeguarding children involved in prostitution (Swann and Balding, 2002) addressed the effectiveness of the *Working together* guidance (DoH, 2000b)) and concluded that most authorities acknowledged the problem and had protocols although some did not acknowledge the hidden nature of abuse taking place off the streets. There were also continuing myths held about children making choices and the amount of harm suffered. Importantly there was no ring- fenced budget for action to prevent or protect the young people. Less than half the authorities provided training on this subject and, as guidance was not prescriptive, local interpretation of the protocols varied widely. The police did not prioritise this work as it was not a police performance target, although areas with vice squads or specialist police provision gained more convictions. Those areas which resourced this issue relied substantially on the voluntary sector for provision (Swann and Balding, 2002).

Social workers must intervene to protect the child, working jointly with police and other agencies implementing section 47 protocols (CA 1989 and DfES, 2006) and using legal safeguards to protect the child and target the abusers. In some authorities a framework addressing three different categories of risk requires varying levels of intervention (LSCB, 2007). Category 1 includes responding to a child who is at risk of being targeted and groomed for sexual exploitation. Category 2 focuses intervention on children targeted for opportunistic abuse through the exchange of sex for attention, accommodation, food, gifts and drugs and where there is concern of use of coercion and control. Category 3 requires action when a child is being regularly sexually exploited and where coercion/control is implicit (Kerrigan Lebloch and King, 2006).

Social workers must work jointly with police child abuse investigation teams and other police teams which may be involved. Police and probation services collate information primarily about known and suspected abusers and social workers collate information mainly about the child, family and community networks. It is only when both perspectives are analysed together that children have the best chance of protection and of seeking justice through the conviction of the abusers. The police may provide crime analysts, especially where there are networks of organised sexual crime against children. Social workers must inform the MAPPA of any known or suspected child sex abusers via their representative on the panel. They must also protect identified children from harm and contribute to MAPPA risk strategies.

For those sexually exploited young people who go missing from home or care, social workers must implement missing children protocols. They must ensure that on the young person's return they are offered someone independent to interview them and/or they are interviewed jointly with police and in a neutral, safe environment.

In working with child victims they must be valued, empowered and informed of their legal rights. These children are already under extreme pressure and it is important to encourage them to talk but not to judge or further victimise them. Children as known or suspected victims of crime, or witnesses to crime, must be interviewed according to the *Achieving best evidence* guidance (CJS, 2007). The social worker must then act as a bridge between the young person and the investigating police and social workers to enable a formal, visually recorded statement to be made. If the child has been photographed or filmed as part of the abuse then the young person may chose to make a written instead of visually recorded statement. In all categories of risk the connection with the young person must be maintained as best as possible. It may be that health or education staff are the only source of professional contact, in which case the protection strategy must preserve this important link and work with those professionals.

When any agency reports a situation of organised abuse, named officers from the police and children's services will be appointed to co-ordinate the case. A senior-level strategy meeting will be urgently convened involving managers. A strategic management group must be set up to take the lead in the investigation, agree staffing, resources including legal advice and media management, and protocols. This group will oversee the operational teams and collate known information about the alleged perpetrators. Collation will include information about any previous allegations/suspicions, inspection reports and employment records. Patterns of abuse will be mapped, including venues, methods and patterns of grooming, bribes, favours and threats as well as identifying and profiling other possible perpetrators. The group will organise liaison with the Crown Prosecution Service with regard to any prosecutions and set up an investigation management group to provide a forum where professionals can meet, exchange information and implement strategy on a daily basis. This group will include representatives from the local authority children's services, police, health, education and probation, will co-ordinate the investigation and provide a safe reporting channel for whistleblowers.

An operational team will:

- make decisions about immediate safety of the young people;
- conduct visually recorded interviews, which may need to be simultaneous to prevent contamination of evidence;
- arrange medical consultations;
- organise forensic retrieval;
- organise any search of premises or computers;
- interview any corroborative witnesses;
- assess photographic/visual evidence.

The senior level strategy group will review the outcome of the operational teams and consider in sequence:

- enquiries and assessment by children's social care about whether a child is in need of protection;
- a police investigation of possible criminal offences;
- consideration by an employer of disciplinary action in respect of the individual/s.

The employers responsible for disciplinary action should await the outcome of the child protection investigation and any police action before progressing to formal disciplinary proceedings. This does not prevent the employee being suspended pending the outcome of the investigations (DfES, 2006, Appendix. 5.2).

CASE STUDY

Becky

Becky, age 14 years and in care, was the subject of a 'Real Story' BBC documentary (BBC, 2006a). Becky made 40 allegations of sexual abuse by more than 25 men over a two-year period. Although she was in a children's home, she continued to be the target of child abusers. She told youth workers, professionals at a child protection conference, a counsellor, residential social workers, social workers, hospital Accident and Emergency staff, a psychiatrist, behaviour management centre staff and police about repeated sexual abuse. She spoke of rape and *sex work*. She said she felt unsafe, even saying that she or her family might be killed and spoke of being punched in the stomach and given drugs and alcohol. She also said that she had to have sex with men to protect others. She demonstrated many signs of sexual abuse. She neglected and harmed herself, attempted suicide, had severe stomach pain, went missing repeatedly and sought refuge in hospital admissions. She told a psychiatrist that she wanted to die. Although the professional network held a child protection conference they defined her as placing herself at risk. She was defined by police and social workers as a nuisance and referred for behaviour management.

Although many different agencies and professionals were involved in this case, Becky was failed by them all. This case illustrated that her voice was unheard and that there was:

- no use of legislation to protect Becky;
- no child protection planning;
- no collation of facts and disclosures indicating abuse – on the contrary a strategy was put in place to *manage the disclosures*;
- no overview of risk to Becky or other children;
- no focus on targeting the perpetrators;
- no investigation proactively to bring the abusers to justice;
- no implementation of organised abuse procedures.

Think about how you might respond to a young woman like Becky. Consider the words you might use as well as your non-verbal reactions and feelings if Becky said the following.

I've done loads of stuff and if they get a bit pervy I just tell them to back off, 's no big deal.

I want a kid, otherwise he'll get my family.

You don't know one thing about my life.

He's my knight in shining armour only he's got a car instead of a horse.

He gives me stuff. We go round his and we have Bacardi, fags and he never lets me go away without putting something in my pocket.

When I'm there I don't feel ugly.

He makes me feel special which is more than anyone else does.

I just want someone to love me.

I've got awful stomach pains.

ACTIVITY *2.9* *continued*

I don't need any help. I can look after myself.

Sleeping with someone for a place to stay isn't prostitution, is it?

I'm disgusting and dirty.

He was really kind to me. I liked the sex.

Why should I tell you? I've told hundreds of times already.

Being on the streets is better than at home.

Comment

Think about the importance of hearing exactly what the young person is saying and seeking clarification through open questions such as:

I wasn't there, please explain that to me.

Describe what took place.

Some children may only be able to describe child abuse using crude language. It is important not to prevent the use of such words but to explore what is meant by them. A young person may well say that they do not feel normal or they feel dirty and it is important to acknowledge the feelings and then explore further what the young person is experiencing. Saying *of course you aren't dirty* would be to dismiss the way they are feeling. Listening to the young person and gaining their trust sufficiently to provide them with the confidence to tell a police officer is a very important social work skill. They may be very frightened of speaking about what is happening and will need much support and may need to meet with the police in a discreet location where they will feel reassured that they will not be seen by the abusers. If a young person uses words you do not understand it is very important to seek clarification and not to make assumptions about the meaning.

Every Child Matters protocol (DfES, 2003) – an analysis of how this might be applied in Becky's case

The Assessment and Progress Record for the Looked After Review is a proforma to be completed by the social worker, with the young person and the carers. The relevant form for Becky would be that for children aged 11–15 years available from the Every Child Matters website. Consider how the following questions from this form may or may not be relevant to keeping Becky safe from harm caused through sexual exploitation.

H4 *Young person understands the risks from drinking and smoking.* Becky smokes and misuses alcohol as a way of escaping from the abuse. She probably knows the risks but at the moment alcohol consumption is part of her survival strategy.

H4 *Young person understands the risks from early/unprotected sex.* Becky does know the risks and has sought health advice but she has asked for protection from the abusers and has not been heard.

H4 *Young person feels able to talk to a trusted adult about health concerns*. Becky does speak to a school nurse but acting in isolation the health worker will not be able to protect Becky. The role of this worker must be maintained and integrated with the child protection plan as she is trusted by the child.

H7 *Young person uses illicit drugs*. Becky uses crack cocaine as the abusers supply this as a way of entrapping her within their network by encouraging dependence on them and possibly her way of surviving the abuse. Strategies to help her to give up the drugs are likely to fail unless the abusers are targeted.

H8 *Young person risks injury or attack through careless behaviour*. The word 'careless' is unfortunate here as Becky is not to blame for the sexual abuse. She is at risk of significant harm through the violence of the abusers but the focus should be on prosecuting the perpetrators rather than pathologising the child.

H8 *Sexual behaviour puts him/her at risk of infection and/or pregnancy/parenthood*. Becky says that she wants to have a baby to get some reward from the endless sexual abuse. This is not her fault but a survival strategy. She is at great risk of significant harm from infections and diseases.

E7 *Young person frequently truants or is absent from school*. Becky hardly attends school because of the power the abusers have over her life. Until this is addressed she will not be able to live the life of a child and gain her education.

B6 *Young person is deliberately hurting him/herself*. This is one of Becky's key survival strategies as when she cuts her arms she feels in control. She uses hospital admissions to seek support.

B14 *Carers try to deal with misbehaviour in a calm, firm and clear way*. This depends on how Becky's behaviour is interpreted. She should not be pathologised as misbehaving but should be seen as a victim of crime.

B18 *Carers try to get to the bottom of things*. The carers will not be able to remove the abusers from the exploitation of Becky. They should provide valuable information to inform an organised abuse strategy and child protection plan.

ID4 *Young person sees herself as unattractive or unappealing*. Becky has clearly stated that she considers herself ugly. Her self-esteem will not improve until she is protected from the sexual exploitation which makes her feel dirty and degraded.

ID4 *Young person has no view of the future or sense of own ability to influence things*. Becky has tried constantly to gain protection without success. She will only look forward to the future when she has gained safety.

ID14 *Positive efforts are made to establish and maintain peer group contacts*. Becky needs help to separate from the peers who are subject to the abuse network. She may need to leave the locality to be safe.

Carers ensure a predictable routine in the home. Becky's life is completely unpredictable as it is ruled by the authority of the abusers.

P5 *Young person is over-friendly with adult strangers.* Becky must be defined as a victim of adult crime and not as willingly seeking out relationships with older men.

Carers point out aspects of behaviour or appearance that are dangerous. Becky is *dolled up* for the abusers. She has no control over their abusive behaviour towards her. Carers must set standards and boundaries of behaviour but until the abusers are targeted by a concerted joint police and social work investigation and intervention, the carers will be powerless to protect Becky.

S7 *Young person runs away and is picked up by the police*. The full details of the police record must be collated with other information as part of the organised abuse enquiry and protection plan and the child given the opportunity to speak with someone independent.

S8 *Young person is hard to get through to about risky and dangerous behaviour*. Becky has tried so many times to report the abuse that she has given up trying.

All the statements to be explored by the social worker with the looked after young person must be considered within the wider joint investigation and child protection planning. There is a risk that this assessment might lead the social worker to pathologise the child and not notice that she is being abused and is suffering significant harm. No protection or care plan will work unless there is parallel action to target the abusers.

Evaluating the safeguards in place for the child sexually exploited

---

ACTIVITY **2.10**

1. *What policies and procedures would you apply if you were Becky's social worker?*

2. *How would you protect Becky and make sure she was safe?*

3. *How would you protect her friends?*

4. *How would you investigate the abusers and bring them to justice?*

5   *Reflect upon what aspects of professional dangerousness apply to Becky's case. What might block you taking effective active to protect her?*

Comment

1. The relevant policies are:

● *Working together to safeguard children involved in prostitution* (DoH, 2000b).

● Section 47 Children Act 1989 – joint investigation with the police.

● Organised abuse investigation because there is more than one child and more than one abuser (DfES, 2006, 6.7).

2. Becky needs a multi-agency child protection plan to keep her safe. This would be devised through local multi-agency protocols or at a child protection conference which would follow from one or more strategy meetings convened according to section 47 (CA 1989) protocols.

3. Each of her friends known to be at risk would be subject to the same procedures. The young people would be visually interviewed using Achieving Best Evidence guidance (CJS, 2007) and paediatric assessments would take place as agreed by the strategy meeting.

4. The organised abuse strategy meeting would collate all relevant information about the alleged abusers and the police would put strategies in place to monitor their activities through surveillance or other means. The police and social workers would collate evidence together in order to inform any criminal proceedings.

Professional dangerousness

In child protection work professionals may unwittingly collude with, or maintain, the dangerous dynamics of abuse and these pitfalls are known as professional dangerousness. The main pitfalls are described below with reference to the professional response to Becky.

Children unheard/parent and carers unheard
Every child abuse inquiry highlights the central importance of listening to the child. Although children do find it hard to speak of abuse it has been shown that prior to a child's tragic death they have often forewarned someone in authority about the risk. Similarly, prior to fatally harming a child, carers often raise the alarm by telling a professional that they are afraid of hurting the child or cannot cope. Becky told over 40 times and was pathologised as inventing accounts. She did not, however, ever retract an allegation which is a common response and a recognised dynamic in child abuse cases (the child abuse accommodation syndrome).

Rule of optimism
Professionals tend to want to believe that all is well for the child. Even when the indicators of abuse are visible there is a tendency to explain them away and be convinced that the child is safe. Professionals thought that Becky was capable of solving her problems and did not define her as a vulnerable child.

Concrete solutions
Professionals respond swiftly to abuse situations with practical solutions such as housing, washing machines, or money rather than by investigating and attempting to verify the alleged abuse. A placement in care was seen to be the entire solution to Becky's situation without a parallel strategy to target the abusers and remove them from her world.

Assessment paralysis
Sometimes professionals feel helpless and incapacitated. Social workers may not respond to children who are chronically neglected or sexually abused within inter-generational networks, believing that nothing can ever change. Decisions made about risk of harm to a child must be constantly reviewed because situations change. The belief that Becky herself was responsible persisted throughout the case. Professionals sometimes feel omnipotent, believe that they know best and will not revisit their perceptions in the light of new evidence. The perception of Becky was not reviewed despite new evidence coming to light.

Stereotyping
Professionals may make assumptions about how families bring up their children, which includes taking no protective action because of a belief that some forms of harm to children are acceptable in some religions or cultures. Becky was stereotyped as a girl who brought the sexual exploitation upon herself and the abusers remained invisible to the professionals.

Closure
Abusive adults may shut out professionals when calls go unanswered, appointments are missed, curtains are closed and doors locked. Child deaths from abuse are often preceded by closure and this may be mirrored by professionals avoiding contact with the adults. As she was not being heard, Becky withdrew from the professional network and became hostile towards it, removing her from sources of help.

Information which is emotional, recent and vivid takes precedence over the old
Inquiries inevitably demonstrate that agencies had a great deal of knowledge about actual or potential harm to the child. New information must be analysed in the context of prior facts and must be transferred as families and/or children move between authorities. Known facts about Becky and the abusers were not collated so that many responses to Becky's situations were based on guesswork.

Non-compliance with statutory procedures
Inquiries commonly report that legislation and policy are sound but that professionals do not comply with their implementation. When child protection procedures are in place, children generally become safe. Organised abuse procedures were not followed to collate and analyse information about Becky's safety and effective joint work with the police did not take place, leaving Becky exposed to further abuse.

Role confusion
In child protection everyone has prime responsibility for the safety of the child and clarity of decisions is essential. Professionals may be unclear about tasks and assume that someone else is responsible for protecting the child. Becky attended a behaviour management unit where the staff should have recognised that she needed the involvement of a child protection team.

Exaggeration of hierarchy
Adults of low status who report abuse may not be heard or taken seriously by professionals, even though they may be close to the child (e.g. neighbours or friends), whereas they will probably listen to the views of a psychiatrist or lawyer. Becky's friends would have had a lot of information about her lifestyle and she also trusted one health worker who should have been identified as a key protector who could have linked Becky with other sources of help.

The Stockholm syndrome
This theory is based on hostage situations where the people taken hostage begin to identify with the cause of the terrorists. It is a survival mechanism common in child abuse cases. If an abuser is intimidating, the worker will begin to take the adult's point of view rather than the child's. Through this dynamic the worker may mirror the child's entrapment, dependence and misplaced loyalty to the abuser. Professionals may have been too frightened to confront those abusing Becky, particularly if the abusers seemed to have contacts within the professional network.

The child's view

No matter how children are enslaved, whoever sells or buys them they face similar consequences from this dirty trade. Young children's bodies are simply not ready for sex. They are fragile and tear easily so the children suffer lesions, bleeding, scarring, infections, sterility and sometimes death ... their mental health suffers too as they are introduced to sexual acts which they often cannot understand but which they may feel devalue their bodies and souls. They become confused with their role in life, their sexuality and come to distrust adults who offer them 'love' and then abuse and abandon them.

(Kane, 1998, p5)

The following quotations are children's voices from a selection of studies.

I don't think for a lot of young people it is a choice. When I first started out, I had to do it. If someone had been there for me, if somebody had listened to me and helped me and supported me in my teens ... I may have been something else.

(Barrett, 1997, p17)

I didn't like any of it to start with, but over time I grew used to it ... they were giving me money and buying me clothes. I regret now what I did but at the time I felt needed and wanted. It seemed better than the children's home.

(D'Arcy and Gosling, 1998, p200)

I didn't like it but I knew it were the only way I could get money without going thieving ... I wanted to stop at age 12 but I didn't know where to start. I never got any help from anyone because I didn't know how to ask for it.

(Melrose, et al., 1999, p62)

All the punters go for the young lads – they call us chickens.

(*Guardian*, 2003)

I hate everything about my body, it's nothing special anymore. It's like it doesn't belong to me anymore.

(Coy, 2005)

All the girls on the beat – it's like the family I never had.

(Coy, 2005)

I looked around at everyone else and I wanted to be like them. I wanted to come home and know I'd got a safe home to go home to where everybody loved me. But I went out looking for love, that's how I got on drugs and with my pimp.

(Coy, 2005)

I just walked round like a zombie. I don't think I had any feelings.

(Taylor-Browne, et al., 2002, p25)

There is no doubt that the risks of harm to sexually exploited young people are high. They experience violence and yet few report to the police through fear of retaliation. Melrose, et al. (1999) found that 48% of their sample had experienced violence at the hands of the abusers and that 44% said lack of money and poverty were the reason that prevented them escaping the perpetrators. The research showed that by the time a child has become involved in prostitution he or she is multiply damaged. Many had learnt to distrust the authorities and were isolated from society, being accepted only among their peer group.

Children exit this form of abuse when circumstances change, such as when they have children, access drug treatment programmes or training opportunities or when they have experienced a particularly violent attack or rape. Exiting can be very difficult because of reliance on drugs and lack of self-esteem. Some girls fear isolation as they would lose all their peer group and have a sense of shame (Melrose, et al.,1999; Taylor-Browne, et al., 2002, p29).

ACTIVITY 2.11

Read the detailed account below from a child interviewed during the Inquiry into the removal of children from Orkney. Think about how you might analyse this account in order to understand what had happened.

She drew a mis-shaped circle with a human figure wearing what she said was a turtle outfit. This figure she told us was Morris. She drew several vertical lines on the circle and said this was people. The 'Morris' figure was drawn 'hooking' a smaller figure which she said was Q. She then drew another figure who she said was J working the music. She drew a table with a box on top and said that was where the music came from. She then described Morris hooking Lakey into the centre and said he sticks his willy into Lakey's bum. M pointed to her own vaginal area whilst saying this. She then said they all stand round clapping and she clapped her own hands quite slowly. She then said that Morris hooks Q and sticks his willy into her (indicating vaginal area again). M then drew a horse and a couple of human figures. We attempted to pursue this drawing but M avoided the subject … She then drew the sun looking down with a sad face and tears and said that the sun was crying.

(Clyde, 1992, p34)

Comment

This extract illustrates the complexities of children's accounts of their experience of organised child sexual abuse. The police officers and social workers interviewed a number of children and needed to make sense of this child's account in the context of other interviews. The children spoke of events which were bizarre and difficult for the interviewers to understand. Their questioning needed to be non-leading with use of open questions to make sure they did not introduce concepts to the child or make assumptions about what words like *hooking* and *turtle outfit* meant or the meaning of their gestures and drawings. Some information provided may have seemed peripheral at the time such as the *music system* and the *people clapping* but became evidentially relevant as the inquiry progressed. This statement is one of a number recorded during the inquiry which demonstrates the level of detail required when listening to children's accounts.

Is the carer proactively protective?

The social worker will need to assess whether or not the parent/carer is protective. They may be involved in the abuse or they may be ineffective carers. A protective carer may be able to assist the investigation. The Coalition for the Removal of Pimping (CROP) suggests a participatory approach that engages parents, recognises their support needs and acknowledges them as a potential resource in interventions (www.crop1.org.uk).

Detailed mapping of shared information about the risk must be undertaken. Protective parents, foster carers and residential staff are well placed to provide detailed information about the adult perpetrators by collating vehicle and meeting places/premises details, telephone numbers, names (including aliases and nicknames) and other information gathered about the young person's behaviour. This will inform police action in targeting abusers and the joint investigation to protect the child. The careful recording of such detail is essential. Parents are frequently defined as neglectful whereas they are also often betrayed, groomed and entrapped by the perpetrators and feel powerless to intervene to stop the abusers' strategies.

Investigating allegations about the sexual exploitation of a child – deciding the threshold for intervention

ACTIVITY **2.12**

The following case studies are designed to aid a questioning approach to the process of protecting children. They usually progress from referral to investigation and action to protect. When reading the case studies structure your thinking and questioning around the points listed in Chapter 1, but do not be limited by this list. Continue to add your own questions and to consider the implications of these in each case.

CASE STUDY

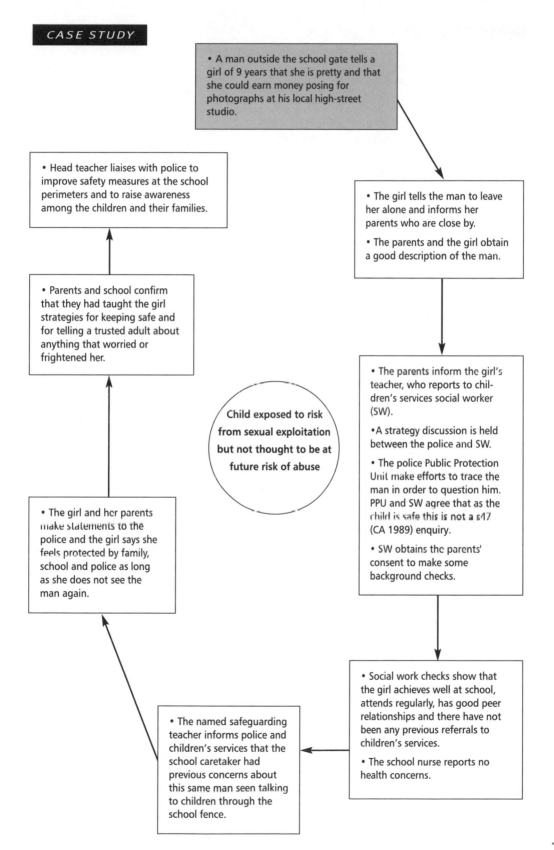

• A man outside the school gate tells a girl of 9 years that she is pretty and that she could earn money posing for photographs at his local high-street studio.

• The girl tells the man to leave her alone and informs her parents who are close by.

• The parents and the girl obtain a good description of the man.

• The parents inform the girl's teacher, who reports to children's services social worker (SW).

• A strategy discussion is held between the police and SW.

• The police Public Protection Unit make efforts to trace the man in order to question him. PPU and SW agree that as the child is safe this is not a s47 (CA 1989) enquiry.

• SW obtains the parents' consent to make some background checks.

Child exposed to risk from sexual exploitation but not thought to be at future risk of abuse

• Head teacher liaises with police to improve safety measures at the school perimeters and to raise awareness among the children and their families.

• Parents and school confirm that they had taught the girl strategies for keeping safe and for telling a trusted adult about anything that worried or frightened her.

• The girl and her parents make statements to the police and the girl says she feels protected by family, school and police as long as she does not see the man again.

• The named safeguarding teacher informs police and children's services that the school caretaker had previous concerns about this same man seen talking to children through the school fence.

• Social work checks show that the girl achieves well at school, attends regularly, has good peer relationships and there have not been any previous referrals to children's services.

• The school nurse reports no health concerns.

CASE STUDY

• A boy of 11 years tells a neighbour that his mother's new partner gives him expensive presents and lets him drink alcohol when his mother is at work.

• The neighbour, who has a child at the same school, shares what she has heard with the teacher.

• The boy also has a brother of 13 years.

• Previous referrals to children's services have been made by neighbours about neglect by the mother. They say that the mother binge drinks following the boys' father's suicide.

• The mother works in the evenings in a pub.

• SW identifies some positive relationships within the extended family.

Concern about children being sexually exploited

• School attendance and punctuality for both boys has deteriorated since the mother's new partner joined the household.

• Both boys are of average ability but seem distracted and show little interest in their work.

• Checks with police about mother's partner under s47 (CA 1989) reveal that no information is available locally or in the town where the boys say he lived previously.

• The school plan to make further referrals should concerns escalate.

• The 13-year-old tells a school nurse that he thinks he might be gay and is being bullied. He wants to go to a local gay youth club.

• He says that his mother's partner tells him he is an attractive boy who could easily find a boyfriend.

• Mother's partner is 15 years younger.

• The named safeguarding teacher refers both boys to the school anti-bullying programme and invites the SW and the boys' mother to a child-in-need meeting at the school.

• The SW decides to make checks with police about the mother's partner without the mother's consent because sharing this information with the family may place the children at risk.

• With the boy's knowledge, the school nurse informs the named teacher of her concerns that the older boy is being bullied about his sexuality.

• She has also noted that both boys now have expensive computer games and iPods.

CASE STUDY

• A boy of 15 years tells the school nurse that he wishes to resume contact with a man he calls 'uncle' wo sexually abused him in the past.

• The abuser was convicted of sexually abusing a number of boys giving them cigarettes, alcohol and somewhere to stay.

• The boy has missed the attention his uncle paid him, believes that his uncle has changed and is truly sorry for what happened.

• The nurse reports to children's services with the boy's knowledge and consent.

• Children's services contact the boy's mother who states that after the abuser was imprisoned, the boy was no longer the subject of child protection procedures.

• She did not believe the initial allegation because he was a friend of the family and she visited him in prison several times.

• Consent from the mother to further checks was not sought as the social worker (SW) decided this might place the boy at risk.

• Child and Adolescent Mental Health Services (CAMHS) have remained involved with the young person and family since the sexual assault and will continue to support the child and assess both parents' capacity to protect the boy from future harm.

• The MAPPA risk strategy states there should not be any contact between the abuser and the boy.

• The Public Protection Unit will monitor his activities.

Suspicion of actual or likely significant harm to a sexually abused child. S47 enquiry

• The school nurse tells the SW he is concerned about the boy's weight gain. In the last year he has become overweight and now has difficulty taking part in school sports activities.

• The father, although separated from the mother, lives close by and tells the SW and police that he is very worried for his son's safety since the abuser returned to the community.

• The SW checks with the school and learns that the boy has a statement of educational needs and extra tuition. He excels at drama.

• He has spoken with his tutor about looking forward to going round to see his uncle with his mates to play music and watch movies.

• SW makes enquiries and holds a strategy discussion with police.

• The abuser is monitored and should he have any contact with the boy there will be a joint investigation and a child protection conference.

• The Multi Agency Public Protection Panel (MAPPA) inform children's services of the abuser's release from prison and recommend s47 (CA 1989) enquiries

• The abuser started a treatment programme in prison which continued in the community provided by the probation service. The abuser is remorseful but still fantasies about sex with children. He is assessed by MAPPA as at low risk of reoffending.

81

CASE STUDY

• The girl is too traumatised to return to the home. The SW identifies an alternative placement as it is not known if the staff member concerned will return to work, although the managers have fully co-operated with the investigation.

• The SW begins to support the girl's application for criminal injuries compensation.

• A 12-year-old girl with cerebral palsy tells her mother during a weekend visit home, that a member of staff from the care home where she lives has upset her.

• She also says he touched her breasts under her pyjamas when he took her on a camping trip and took videos of her with his mobile phone.

• The girl lives in a small residential care home 100 miles from the family home, with eight other disabled children.

• Other authorities with placements in the home are informed of the allegation. A strategy meeting is organised by the authority where the home is and all relevant authorities are invited.

• Child protection planning takes place at a local level for every child who attends the residential home.

• Given police and SW knowledge of prior allegations within the children's home, and the production of images of the child, organised abuse procedures (DfES, 2006) are implemented.

• Consideration is given to pursuing criminal proceedings.

• The mother reports what she has heard to the child's social worker (SW) in the local disabled children's team who makes a referral to the police child abuse investigation team (CAIT).

• The staff member concerned is suspended by the director of the home, pending investigation.

• The police visit the mother to take a statement.

S47 investigation of a sexually exploited child

• During an interview with the police and SW the mother states she believes her daughter's allegation.

• The mother is herself a survivor of sexual abuse.

• The daughter was also physically abused while in nursery school and her mother is knowledgeable about safety issues.

• The mother has three younger children and the allocated social worker arranges family support so the girl can remain at home during the investigation.

• A residential worker tells the police that the two staff previously dismissed were still visiting the home and were friends of the alleged abuser. He also said that the alleged abuser was not qualified and only got the job through fake references.

• A paediatric examination takes place, with the girl's consent, which confirms some minor physical trauma to her vaginal area which the paediatrician said was not inconsistent with the girl's account.

• A strategy discussion is held between police and children's services and a joint investigation is agreed.

• The police officer and the SW contact colleagues in the area where the children's residential home is located and a strategy meeting is convened.

• There have been two other abuse investigations at the home in the past two years about two staff members who were dismissed for gross misconduct.

• The girl is interviewed according to ABE guidance (CJS, 2007), with her own and parental consent, by a police officer and SW and an intermediary who understands the girl's communication needs. She discloses that the staff member, who she named, also *gives kisses on the lips and puts his finger inside her bottom.*

82

CASE STUDY

• At the strategy meeting it is decided that should she run away from the new placement, an application for secure accommodation will be considered.

• In line with local child sexual exploitation protocols, and in order to assist prosecution, all multi-agency information is to be collated to inform the police investigation and child protection planning.

• An application for criminal injuries compensation is made.

• A 14-year-old girl is found in bed with a man of 52 years following a raid on a massage parlour and is placed in police protection.

• Four other young people are also discovered at the scene.

• The police use their powers of protection to remove her and inform children's services immediately.

• A strategy discussion takes place between police and children's services and a joint investigation is agreed.

• Children's services records state the girl is currently missing, has been reported missing many times and began to run away from home and foster care from the age of 13 years.

• Police have found her in various parts of the country including coastal resorts.

Immediate action to protect a child from sexual exploitation

• Further social work (SW) checks show that the girl has been missing from school for over a year. Previously, she was achieving well and is described as sociable and popular with other children.

• The girl's mother has severe mental health problems, a history of alcohol misuse and cannot protect her daughter.

• The girl's father is in the army and away from home for long periods.

• Children's services decide not to seek consent for the checks as this would not be in the child's best interests.

•The SW obtains an Interim Care Order with directions for a paediatric assessment including drug screening and a visually recorded interview.

• A placement in residential care, a long distance outside of the authority, is identified.

•A strategy meeting is to be convened as soon as possible.

•The outreach worker visits the girl in her new placement.

•Organised abuse procedures (DfES, 2006) will be implemented by police in relation to all the children removed from the massage parlour.

• The foster carer tells the SW that she cannot manage the girl's behaviour or stop her running away and that older men persistently call at the house and wait outside in cars.

• There have also been several threatening and abusive phone calls from men to the girl.

• The SW interviews the girl at the police station who says she will continue being a *sex worker* and that it is her choice. She also says she can look after herself.

• A worker in an outreach service has engaged with the child and reports to the SW that the girl smokes crack cocaine and has unsafe sex.

•The SW telephones the parents to inform them that their daughter has been found, that she is to be interviewed and an Interim Care Order is to be sought.

83

Now return to the four cases on in Activity 2.8 and try constructing some diagrams for these cases. What factors might make these children more or less safe?

C H A P T E R   S U M M A R Y

This chapter reflects concern at the considerable reduction in the numbers of cases of child sexual abuse defined as requiring protective intervention. We have highlighted that anti-oppressive practice, concerned with the abuse of power, requires that children who are sexually abused receive a protective social work response. Many forms of child sexual abuse, including within the context of organised abuse, are presented to demonstrate the inadequacy of the current level of social work response. The importance of listening to children who disclose abuse is a particular focus. This chapter studies the strategies used by child sex abusers and supports joint investigation in which social workers become well informed about how perpetrators, including women and children, target vulnerable children. The difficulties in the use of mechanistic protocols for risk assessment in cases of child sexual exploitation are explored. An in-depth study of the subject of child sexual exploitation includes information about professional dangerousness and exploration of the use of ECM protocols.

FURTHER READING

Bray, M (1997) *Poppies on the rubbish heap. Sexually abused children. The child's voice*. London: Jessica Kingsley.
A sensitive account of working therapeutically with children who have been sexually abused.

Calder, M (2008) *Complete guide to sexual abuse assessments*. Lyme Regis: Russell House.
This important text offers a wealth of information about conducting, and evaluating sexual abuse assessments.

Cooper, T (2006) *Trust no one*. London: Orion.
One survivor's account of abuse in the care system.

Davies, L (2007) Responding to the protection needs of traumatized and sexually abused children. In Hosin, A (2007) *Responses to traumatized children*. Basingstoke: Palgrave, pp203–27.
This chapter outlines the protective procedures and therapeutic interventions required for responding to child sexual abuse.

Malone, C, Farthing, L and Marce, L (eds) (1997) *The memory bird. Survivors of sexual abuse*. London: Virago.
A collection of personal accounts of abuse and individual survivors' routes to recovery.

Melrose, M and Barrett, D (eds) (2004) *Anchors in floating lives: Interventions with young people sexually abused through prostitution*. Lyme Regis: Russell House.
Knowledge from research and practice examples are presented in a very readable format.

Nelson, S (ed.) (2008) *See us – hear us. Schools working with sexually abused young people*. Dundee: Violence is Preventable.
A book based on research with young people who have been sexually abused and who talk about their experiences within the educational system. It explores what worked well and how schools could improve, and is aimed at schools and youth organisations.

Social Work Inspection Agency (2005) *An inspection into the care and protection of children in Eilean Siar*. Edinburgh: Scottish Executive.
This inspection report makes 31 recommendations for all agencies that deal with the protection of children.

WEBSITES

www.ceop.gov.uk
Child Exploitation and Online Protection Centre (CEOP) is a police initiative aiming to track and prosecute abusers either directly or in partnership with local and international forces. It provides a 24-hour online reporting facility for children and adults about internet child abuse.

www.cica.gov.uk
Criminal Injuries Compensation Authority. The CICA is responsible for administering the Criminal Injuries Compensation Scheme throughout England, Scotland and Wales. Compensation is paid to eligible applicants who have been the victim of violent and sexual crimes.

www.crop1.org.uk
The Coalition for the Removal of Pimping is a voluntary organisation working to end the sexual exploitation of children.

www.cwasu.org.uk
Child and Woman Abuse Studies Unit, London Metropolitan University. A centre for independent research, training and consultancy from a feminist perspective.

www.fco.gov.uk/forcedmarriage
The Forced Marriage Unit of the Foreign and Commonwealth Office offers confidential advice and assistance to those who have been forced into marriage overseas, are at risk of being forced into marriage, people worried about their friends or relatives.

www.howitis.org.uk
Howitis is an initiative between the NSPCC and Triangle providing a library of images about feelings, rights and safety, personal care and sexuality to assist communication with disabled children and young people in abusive and in other situations.

www.kidscape.org.uk
Kidscape is a charity established specifically to prevent bullying and child sexual abuse. It provides practical skills and resources to help keep children safe from harm.

www.matters2me.org.
A DVD to tell children, parents and carers about risks from online abuse, grooming and bullying.

www.missingpeople.org.uk
Missing People is a charity working with young people who run away or go missing. It supports families and provides information about unidentified people.

www.stopitnow.org.uk
Stop it Now is part of the Lucy Faithful Foundation charity and is a campaign providing the public with information and raising awareness about child sexual abuse.

Chapter 3
Neglect

5.7 Skills in working with others
- consult actively with others, including service users, who hold relevant information or expertise;
- act with others to increase social justice by identifying and responding to prejudice, institutional discrimination and structural inequality;
- challenge others when necessary, in ways that are most likely to produce positive outcomes.

7.3 Knowledge and understanding
- ability to use research and enquiry techniques, to collect, analyse and interpret relevant information;
- a developed capacity for critical evaluation of knowledge and evidence from a range of sources.

Introduction

The unwanted and unsung heroes and heroines of British society, who suffered at the hands of 'care' and 'don't care' with thousands of other 'unwanted' children. That these children grew up to make something of their lives from the chronic neglect that was the 'care system' is a tribute to their courage and fortitude ... Society pays for its neglect. Children become adults.

(Frampton, 2003, p290)

Children who have experienced extreme neglect and damage do not produce outcomes the way we expect them. Nevertheless their success is palpable. They are dignified individuals who are making their way back from emotionally dark places.

(Batmanghelidjh, 2006, p11)

This chapter focuses on protection of children from neglect. It begins by looking at definitions and moves on to consider the knowledge required to make professional judgements. The complexities of this form of abuse will be examined to support an informed approach to individual children's circumstances. Research into children's views and survivor perspectives provides a basis for sound decision-making. Four case studies provide opportunity for further application of knowledge to practice. The chapter concludes with case examples of neglect involving children left at home alone, which will take the reader through an investigative process, escalated through five levels of social work intervention to support in-depth analysis.

Definition of neglect

the persistent failure to meet a child's basic physical and/or psychological needs likely to result in the serious impairment of the child's health or development. Neglect may occur during pregnancy as a result of maternal substance misuse. Once a child is born, neglect may involve a parent or carer failing to:

- *provide adequate food, clothing and shelter (including exclusion from home or abandonment);*
- *protect a child from physical and emotional harm or danger;*
- *ensure adequate supervision (including the use of inadequate care givers);*
- *ensure access to appropriate medical care or treatment.*

It may also include neglect of, or unresponsiveness to, a child's basic emotional needs.

(DfES, 2006, 1.33)

Learning about neglect

Think about what persistent, basic *and* serious *mean in the context of the definition of neglect in* Working together (DfES, 2006, 1.33).

Comment

It is important to point out that this guidance specifies *persistent* as an essential component of neglect, yet of course one single incident of neglect could be fatal, for example, when a child falls from an open window or suffers burns from an unguarded fire. Dickens points out that *a one-off failure to provide adequate clothing would not meet the criteria: but there are hard questions about how many would, what period of time and in what circumstances* (Dickens, 2007, p81). Gelles states that it is often unclear *whether neglect is due to a parent's omissions or due to absence of social, economic or psychological resources.* Where should the blame lie – with the family or with society for structural deficits and gross inequities based on wealth, age, class, gender, ethnicity and disability (Gelles, 1999)?

Inequalities such as infant mortality rates vary considerably across the country. A child born in central Birmingham is eight times more likely to die before their first birthday than a child born in mid-Surrey, which could be said to illustrate the level of societal neglect of some communities. Babies from ethnic minority groups are particularly likely to have lower birth weights (CRAE, 2006, p34). Neglect is often located within poor and disadvantaged communities, yet families within these communities are more visible to the authorities and more likely to be officially judged than children of wealthier families. The eradication of poverty would ease stress on poor families but neglect is more to do with cyclical modes of thought and behaviour than cyclical experiences of poverty (McSherry, 2004). Therefore ending poverty would not lead to ending child neglect. Tanner and Turney comment that judgements about neglect are typically value laden about standards of care, *a position compounded by social workers' unwillingness to pathologise families who may already be disadvantaged by poverty* (2003, p3).

Gaudin draws attention to the disproportionate effects of poverty on black and ethnic minority groups in the US, noting that *ethnic and cultural differences in child maltreatment are small or non-existent when families have adequate social and economic resources, but the combination of racial discrimination and poverty places unusual stresses on families of colour that frequently overwhelm their coping resources* (Gaudin, 1993, p19 cited in Tanner and Turney, 2003, p30). Yet in studies relating to neglect, ethnicity of the subjects, published in three key journals, was recorded in only about half and analysis and design of the studies omitted ethnicity in three-quarters (Tanner and Turney, 2003, p30).

Although the guidance does not specify *failure to thrive* in children this may very well be caused by neglect or there may be clear medical reasons. Failure to thrive is defined as when weight, height and head circumference of the child are significantly below age-related norms and the child's wellbeing causes concern (Iwaniec, 1995). Unless there is reason for immediate protection of the child it is usually only when a paediatrician has given a view that the cause is non-organic (i.e. a child whose growth and development are not what would be expected in relation to normal milestones and this lack of development is not due to genetic or physical causes) that child protection procedures will begin. Some failure to thrive is caused through understimulation as well as poor feeding. Percentile charts are an essential tool in monitoring the growth and development of children and for assessing changes while the children are in different environments. Health professionals present these at all child protection meetings and provide an analysis of the meaning of the statistics which correlate information about the child's height, weight and head circumference over time (DfES, 2006,1.33).

Some facts about neglect

- In 2007 there were 12,500 children and young people who were the subject of a child protection plan under the category of neglect. Neglect comprised the largest category (DCFS, 2007).

- Some 30% of children who die from child abuse die from neglect mainly by female carers (Reder, et al., 1993). Children who die in house fires are often found to have suffered neglect by having been left alone (Squires and Busuttil, 1995).

- Neglect may coexist with other forms of child abuse. Farmer and Owen (1995) found that in a third of neglect cases physical abuse was also a concern; in a fifth of physical abuse cases there were also concerns about neglect; and in a quarter of sexual abuse cases there were also neglect concerns (Farmer and Owen, cited in Tomison, 1995).

- It is important not to assume a direct causal link between neglect and poverty. Many parents who are poor do not neglect their children and carers in high socio-economic classes may neglect their children (Burke, et al., 1998).

- Babies and young children are particularly vulnerable to all forms of child abuse but there is little known about teenagers and their deaths from neglect. There are very few serious case reviews concerning children over the age of ten years who die as a result of child abuse (NSPCC, 2001a).

- Children who run away from home and live on the streets may die from hypothermia, drug misuse, self-harm or disease but their deaths will not be analysed as resulting from child abuse. Two-thirds (68%) of young people who have run away overnight said they had not been reported as missing to the police by their parents or carers (Rees and Lee, 2005, p22).

- On average each young offender institution provides only eight hours of education for the young people per week (CRAE, 2006, p56).

- Vouchers given to low-income families to purchase milk, fruit and vegetables are not available to asylum-seeking families (CRAE, 2006, p48).

- 1.3 million children (1 in 11) in the UK are living with parental alcohol misuse (Turning Point, 2005).

- It is estimated that 2.3% of under 16 year olds are affected by parental drug misuse (www.drugs.gov.uk/publication-search/acmd/hidden-harm).

- In a sample of neglectful families, alcohol was present in 75% of cases. In many the children were left to look after themselves, food was in short supply and clothing unwashed. The children were socially isolated (Iwaniec, 1995, p13)

- Of the 98,730 households in temporary accommodation, 74% include dependent children (ODPM, 2006, cited in Beckett, 2007, p173).

CASE STUDY

Paul

Paul was born in 1991, the youngest of seven children – four boys and three girls. He died aged 15 months of pneumonia, blood poisoning and septic lesions brought about by severe neglect. In the last few days of his life he had been left in a pram in urine-soaked clothes. The home had very few of the items most families would consider basic – sheets on the bed, carpets, soap or toothbrushes. The toilet had overflowed and the children lived on what they could scavenge from the rubbish bins of shops. The parents were convicted of manslaughter.

The children were never the subject of child protection procedures, yet there were over 150 instances over 12 years of concern to professionals, including failure to thrive, inappropriate feeding, poor school attendance, unkempt and dirty presentation, poor hygiene, developmental delay and lack of self-esteem. The children had been seen begging and furnishings provided to the family were subsequently sold. In 15 years, 30 operational units from police, social services, health, probation and education were involved. The 150 indicators were only collated after Paul's death because child protection forums for sharing information were not implemented.

The family were poor and financial assistance was provided over the years as well as practical support, such as allowing the children to take a shower at school. The children were not defined as suffering significant harm but as a low-income family needing support. The long-term impact of the neglect was not appreciated.

There was a professional unwillingness to impose middle-class values on the family. The Area Child Protection Committee (ACPC) at the time said a heavier touch had been needed where professionals should not have been afraid to insist on minimum standards of physical and emotional care for these children (Ibbetson, 1995). It was also clarified that neglect caused by financial poverty may coexist with neglect due to emotional poverty and the relief of the former does not relieve the latter. The Inquiry reported that the major input by professionals had been to the adults in the household and not to the children. Paul's name featured little in the case records. It was almost as if he did not exist, not only within the family, but also to the professional agencies (Bridge Child Care Development Service, 1995, p181).

Disabled children and neglect

Sullivan and Knutson (2000a, p1257), who analysed records of 40,000 children in the US, found that disabled children were 3.8 times more likely to be neglected than non-disabled children.

I worry that we accept levels of neglect and really poor quality of care that we wouldn't if it was an able-bodied child.

Social worker (NSPCC, 2003, p9)

Disabled children are not a homogeneous group and should not be grouped together for the narrow application of theory and research evidence. Disabled children are not only the responsibility of specialist practitioners, and should not be viewed as a *breed apart* (Cross, 2001, p148). Each child must be seen as an individual with an impairment or disability that is part of their identity and not as a tragic case requiring sympathy (Mason, 2000).

The limited information available about the circumstances of disabled children in the UK is out of date. It is not known how prevalence or pattern of disability, for example, increase in numbers of children with complex health needs and children diagnosed with autistic spectrum disorders. It is known that most disabled children have more than one disability, with severely disabled children commonly having physical, sensory and learning disabilities (Gordon, et al., 2000).

ACTIVITY 3.2

Why do you think disabled children are particularly vulnerable to neglect?

Comment

Utting (1997), in his review of the safeguards for children in care, noted that disabled children, as well as being more vulnerable to all kinds of abuse than non-disabled children, are also vulnerable to specific forms of neglect. These include over- or under-medication, poor feeding and toileting arrangements and lack of supervision or stimulation. Communication difficulties may also make it difficult for a disabled child to tell others about abuse or to present evidence in court. *These factors taken together increase their vulnerability and make them targets for abusers since the risk of disclosure is low and the risk of a successful prosecution even lower.* He also found that disabled children were more likely than non-disabled children to be in residential placements (Utting, 2005, p83).

Research has also shown that disabled children are neglected through the lack of resources and support services, particularly for black and ethnic minority disabled children and their families (NSPCC, 2003, p28). Abbott, et al. (2001) in a survey found that one in four local authorities did not define the children they place at residential schools as *looked after*. Little evidence was found of the children's own wishes and feelings being ascertained. *The low priority accorded to them by social services and the lack of clarity about their looked after status means that social workers often do not play much of a role in safeguarding their interests* (NSPCC, 2003, p48).

A number of barriers can get in the way of protection for disabled children. *Children are left in situations where there is a high level of neglect ... because a professional feels the parent, carer or service is doing their best* (NSPCC, 2003, p34). Sympathy with the family at times may lead to collusion and the signs of abuse may become attributed to the disability rather than to neglect. Social workers may also be unfamiliar with best practice for particular children's needs. There may be an over-reliance on the main carer for information and it is important to contact a number of different sources to gain a full picture of the child's needs.

There may be specific indicators of neglect in relation to disabled children such as:

- segregation;
- confinement to a room or cot;
- misuse of medication or sedation;
- ill-fitting equipment such as poorly-fitted splints;
- overzealous behaviour modification, e.g. through deprivation of food or liquid, clothing or medication;
- misapplication of regimes;
- treatment without proper analgesia;
- invasive procedures without consent.

(Barker and Hodes, 2007, pp64–5)

The systems designed to protect all children may fail disabled children. For instance, disabled children subject to child protection plans were less likely to be placed on the Child Protection Register before this was abolished (Cooke and Standen, 2002). There is a risk of them slipping through the protection net because of the split between the specialist disability and the children's teams. A coalition of charities has set up a campaign group entitled Every Disabled Child Matters, recognising that the Every Child Matters agenda (DfES, 2003) is not inclusive of the needs of disabled children (www.edcm.org.uk).

Neglect of children at different ages

ACTIVITY 3.3

Social workers sometimes think that children are more vulnerable to abuse at particular ages. At what age do you think children are more likely to experience neglect?

Comment

Most child abuse inquiries about children who have died or have been seriously injured as a result of neglect concern young children. However, children of all ages may be subject to neglect.

In the UK an estimated 1 in 50 children are forced to leave home before the age of 16 years. These children are unlikely to receive services and are more aptly described as *throwaways*. Once on the street they are at great risk of neglect and serious harm. One in seven is hurt or harmed and one in nine sexually assaulted. About two-thirds of children who run away overnight are not reported as missing (Rees and Lee, 2005).

Thinking about types of neglect

Separation

Child evacuees

The long-term impact of separation on a child has been documented in research carried out with wartime evacuees. Although there are no official estimates of numbers, records show that about 3.5 million children and mothers in the UK were evacuated during the Second World War and were separated for up to six years before returning home. Over 60 years later the emotional and psychological trauma, stress and anxiety experienced as children are now re-emerging for people in older age. For many their lives would have seen them coping but as their independence is threatened the impact of their childhood experiences of insecurity and trauma is re-appearing. *For most, the simple separation from their own families will have been enough to set in place the chain of events that would lead to psychological problems six decades later* (Dobson, 2003).

Child migrants

Humphreys (1996) researched the impact of separation from UK birth families on the child migrants when thousands of children were sent to the colonies during the 1940s and 1950s as cheap labour for farms and construction industries as well as for domestic labour. Her account *Empty cradles* gives the history of these tragic events and survivors' accounts of the abuse and emotional deprivation experienced.

Children in the midst of parental divorce and separation

When parents are separating, children's needs and wishes can become lost within the parental trauma and conflict. Three million children in the UK experience their parents separating or divorcing. Douglas makes the case for these children to be defined as children in need. He says that *children's resilience though real is often over-stated* and that children experience the same emotions as a parent at these times, such as loss, grief, rejection, guilt and a sense of abandonment (Douglas, 2006, p36). Goldson (2006) stated that the vast majority of separating parents do not wish to harm their children but many do as they become preoccupied with their difficulties and there is disruption of the child's world. She found that children when involved in the mediation process with their parents found a voice and reported a decrease in anxiety about the emotional and practical issues facing them as their family life was rearranged. The parents also reported their children to be less anxious.

Brothers and sisters separated in the care system

A survey by A National Voice (2006) was conducted with 112 children in care between the ages of 10 and 25 years to examine issues relating to sibling contact. In the sample, 91% had at least one birth sibling and 54% had at least one foster sibling; 84% of those with birth siblings and 64% of those with foster siblings did not live with them; 75% of those with birth siblings and 35% of those with foster siblings had problems seeing them. The survey found that 75% of respondents with birth siblings and 37% of those with foster siblings would like to see them more frequently. The children said that the main blocks to sibling contact were:

I'm too young to go by myself.

They are too far away.

I do not know where they are.

There is no one to go with me.

It costs too much to go to see them.

Social workers have a central role in maintaining contact between siblings in care yet the children had the following comments about the help provided by social workers:

I only got help because I rang all the time not actually because they thought it was important.

They tried sorting it out but it didn't work.

They provided money.

Social worker said they would help us step by step but they just gave me his number and told me how to get there.

(ANV, 2006, p4)

Children deported from the UK

Home Office statistics do not state clearly the numbers of dependent and unaccompanied children being deported each year. From the total number of deportations, the percentage of minors among dependants indicates that around 1,500 children are removed from the UK each year. The main destinations of deportees are Iraq, Serbia, Montenegro, Afghanistan, Iran, Turkey, Nigeria and until recently Zimbabwe. A number of these children were born in the UK or have spent the greatest part of their lives in this country. Most of these children had formed friendships which were broken and have had their education violently disrupted, while for all of these children the future will be uncertain as there is no guarantee of child protection in their own country. In some of these destinations returned asylum seekers are punished with imprisonment, torture or murder. The Stop Deporting Children Campaign demands that the government puts children's rights and needs before the needs of immigration control (www.standup4children.org/).

The Children's Commissioner for Scotland expressed her concerns: *What can happen is immigration officers and police, big groups of them, 11 to 14, go to a family's house at seven o'clock in the morning, sometimes earlier, and waken the children in their beds. I would describe it as completely inhumane, I think we're terrorising these children and families* (BBC News, 2005). A Code of Practice for Keeping Children Safe from Harm states that immigration authorities will fully take part in the Local Safeguarding Children Boards (Border and Immigration Agency, 2008, 3.6.13).

Institutional and organisational neglect

Neglect may also be a form of *secondary abuse*. This is abuse caused by the systems designed to protect children. Key examples of such neglect are children abused within institutions or while in care. Frampton provides an account of his childhood in care in the 1960s, which he describes as *the social dustbin* and as chronic neglect. *I unconsciously but stubbornly followed my instincts, side stepping danger, drawing back from cliff edges, unsafe situations and unsafe people* (Frampton, 2003, p235). Children in care having multiple placements are an example of neglect by the systems designed to protect (Beckett, 2007, p197). In 2007, 790 children experienced between 5 and 19 placement moves and 130 experienced over 10 (Adonis, 2008). It is important to realise that the care system may not always provide the high standard of care required for vulnerable children; however, this factor must never deter professionals from being prepared to remove children from harmful situations.

In 1991, Frank Beck received five life sentences for sexual and physical assaults against children between 1973 and 1986 in children's homes in Leicestershire. His regime involved so-called regression therapy, which included the humiliation of children and promotion of aggression which resulted in restraint.

> *The kids were in their early teens – the older kids had drinks in bottles with dummies. It was an attempt to dig down to the supposed roots of children's problems by returning them to a state of infancy. Younger children might be dressed in nappies and fed from bottles. Social workers might cut up the food on their plates as if feeding infants. Children would be given toys designed for younger children ... children were provoked into violent temper tantrums, physically restrained often by several social workers and sometimes choked around the neck with a towel ... children were dressed and undressed by staff, kept in pyjamas for days. They were spoon fed, read bed time stories for children of three or four.*
>
> (D'Arcy and Gosling, 1998, p28 and p8)

The regime promoted by Beck illustrates *the way in which theoretical labels and concepts were used to confer credibility and intellectual respectability on abusive practices* (Stanley, et al., 1999, p20).

Harbert wrote a novel based in part on his experience of being a director of social services when he felt quite unable to protect the children in his care because of the role of local politicians, unions and local authority executives. The novel, *Bent twigs*, provides an insight into the powerlessness of children in the care system and the struggle of professionals trying to provide them with high-quality care and safety (Harbert, 2005).

An example of organisational neglect is the lack of local government strategies for homeless young people. The CRAE report (2006) cited the fact that, in a study of 100 authorities, Centrepoint, a refuge for homeless young people in London, found that over half did not say how they would house 16- and 17-year-olds and 32% had no places for supported accommodation for this age group. Similarly, young people in the same age group have difficulty accessing any psychiatric services. Most only obtain help following a crisis situation and wait between six months and a year for any other appointment (Young Minds, 2000).

Asylum-seeking children and children in detention centres

> *Life in camp every single day is becoming more boring. It is. I'm here three weeks and it's like brain damage, because you're trapped inside. It feels like I've done something wrong to be in a prison. I can hardly eat, only once a day, because, honest, I'm very, very depressed.*
> (Saida, aged 13 years while at Yarls Wood Detention Centre. She was eventually deported). **www.standup4children.org/chlstory.html**

Immigration officials, and staff in detention centres, do not have a duty under section 11 (CA, 2004) to have regard to the welfare of children. There is concern about the neglect of children in detention centres for asylum seekers. In interviews, children at the Yarls Wood Detention Centre children said they were *upset, I felt I was in jail,* and *frightened by the big and noisy shoes worn by the officers.* Only 4 out of the 13 children said they felt happy. In particular there was concern about the length of time children were detained. A quarter of the children were kept between 20 and 112 days (Bonomi, 2006). Save the Children estimates that around 2,000 children are imprisoned in detention centres each year. An inspection of Yarls Wood reported critically on the detention of disabled children (Dawar, 2008).

The Chief Inspector of Prisons and the Children's Commissioner have raised concerns about the lack of child protection in the detention centres. There are particular concerns about neglect of asylum-seeking children in relation to health care. The Refugee Council reported numbers of girls denied access to maternity care and many had given birth at home without any medical care (CRAE, 2006, p34).

Parents of children who have been refused the right to remain in the UK are denied public funds and therefore access to services. This even affects women fleeing violence who are now denied a place in a women's refuge. The impact on the children is devastating and social workers should never be placed in a situation where they remove children from a family because, as a result of this harsh and oppressive policy, a family is unable to provide for their children. The Campaign to Abolish No Recourse to Public Funds has a leaflet available from **www.southallblacksisters.org.uk/downloads/**

Children in custody

Neglect issues were raised by the Chief Inspector of Prisons in her annual report (HM Chief Inspector for Prisons, 2006). Over a third of children said they felt unsafe in custody, a quarter said they had been insulted or assaulted by a member of staff and a third said that no staff member had checked them in the past week. One child in 50 reported sexual assault by staff. The UK incarcerates more children than any other European country. In 2008 there were 3,037 children in custody in England and Wales. Of these, 85% were in prison custody and 19% were on remand. Children in penal custody are known to be among the most disadvantaged. Over a quarter have the literacy and numeracy ability of an average seven-year-old, 85% show signs of mental health problems, over half have been in care or involved with social services and 41% have been excluded from school. During 2004, 3,337 children assessed as vulnerable were nevertheless sent to young offender institutions (CRAE, 2006, p55). Up to 1,000 young people per year are remanded to custody because they lack somewhere suitable to live (Howard League, 2008).

Children in the armed forces

Of all new recruits to the armed forces in 2004–5, 35% were under 18 years. In March 2006 the Deepcut Review highlighted concerns about the care of young recruits following the deaths of four army trainees in the barracks at Deepcut, Surrey (Blake, 2006). There is no legal reason why these young people are not covered by Children Act legislation yet there were no serious case reviews on the two young people who died under the age of 18 years. CRAE argues that child recruits should have the same safeguards as other young people in institutional settings including a right to maintain family contact, access to advocacy and advice, the opportunity to raise child protection concerns with external agencies and access to external inspectors (CRAE, 2006, p52).

Children trafficked for domestic labour

Mende Nazer was a child slave in London until 2002 and describes her suffering:

as the weeks passed I became more and more depressed. I was a stranger to the children. I was completely isolated and alone. I stayed in the house and worked from early morning to late at night – unloved and uncared for. I was trapped in the middle of this strange city that I had been told was dark and dangerous. All I did was work, work, work. The only thing I looked forward to was sleeping in my cold room.

(Nazer and Lewis 2004, p263)

Trafficking involves the exploitation of children through force, coercion, threat and the use of deception and human rights abuses such as debt bondage, deprivation of liberty and lack of control over one's labour. It includes the movement of people across borders and also the movement and exploitation of people within borders (DfES, 2006,11.76). Children may be trafficked to the UK, within the UK or in transit through the UK to another country for financial gain. The UK is a destination country for trafficked children for domestic service and benefit fraud. Some enter the UK as unaccompanied minors or as students or visitors. They may be brought in by adults who claim to be their carers and some girls may be brought in through being tricked into bogus marriages. The UK is a transit country for children sent to Italy, Canada, US and Ireland. Some trafficking is by organised gangs, in other cases by individuals. Exploitation includes children being used for domestic labour, sexual exploitation, restaurant work, drug dealing, begging, benefit fraud, forced marriage, ritual killing and the trade in human organs.

Traffickers will often subject the children to physical, sexual and emotional violence. There have been reports of particularly West African children being threatened with ritual curses and threats may be made against their families in their home country (Home Office, 2008). Children may enter the UK as students, tourists or unaccompanied minors. Once in the care systems they may be removed and abducted by the traffickers and go missing from professional protective systems.

Children may be recruited to escape poverty, warfare, discrimination and/or a lack of education, with the parents not realising the risks to the child; but also parents may sell their children for profit. Even before they travel, children can be subjected to various forms of abuse and exploitation to ensure that the trafficker's control over the child continues. The child's identity documents may be confiscated, the child may be locked up and isolated and some are told that they must repay the debt of the air fare, accommodation and food and must work to pay this off. Voodoo is sometimes used to frighten children into thinking that if they tell anyone about the traffickers, they and their families will die.

In one study, 80 cases of known or suspected child victims of trafficking were identified in the north of England. 60% of these children (48) had gone missing from care and had never been found. Many of the children had not been investigated, identified or recorded as a victim of trafficking at the time they went missing (Beddoe, 2007, p25). In 2007, the DCSF reported that 160 children had gone missing from care and remained missing. More than 100 other children had been missing for over four years who should have been in care. Of course, many children who go missing are not reported to the police (Brady and Owen, 2008).

ACTIVITY 3.4

Read the list of the key indicators of trafficking stated below and consider which applied in the case of Victoria Climbié.

Key indicators relating to trafficking include children where the child:

1. *Does not appear to have money but does have a mobile phone*
2. *Is driven around by an older male or 'boyfriend'*
3. *Is withdrawn and refuses to talk*
4. *Shows signs of sexual behaviour or language*
5. *Shows signs of physical or sexual abuse, and/or has contracted a sexually transmitted infection*
6. *Has a history with unexplained gaps and moves*
7. *Is required to earn a minimum amount of money every day*
8. *Works in various locations*
9. *Has limited freedom of movement*
10. *Appears to be missing for periods*
11. *Is known to beg for money*
12. *Is being cared for by adult/s who are not their parents. The quality of the relationship between the child and their adult carers is not good*
13. *Has not been registered with or attended a GP practice*
14. *Has not been enrolled in school*
15. *Has to pay off an exorbitant debt, perhaps for the travel costs, before being able to have control over his/her own earnings*
16. *Hands over a large part of their earnings to another person*
17. *Is excessively afraid of being deported*
18. *Has had their journey or visa arranged by someone other than themselves or their family*
19. *Does not have possession of their own travel documents*
20. *Has false papers, and these have been provided by another person*
21. *Is unable to confirm which adult is going to accept responsibility for her/him*
22. *Fits current profiles for those at risk of exploitation*
23. *Has entered the country illegally*

(LSCB, 2006, 10.1, and LSCB, 2007, 5.43.9)

Victoria Climbié was taken by Marie Therese Kouao from her family in the Ivory Coast via France to London under a false name and a false passport and her parents did not retain contact with her. She stood to attention and was deferential in the presence of Kouao (described as a master–servant relationship), who was seen to neglect Victoria. Victoria was known by a number of different names. She was noted as having unexplained injuries by two different hospitals and she was not registered with a school or doctor. There were allegations of sexual abuse by the aunt's boyfriend and signs of sexual abuse were noted by the first pathologist although the second pathologist cast doubt on these findings..

Comment

The following indicators applied in the case of Victoria Climbié:

3, 4, 5, 6, 10, 12, 13, 14, 18, 19, 20, 23

Garrett (2006) presents an argument for seeing the case as a global issue. He considers transnational migration as a core aspect of the tragedy of Victoria's death. The Inquiry, with a limited frame of reference, defined the murder of Victoria as the result of child abuse by carers in the UK. The possibility of trafficking and Victoria's origins and history in Africa and France were not investigated in any depth by the Inquiry team. This was a lost opportunity in terms of developing understanding of events in Victoria's short life and in gaining knowledge about the global transit of children.

Trafficking for exploitation, which includes for forced labour and the removal of organs, was introduced in the Asylum and Immigration Act 2004. If trafficking is suspected the police child abuse investigation team (CAIT) must be informed and social workers must work jointly with the police in the investigation of these serious crimes. Detailed guidance is available from the Home Office (2008) and in *Working together* (DfES, 2006,11.76–80). The child must be given a safe place to stay and be provided with support services and legal advice. Social workers must work with police to identify the traffickers and to locate relatives in the country of origin, making judgements about what is in the child's best interests – to remain in the UK or return to their home country. Children in care must be monitored for signs of meeting traffickers such as through checking phone calls. The child will need to be supported in not going with the trafficker.

Considering the significance of physical and behavioural indicators of neglect

Social workers need to recognise specific signs which may indicate neglect. Although some indicators will be definitive, most will need evaluation through the child protection processes and multi-agency debate. On their own or grouped together they may be indicative.

RESEARCH SUMMARY

Robinson (1999) found that there was a wide range of difference in professional judgement about the relevance of specific indicators of neglect. Professionals, social workers, health visitors, paediatricians, police and psychologists, could only reach agreement on 11 out of 33 possible indicators.

Levels of inter-professional agreement on indicators of probable or definite neglect were:

non-compliance with specific medical care 96%;

inadequate or dirty clothing 88%;

child wandering or unsupervised 85%;

child dirty or smelly 81%;

poor child health surveillance and immunisation uptake 70%;

domestic violence 69%;

severe dental decay 68%;

not registered with GP or dentist 60%;

frequent accidents or injuries to child 60%;

poor feeding or sleeping patterns 55%;

refusal to accept social services input 53%.

ACTIVITY 3.5

Do you think the following are signs of neglect?

Obesity

Behavioural problems

Lack of age-appropriate toys

Poor attendance at school or nursery

Global developmental delay

Frequent out-of-hours GP consultations

Frequent hospital admissions

Poor concentration or learning

Speech delay

Not taken to optician regularly

Poor self-care

Involuntary wetting

Involuntary soiling

Non-attendance for medical appointments.

Comment

Robinson found that the professionals reached less than 20% agreement on the above factors. Here are some examples of the complexities of making judgements about some of the neglect issues raised in the research.

Obesity may be the result of neglect if a carer continually feeds a child inappropriate foods and takes no notice of medical advice. The child may be defined as at considerable risk of significant harm because of the medical and psychological risks. But there may be many other reasons for obesity such as medical conditions or depression. A child may choose to look obese in order to be unattractive to a child sex abuser and therefore there may be psychological reasons for the condition.

Doctors speaking anonymously to the BBC said overfeeding a child should be considered neglect in extreme cases:

> We're very lily-livered about this as a society ... I have seen an obese child taken away from parents return to a normal body weight in a few months ... I've seen a 10-year-old who could only walk a few yards with a walking stick. Her diet of chips and high fat food could firmly be laid at the parents' door. I believe they were killing her slowly ... Seeing a 10-year-old with diabetes and high blood pressure. He is at risk of heart disease in his 20s – the family will not make changes.
> http://news.bbc.co.uk/1/hi/health/6749037.stm

Although 70% agreed that poor health surveillance was a sign of neglect, this factor was linked with immunisations. Parents have a right to refuse immunisations for their children. This is a clear matter for parental choice and in itself is not a child protection concern. Parents have a right to seek alternative health remedies for their children and this might include alternative forms of vaccination. Severe dental decay may indicate neglectful parenting but it may be the parent does not realise, for example, that apple juice in a baby's bottle will have an acidic effect on the teeth and they think they are acting in the best interests of the child. If a parent did not seek medical advice and refused to provide the child with treatment, this would be neglect. Frequent hospital admissions could indicate a parent who is very anxious and seeking support about their child's health. Perhaps they had a previous child who died or was seriously ill and a plan to support them could be put into place.

Other behavioural indicators of neglect not included in the research might also be:

- constant hunger;
- lethargy, listlessness and fatigue;
- alcohol, drug and/or substance misuse;
- rocking, head banging;
- begging or stealing;
- avoiding school;
- avoiding going home;
- inappropriate responsibilities – e.g. housework, caring for parents/siblings;

- self-harm;

- angry outbursts, harmful to others or damaging property;

- running away;

- eating disorders.

Children as carers need a great deal of support if their needs are to be met. Scott (2007) identified hundreds of thousands of children in Britain who nurse sick or disabled parents with little support or respite care.

Responding to the need to protect a child from neglect at an early stage

Neglect, like all forms of child abuse, is damaging. In comparison with physically abused children neglected children have more severe delay in cognitive and social development, and limited peer interactions and tend to internalise rather then externalise their problems. Persistent neglect has significant neuro-developmental consequences for young babies, potentially affecting all areas of cognitive, social and emotional functioning. In addition, the effects seem to be cumulative (Hildyard and Wolfe, 2002). Daniel (1998) suggests that the three key factors contributing to childhood resilience and survival in the face of negative life events are a secure base, self-esteem and a sense of self-efficacy. *Thus the experience of neglect is most likely to undermine the very factors that underpin emotional wellbeing and that act as a buffer from the emotionally damaging effects of adverse experiences* (in Tanner and Turney, 2003, p27).

RESEARCH SUMMARY

Tanner and Turney point out that much research on neglect focuses on the perceived failures of mothers without equivalent attention to the role of fathers. The following study is such an example although it provides some useful findings (2003, p30).

A 20-year study followed the progress of 44 children aged 3 months–7 years who had been diagnosed with non-organic failure to thrive and who had received psycho-social intervention. All children had weight below the third percentile and a history of inadequate weight gain with no medical reason for the condition.

The children initially showed delay in social and language development, depression or severe inhibitions, fear and refusal to eat solid food and at meal times the children vomited and screamed. The mothers initially showed high levels of general anxiety as well as in parenting, low self-esteem, depression, difficulties in feeding their child, derived a lack of pleasure in the mother/child interaction, were socially disadvantaged, had conflictual parental relationships and lacked social support.

Those with higher self-esteem and cognitive attainment, increased social support and more positive relationships tended to have positive outcomes. If the failure to thrive was due to ongoing abuse the outcome was poor.

However, it was not the case that children who suffered abuse were inevitably doomed to a bleak adult life. Even when there was severe cruelty during childhood the results suggest that given the right circumstances these individuals later developed into socially competent and well functioning adults and parents (Iwaniec, et al., 2003, p225).

Of the 16 children who had suffered abuse, seven had positive outcomes. All seven had experienced positive change during childhood or later teenage years. Those who showed poor outcomes had faced further negative life events (Iwaniec, et al., 2003).

Stone found in a study of 20 neglect cases that caregivers were ill equipped, emotionally or practically, to care for children. Twelve out of the 20 had experience of the care system or prison and substance misuse, mental health problems or learning disabilities were common, each factor being present in half of the cases. *Parents were noted to be preoccupied with their own unfulfilled needs* (Stone, 1998, p8).

Neglected children may become easy targets for child sex abusers. If social workers intervene effectively at an early stage to prevent children being homeless, isolated, hungry, cold, ill and uncared for, they may prevent the downward spiral of abuse and there will be fewer children in the pool of vulnerable children so readily available to child sex abusers. Batmanghelidjh writes of attending the funerals of young people she has met through her work with neglected children: *Children who were too alone on the streets, who were prey to the perverse, who had been murdered or committed suicide. There was no one to carry the coffin or fill the hole with earth at the graveside, apart from other similarly desolate children, who looked bleak. It could have been any of them in that coffin* (Batmanghelidjh, 2006, p11).

Howe (2005) writes of the devastating impact on children's behaviour of inconsistent and neglectful parenting often linked with parental drug and alcohol misuse, domestic violence and depression. He describes characteristics of the uncaring environment: *hungry and frightened, confused and alone, with no one to turn to, to soothe you, to make you feel safe and to help you make sense of all that is happening, leaves the essence of your very being as no more than a cauldron of undifferentiated fear and distress* (Howe, 2005, p145). Bancroft, et al. (2004) describe the impact of parental substance misuse as often leading to neglectful situations such as fires caused through leaving electrical appliances on or dropping cigarette butts.

Neglect often coexists with other types of significant harm. According to Stevenson, the link between neglect and emotional abuse is particularly strong (Stevenson, 1998, p14). Parents can be given opportunities to learn parenting skills and to experience some of the parenting they may have missed in their own childhoods as well as be assisted in developing supportive community networks. Schemes such as Home Start, Sure Start and Newpin can help some abusive parents to improve their parenting but some cannot be helped within the timescale of the child's childhood (Bridge Child Care Development Service, 1999).

How long would you wait for parents or carers to change their neglectful behaviour?

Research informs of the importance in neglect cases of long-term focused protective work. Consider how this approach fits with the common assessment (CAF) and the initial assessment (seven days) and core assessment (35 days) recommended in the Framework of Assessment for Children in Need and Their Families (DoH, 2000a).

Comment

Given the serious impact of childhood neglect, it is important to intervene to protect within the timescales relevant for the child. On its own, neglect powerfully and negatively affects children's lives and must not be viewed as an add-on to something considered a more serious incident (Tanner and Turney, 2003, p30). Given that there may not be an incident as such to trigger an immediate protective response, a long-term approach might lead to drift and lack of intervention in time to provide the child with a positive life experience. Tanner and Turney warn against social workers waiting for a clear cut incident before action can be taken as

> *this may consign a child to an extended period of significant harm living with the corrosive effects of long term chronic neglect. This is not a recipe for unplanned interventions, but rather for rigorous, multi disciplinary assessment that takes account of the impact of neglect on the child's cognitive, social, emotional and physical development and for early intervention to stem and hopefully correct these adverse consequences.*

> (2003, p30)

They go on to state that, as neglect usually has a number of causes, intervention may need to be at a number of levels and therefore needs to pay attention to *a range of practical, emotional and social/structural factors* (2003, p31). Long-term work, in cases of chronic neglect, may take 12–18 months and must be purposeful and focused within child protection protocols. *We must make sure that children do not become hostages to fortune – left in limbo whilst work is done with their parents* (2003, p32). A section 47 (CA 1989) investigation is not time-limited in the same way as assessment protocols. The timescale must be that which is required to make sure the child is safe.

What blocks might there be to professional intervention to protect a child from neglect?

Comment

The decision about when incidents of neglect become a chronic and harmful situation for a child is a matter of professional judgement. Neglect is less likely to activate a child protection response than physical and sexual abuse (Reder, et al., 1993). This is sometimes referred to as the *neglect of neglect* syndrome. Neglect cases tend to be filtered out of the protective system (Gibbons, et al., 1995). There does not have to be a significant event to satisfy the grounds for neglect but rather evidence of the harm the child is suffering. Dickens uses the term catapults – the various legal and procedural imperatives that justify action to protect a child. Dickens found that the 'catapults' seemed to be a specific event or change in circumstances (e.g. when the mother became terminally ill), and rarely did a social worker decide that enough was enough and make a decision to act *solely on the basis of accumulation of long standing concerns* (Dickens, 2007, p83). In the context of long-term work a professional may become overwhelmed with a sense of helplessness reflecting family dynamics. Neglect is not usually

> *a single event but a process or way of life characterised by unremitting low-level care for children and often an ingrained sense of helplessness within the family. Over a period of time, particularly when nothing much changes, the social worker may find themselves getting 'drawn in' and becoming used to that level of care that if encountered in a new situation would strike them as unsatisfactory. In a sense the worker stops seeing what is happening to the child and becomes quite stuck.*
>
> (Tanner and Turney, 2003, p26)

Professionals often think in terms of reasonable parental behaviour but Dickens found that there were different views about what was reasonable in all the circumstances of a particular case (Dickens, 2007, p79). Clusters of indicators of neglect must be collated and the sum total may trigger the need for a section 47 (CA 1989) enquiry. However, different aspects of neglect may not coincide at the same time and priorities will shift as professionals see an improvement in one area of parenting and deterioration in another.

> *Perceived negatives in one aspect of a child's life may be thought to be balanced out by [perceived] positives in another. For example, if a child's physical appearance, hygiene and health care are a cause of concern but school attendance and performance is good then agencies may see the positive effect of school as balancing out the negatives of other concerns.*
>
> (McSherry, 2007, p5)

It is important that perceived positives do not distract professional attention from careful risk assessment of significant harm.

The *Paul: Death through neglect* Inquiry report stated *the diagnosis and detection of neglect is dependent on establishing the importance and collation of sometimes small, apparently undramatic single pieces of factual information which, when seen together, are of considerable significance* (Bridge Child Care Development Service, 1995, p4).

Chronic neglect can also lead to defensive practice where *individual thought and initiative is stifled, responses become routinised and threshold of response increased* (Tanner and Turney, 2003, p30). Professional judgement and analysis may become compromised through a conveyor-belt or mechanistic approach.

ACTIVITY 3.8

The core assessment proforma available on the Every Child Matters website is an example of a mechanistic approach which does not encourage questioning and may cloud professional analysis and discretion. Consider how the following questions from the core assessment form may or may not be relevant and/or useful to the investigation process in protecting children from harm caused by neglect.

Every Child Matters protocols (DfES, 2003) – an analysis

P1 *Child is not provocative or challenging in appearance or behaviour*. What does this mean? For instance children are encouraged to say no to abuse, which would be recognised as an acceptable challenge. Is refusal to wear school uniform an unacceptable challenge or an indicator of a child's high level of self-esteem and confidence to challenge adults?

P7 *Parents/carers ensure that child's personal hygiene is adequate.* What if there is no hot water or bath or if the child wets/soils themselves constantly?

P8 *Parents/carers teach appropriate behaviour*. What is appropriate behaviour? Who is defining it and how?

P12 *Parents'/carers' relationships with neighbours and those in authority are generally harmonious*. What if parents/carers challenge authorities over human rights or political issues such as sending young people to war – their relationship to those in authority may not be harmonious but they would argue that they have the moral high ground.

FE1 *A member of the household experienced a stressful childhood.* (e.g. childhood abuse; period in care). Survivors of child abuse and care leavers who may not have any history of child abuse may consider the inclusion of this question as discriminatory. However Corby (2006, p144) urges caution in using a previous history of child abuse as an indicator of a child being at risk as there is very limited knowledge about this. Sheppherd (2003) concluded that *the experience of abuse as a child leaves parents at considerably greater risk of having parenting problems with their children, the relationship between the two is far from inevitable. It is the combination of childhood abuse and continued poor life experiences which increases the chances of an individual becoming an abusive parent* (Sheppherd, 2003).

FE2 *The family suffered a traumatic loss or crisis which is unresolved (e.g. bereavement).* What is a resolved bereavement response? There are many possible responses to such life crises.

FE5 *Does a member of the household experience:*

poor mental health

poor physical health

behaviour problem

physical disability

learning disability

sensory impairment

problem alcohol/drug use?

Each category could mean a vast range of possibilities for positive or negative child care. What is a *behaviour problem*? As there is no correlation between physical disability or poor physical health and neglect of a child this question is discriminatory if used where there is an allegation or suspicion of child abuse. Booth and Booth (1993) studied 20 parents with learning difficulties parenting 50 children. Poverty, social isolation and poor housing featured more importantly as influences on parenting than the learning difficulty (cited in Corby, 2006, p40).

FE8 *The wider family provide:*

   practical help

   emotional support

   financial help

   information and advice.

What if there is no wider family? What if the family has a history of generational abuse and withdrawal from them is protective?

F12 *Parents'/carers' relationships with others provide a good example to the child.* What if the parent's employment is as a sex worker? What constitutes a good example?

It has been shown by Farmer and Owen, (1995) that professionals are often reluctant to change their original plans (Department of Health, 1995). Review of planning in the light of collating known evidence from case files and analysis of chronologies is crucial. There may be previous incidents or the child and their siblings may have previously spoken about abuse. Where children have died from neglect, such as Paul, professionals have continually provided short-term solutions such as material support and the case had not been re-evaluated in the light of many subsequent referrals (Bridge, Child Care Development Service, 1995).

Delay in neglect cases presents considerable risk. Families who move home frequently and where new professionals are constantly involved may not receive intervention to protect even though such families may continue to attract professional attention. An attitude of co-operation by the family may lead professionals to want to continue to offer support but in doing so they may minimise the evidence of the impact of neglect on the children. Endless checklists can lead to dangerous practice as indicators of neglect are catalogued but do not necessarily lead to action and protective planning.

The social work response

ACTIVITY **3.9**

Deciding to what extent a child is at risk is based on professional judgement and the application of knowledge to individual cases. Here are four cases to which the authors have had to provide a protective social work response. Make a decision about which of the categories of response apply to these cases:

A *The child is not thought to be at any risk of child abuse.*

B *There is concern about neglect of a child.*

C *There is suspicion of likely or actual significant harm to a child. (s47 enquiry, CA 1989).*

D *A section 47 (CA 1989) investigation of child abuse is indicated.*

E *Immediate action to protect. Evidence of actual significant harm and/or criminal offence.*

---

1. *Three children in a home where all the windows are boarded up and they are living constantly in complete darkness – a reflection of a parent with unresolved grief who is hiding from the world.*

2. *Four young children in a flat where each room is piled high with old newspapers, food cartons and clothes to the extent that the children have severely limited space within which to move about – the mother has obsessive compulsive behaviour and is unable to throw anything away, which is a response to severe loss in her life.*

3. *The social worker and health visitor on a joint visit notice, in the bedroom of a 3-year-old boy, a wire cage above his cot preventing him from escaping while his parents are out at the local pub.*

4. *A 12-year-old boy in a foster placement is left alone sleeping in a shed out in the garden and not allowed to eat with the family.*

In relation to these cases:

- *Think about what criteria you would use in making judgements about neglect.*

- *Think about what might influence your selection of these criteria.*

- *How do you differentiate between situations that include risk but do not reach a threshold of actual dangerousness?*

- *At what stage is professional intervention indicated?*

- *What level of intervention is appropriate?*

- *When does neglect of a child become a crime?*

- *When is immediate action needed to protect the child from harm?*

- *Are there other children who may also be being abused?*

Comment

Perhaps you based your decision-making on your:

- experience as a child, as a parent or from your observation of and interaction with children;

- professional experience of a particular case;

- cultural or religious perspective of family life;

- knowledge of the law and child protection policy and practice guidance;

- knowledge of lessons learnt from child abuse inquiries and serious case reviews;

- understanding of the concept of neglect;

- knowledge base of the subject from research findings;

- media reporting.

Each of the above cases did require a proactive social work intervention ranging from family support to section 47 (CA 1989) enquiries and investigation to legal safeguards. The detailed analysis below will assist your later reflection on your decisions in the above scenarios.

Making judgements when a child is left home alone

The media can portray home-alone cases by demonising mothers and ignoring the fathers' role, and research frequently emphasises the role of women as mothers in neglect cases without equal consideration of neglect by fathers (Tanner and Turney, 2003, p30). This focus may impact on professional responses and lead to a heavy-handed approach (Garrett, 2001). In contrast, the Hollywood image is not of risk of harm but of a plucky child who fends for himself. The decision to leave a child at home without adult supervision may be reasonably made by parents as a way of encouraging the child's sense of independence and the child may find the experience enjoyable and rewarding. What constitutes neglect varies considerably across cultures. For example, for Laotian and Cambodian refugees in the United States it was noted to be unremarkable to assign the care of younger siblings to a child of 8 years old (Korbin and Spilsbury, 1999).

The extent of home-alone cases

The numbers of children routinely left alone would indicate a level of intentional or unintentional parental neglect. In early 1994 research indicated that a fifth of all 5–10 year olds were being left alone after school or in the holidays: a total of approximately 800,000 children (Garrett, 2001, p654). Children left home alone is a common reason for referral to children's services. A study of 18–24 year olds found that 5% had experienced serious absence of supervision as children defined as left alone overnight under the age of 10 years (Cawson, et al., 2000, p51).

The law

> *Government should make sure that children and young people are protected from abuse, neglect and being harmed by the people looking after them.*
> (United Nations, 1989, Article 19)

The Children Act 1989 requires intervention if children are suffering actual or likely significant harm. There is no law which states at what age a child can be left home alone. That there is such a law or agreed age limit is a misconception that is made by professionals and non-professionals alike. The relevant legislation is the Children and Young Person Act 1933, which applies to anyone *over the age of 16 who has responsibility for a child under that age and wilfully neglects or exposes the child in a manner likely to cause unnecessary suffering or injury to health*. However, for the police to pursue a prosecution the situation usually has to be extremely severe, such as young children left alone while their parent or carer goes on holiday.

It is far more common for social workers to be addressing less clear situations of harm and having to make judgements about whether or not to treat the case as a child in need (s17, CA1989) or a child in need of protection (s47, CA, 1989). In Scotland it is against the law to leave children under 12 years old alone. Views about at what age children should be left alone for a short period range from 6 to 16 years (Christopherson, 1983, in Garrett, 2001, p646). Police guidance says that *common sense must apply and the child be capable of looking after itself* (www.met.police.uk/askthemet/480.htm), whereas the London Child Protection Procedures refer to an overly high threshold of evidence of neglect if a child is *abandoned or left alone for excessive periods* (LSCB, 4.2.26). The consequences of children being left alone can be very serious indeed and the question must always be considered as to whether the child may need immediate protection through removal from the home or should be the subject of section 47 enquiries.

The NSPCC recommend never leaving babies or young children alone for any length of time, or most children under 13 years for more than a short period. They recommend that no child under 16 years be left overnight (NSPCC, 1993). However, prescriptive age limits may distract from case-specific decisions. It is usually the police who first become aware of a child left alone, make an assessment of any immediate risk to the child, intervene to protect and refer to children's services.

The jigsaw of information – working together to protect children

---

CASE STUDY

Children left home alone

There is a spectrum of abuse of children left home alone. Being left alone may be one sign among a cluster of very serious indicators of harm. For instance, Victoria Climbié was left alone bound in a bin bag in the bath but this aspect gained little attention among the other forms of abuse she was subjected to. Tahla Ikram, age 17 months, died following systematic abuse and multiple injuries inflicted over time and untreated. He had been in care previously, having been left at home alone (*Guardian*, 2007). In contrast, a case which has attracted public sympathy and debate about this issue is that of Madeleine McCann, age 3 years, who disappeared after being left alone with her younger siblings while her parents ate dinner at a holiday resort (Hamilton, 2007). Another case where tragedy followed is that of a mother, called to work as a psychiatric nurse, who left a boy aged 9 and a girl 13 years home alone and following an arson attack the boy died and the girl was seriously injured (Allen, 2004). In another case, a mother was convicted after leaving her daughter aged 14 years alone for six weeks so that she could go abroad to see her boyfriend. While she was away, her daughter ran out of money and had no one to turn to and children's services intervened (BBC News, 2008).

In making decisions about intervention in cases of neglect, a range of agency checks needs to be made. Immediately the police and social worker exchange information through a strategy discussion and decide whether the child is in immediate danger. Prior to a strategy meeting, and as part of a section 47 investigation, information is sought from other agencies.

A teacher may have noticed other indicators of neglect such as the child's lunch box containing little food, or a child not being dressed appropriately for the weather, or having little concentration in class. The housing department may have information about environmental health issues such as complaints from neighbours about rubbish or infestations. Probation or police may know about family members with criminal histories relevant to the care of the child or of domestic violence or substance misuse in the home. Health professionals may have the early history of the child even pre-birth which has been shown to be particularly relevant to the assessment of neglect (Reder et al.,1993). Importance must be awarded to information from professionals who know the child well, such as a nursery teacher or school nurse. It is often neighbours, relatives and friends who have a wealth of information and if they report neglect their voices should be heard. They may be being malicious but checks must be made on the authenticity of their perceptions of the child's safety. It is important to remember that in a section 47 (CA 1989) investigation it is not necessary to obtain parental permission for making these checks although it is good practice to do so if this does not place the child at further risk of harm.

The jigsaw of information will need to be collated from the agencies and evaluated. Perhaps the case can be de-escalated if there are few concerns or it may be obvious that a section 47 (CA 1989) investigation will lead to decisions regarding formal interviews of the child and family, paediatric assessments, a child protection conference or other protective action such as a legal order to remove the child to safety.

If the police are pursuing a criminal investigation under the Children and Young Persons Act 1933, it will be important for them to obtain forensic evidence such as photographs, medical evidence of any impact of the neglect, items of clothing or bedding, mobile phone messages and computer e-mails. They may also need to interview witnesses such as siblings or neighbours to see if they corroborate the child's statement or other evidential findings. Social workers can assist the police by being aware of these possibilities and making sure that they preserve such evidence and do not contaminate what may become a scene of crime. The police may want to interview the parent under caution as a suspect of crime. Any social work interview of the parent must be agreed with the police to make sure that there is no interference with the criminal investigation.

The child's view

An essential part of the jigsaw of information required in decision-making is the child's view.

In the case of Paul, the inquiry stated:

> we would like to conclude by asking all professionals working with children and families, their managers, policy makers and politicians to make sure that the child is the focus of their work and to ensure that the child's views and needs are at the forefront of all decision making.
>
> (Bridge Child Care Development Service, 1995, p210)

A comprehensive account of children's views of neglect is available from Gorin's research (2004). She made the following findings.

- Children are often more aware of problems than parents realise, but they don't always understand what is happening and why.
- Children whose parents have experienced domestic violence, substance misuse and, to a lesser extent, mental health problems report witnessing or experiencing violence themselves, sometimes very extreme.
- Children worry about their parents more than may be recognised, particularly if they fear for their parents' safety.

- Some children, particularly boys, will not talk to anyone about their problems and many children report coping by distracting themselves.

- Children mainly use informal support, and are most likely to talk to parents (more often mothers), friends, siblings, extended family or pets.

- Children do not know where to go to get assistance and rarely seek the help of professionals initially.

- Experience of contact with professionals is mixed. Children's concerns include professionals not believing them, not talking directly to them and not acting to help them when asked;

- Children say they want someone to talk to, who they trust, who will listen to them and provide reassurance and confidentiality. They want help to think through problems, without necessarily taking full responsibility for decisions.

- Children's most persistent plea is for more age-appropriate information to help them understand what is going on in their family.

It is essential to obtain the view of the child who would usually be interviewed on their own. Within a section 47 (CA 1989) enquiry the parent's permission is not required but should be sought if possible unless to do so would place the child at risk of harm. The decision about interviewing the child and parents is made during a strategy discussion with the police. If the neglect is very serious and the police consider that a crime may have been committed, then the child must be interviewed by a police officer and social worker according to the Achieving Best Evidence guidance (CJS, 2007). This would usually be a visually recorded interview. It may be agreed that the social worker should interview the child. If the child says that they feel completely safe, there must be evaluation of the child's view. Even if the child feels safe, and even if they are of an older age group, this does not mean that they are protected from harm. The child's view may not be the same as their best interests. A carer may have told them what to say to keep professionals at a distance and the child's view may not reflect the degree of risk as, for instance, they may be trying to protect a vulnerable parent from professional intrusion. The Inquiry report into the death of Paul stated that *professionals need to be aware that neglected children are attached to their parents and may deny or minimise their problems* (Bridge Child Care Development Service, 1995, p198).

Sometimes children who are repeatedly neglected will define their situation as normal and on interview present as confident and content with their lives. It is important to remember that children often retract initial allegations about abuse and a child who has complained at school about being hungry or cold at home might state the very next day that everything is fine. Social workers must be vigilant that the rule of optimism, which is the overwhelming desire to think that the child is unharmed, does not prevent them being open to the possibility that the child is suffering significant harm. In the case of Paul, despite gaining reports of the children suffering extremely neglectful home conditions, the social workers defined them as a *dirty but happy*, a loving family with their problems mainly stemming from housing conditions (Bridge Child Care Development Service, 1995).

A child of 14 years might feel safe left in a flat where he could contact the warden at any time while his mother went shopping for a short while. Compare this with a child of the same age hiding in the cold in the garden because he heard a noise that scared him when left alone all evening while his parents were out at a meal with friends. It cannot be assumed that an older child can cope with being left alone or that a younger child is behaving older than their years and therefore not in danger. Sarah Vine was left alone age 8 years and says:

> There is another factor, too. Being left alone in the house was scary. I never let on to my parents how scary, as I didn't want to disappoint them. But I was pretty terrified. I would lie in bed, wide awake, listening to the strange noises of the night, analysing every squeak and rustle, until I heard the welcome crunch of their car's tyres on the driveway – at which point I would finally succumb to sleep.

(Hamilton, 2007)

A disabled child is more likely to be dependent on others for their care and so left alone they may be at an increased risk of harm. A child with certain learning or physical disabilities may not understand levels of risk, how to protect themselves and seek help or because of limited mobility they be unable to escape swiftly situations of danger. However, it may be that a disabled child has safeguards in place for their needs and feels entirely confident about being home alone in certain situations and the child's own perception is agreed by those specialists who know them well, who must always be consulted.

Is the carer proactively protective?

Parents and carers who are compliant with the social worker and even remorseful may certainly be genuine but they may be trying to conceal an abusive situation. This is why it is important to collate information, systematically piece the jigsaw of events together and analyse whether the various responses are consistent with the child's explanation of events and accounts from witnesses. When Victoria Climbié suffered burns to her face and head, there were three different explanations given by a kettle, a cup and the tap. Such inconsistencies must raise questions about whether or not an accident was in fact deliberate harm. Victoria also suffered other forms of neglect. She was left in hospital with no visits, clothes, toys or food brought in to her. Ninety per cent of child abuse investigations conclude with the child remaining within the home (New Philanthropy Capital, 2007, p19). The carers may need support and assistance to keep their child safe and then a risk assessment will be needed to consider the parental capacity for change. The carer may not be physically and/or psychologically capable of changing their parenting. It may be important to obtain a specialist psychological, psychiatric or medical report in order to assess the parent's capacity to be a proactive protector of the child.

The carer's attitude to the social worker is of significance. *I just popped out for 5 minutes to get medicine for the sick baby,* will evoke a different professional response from an avoidant reaction such as, *why don't you go across the road and see Mrs X who hits her kids.*

Every time police attend a child left home alone they send a referral (police form 78) to children's services informing that a child has come to their notice. Though parents say the incident was one-off it must be considered that even an isolated incident can constitute significant harm to a child. Social workers will need to decide the extent of the risk.

It is also important to evaluate whether or not the action was deliberate or unintentional. The impact on the child may be equally harmful but a carer who is obviously very anxious about the safety of their child and says the train from work was delayed will evoke a different professional response from one who seems uncaring and is absent because of an erratic lifestyle associated with drug misuse which places their needs above those of the child. In the first case it would be important to check out the details of the parental account and also consider what precautions were taken to allow for such an eventuality. Perhaps a relative or friend had been contacted to care for the child meanwhile. The parent may be struggling themselves through illness or disability or they may have language or communication difficulties. The social worker needs to evaluate the parent's need for support in being an effective carer, but also be prepared to acknowledge that the child may nevertheless be neglected intentionally or unintentionally.

Social workers may be told by carers that it is normal in their particular culture for children to be left to care for other children in the family or for children of a young age to be deemed responsible and mature enough to be left alone. The question in this instance is whether or not you have checked this cultural perception to be an accurate reflection of a specific value system. Even within a particular community, practice may differ between families. It is important not to make assumptions. Professional judgement again is required and sensitivity to assist the family to understand the risks posed by life in the UK for a child unsupervised and isolated.

ACTIVITY 3.10

Think about the following parental responses to a professional interview to investigate an allegation about neglect and how you might respond to adults who:

are compliant: You are quite right – she wasn't old enough to be left alone – things haven't been right in this house for some time.

see themselves as experts: We are professionals ourselves, we can judge when he can take care of himself. We will sort it out. It's just been a difficult time. We don't need your help thank you.

are angry: We don't want you snooping round our house coming in when we're not here. Who do you think you are?

are avoidant: No you can't come in. We are busy feeding the kids. We'll come to your office tomorrow when they're in school.

Comment

Morrison provides an excellent method of evaluating parental responses to professional intervention referring to possible reactions and how these may be risk assessed (in Adcock and White, 1998, pp140–1). For instance, a parent might respond in one of the following ways.

I accept my child has been placed at risk by leaving her at home on her own.
At this stage the child will need a protection plan in place because there is insufficient evidence of change.

I know I neglected her, she is too young to be left on her own but she had just driven me mad not taking her bottle.
The parent does admit that they are in some way responsible for the neglect but they locate the problem in the child's behaviour. Such an admission does not indicate that they accept responsibility. The risk to the child remains because the child's behaviour might once again prompt an abusive parental response.

I feel bad about leaving her on her own. She's too young really.
The parent feels uncomfortable about the neglect. Yet, while evoking some sympathy in the social worker, caution must be taken as this could indicate false compliance as a result of the agency intervention.

We can't go on working these long hours and caring for my elderly Mum, the kids are suffering being left so much.
The parent does realise the need for change and may well do whatever the professionals ask but they still may not see a way through and have little idea of how to achieve the changes needed.

I know I can manage to improve things. I'm going to start sharing child care with my neighbour so they aren't left alone any more.
The parent has a plan for change and shows motivation. The social worker will need to support the parent in making the change.

Even though I do not want my child to have a child protection plan, I recognise it will help me get support in working out how to manage my kids better and not to leave them to get their own supper.
The parent realises they have to make decisions and accept professional support. This is a basis for working in partnership with the parent.

From next week I'm going to organise a child minder for when I can't get back in time.
The parent is determined to change and the social worker needs to respond to their motivation and determination so that the momentum is not lost. It is the time to identify clear goals, how the parent and worker may achieve the goals and what rewards and changes there will be when the goals are met.

It is important not to make contracts too early when the parent is at the start of this process and small stresses may trigger the parent's sense of being out of control again. It is commonly a process of evaluation and re-evaluation and a distinction must be made between lapse and relapse. *Lapse* is when a high-risk situation happens and the parent puts the relapse prevention plan into action, e.g. respite help, assistance from extended family, etc. *Relapse* signifies a return to abuse and child protection measures need to be in place.

Family group conferences

Family group conferences (FGCs) are facilitated by children's services as a way of working with families where plans and decisions need to be made. *Working together* states that an FGC must not replace or remove the need for a child protection conference (DfES, 2006, 10.2). If the child is thought to be at risk of significant harm the FGC must always be held within child protection procedures. The FGC has four parts. At the convening stage an independent co-ordinator, such as a community leader, meets with the social worker to clarify the concerns and meets the family to define the family network with them. A conference of all extended family members, friends, and community representatives is arranged by agreement in relation to dates, food and venue. At the information-giving stage the social worker will present their concerns to the group. The private family time stage involves the family meeting in private to respond to professional concerns and to make a plan to safeguard the child. Children should be invited to take part – perhaps with someone of their choosing to act as an advocate for them, such as a teacher or friend. At the agreement stage the family present their plan and this is accepted by the professionals unless to do so would place the child at risk. The FGC is best used following section 47 (CA 1989) enquiries where there are concerns about the care of a child but where these have required the implementation of further child protection procedures. Sometimes a child protection conference decision will be for an FGC to take place in order to progress the agreed child protection plan with the family.

Evaluating the safeguards in place for the child left alone

It is very important for the social worker to visit the home and make a detailed assessment of the living conditions – this will mean looking in the kitchen, bedroom and other rooms and outdoor space.

ACTIVITY **3.11**

What do you think are important questions that might be asked about safeguards in the home when investigating the case of a child left home alone?

Comment

You might have considered some of the following factors.

- Does the child know how to use a telephone, do they have credit on their mobile or can they contact a neighbour in an emergency?

- Is there an alarm? Can the child exit the home easily in an emergency?

- Are basic safety precautions installed in the house such as stair gates, cooker guards, fireguards, socket covers and smoke alarms? Are medical and toxic substances stored safely?

- Is the child of sufficient age and understanding to know what might constitute an emergency such as a smell of gas or the sound of a smoke alarm?

- Is there sufficient food available? Is there an unreasonable expectation for the child to cook food? Is there food in the fridge?

- Is there light? Has the gas/electricity/water been cut off?

- What is the general level of hygiene? Are the children's beds clean and dry?

- Are harmful substances out of the child's reach eg. alcohol or drugs? Are they exposed to risk from the paraphernalia of drug misuse such as syringes?

- Does the child have access to inappropriate material such as pornography?

- Are the children protected from online abuse?

- Are there pets? Do they pose a risk to the child? Are the pets well cared for?

- A strong test of a child's comprehension of how to keep themselves safe is whether or not they open the door to strangers. A reluctant child may indicate that they know that you are a stranger and they have been told that they should not let you in.

- Are there adults who pose a risk to the child who can gain access to the vulnerable, alone child?

- Is the child at risk of harm from their own behaviour? Without adult supervision are they likely to cut themselves with a knife, run into the road or cause a fire?

Children locked in rooms while alone indicates significant risk of harm. This is a single factor which research clearly demonstrates to have been a factor in many cases where a child has died from child abuse (Reder, et al., 1993, pp107–8).

In cases of chronic neglect where work with the family may take some time, it is important to clarify with families and the professional network what would be considered to be successful outcomes and how these are evaluated. Social workers may use the model of *managed dependency* to enable parents to relearn and reconfigure previously damaging experiences of relationships which impact on their parenting skills (Tanner and Turney, 2003, p32). In long-term intervention it is essential that the focus on the child is maintained and a relationship developed.

> *In our experience, social workers often report very little direct or meaningful contact with children beyond what is statutorily required and may not feel they have the time or skills to develop a relationship with them … Whilst trying to bring about change in the parents, critically we also need to be trying to bring about change for – and with – the child.*
>
> (Tanner and Turney, 2003, p32)

Investigating allegations about a child left home alone unsupervised – deciding the threshold for intervention

ACTIVITY 3.12

The following case studies are designed to aid a questioning approach to the process of protecting children. They usually progress from referral to investigation and action to protect. When reading the case studies structure your thinking and questioning around the points listed in Chapter 1, but do not be limited by this list. Continue to add your own questions and to consider the implications of these in each case.

CASE STUDY

• A 12-year-old girl and a 3-year-old boy are left home alone in a flat within a terraced house.

• A neighbour informs the police who stay at the house with the children.

• The police inform children's services social worker (SW), who makes checks.

• There are no previous referrals to children's services and no concerns from health services.

• The police agree during a strategy discussion that children's services conduct a single-agency enquiry and initial assessment.

• SW visits the house where mother has returned.

• The school staff monitor the children and children's services will provide assistance with child care.

• SW contacts the school and finds out that both children attend school/nursery school regularly and are achieving well.

Child left home alone and not thought to be at any risk of abuse

• SW interviews the mother who says that she had tried to find suitable supervision for the children.

• An upstairs neighbour was easily contactable and available to the children.

• The mother tells the SW that she was out shopping very close to home and was only away for a short period.

• Mother gives her consent to the SW to check with other agencies.

• The SW notes that the children have access to warmth, food and a safe home environment.

• SW interviews the girl on her own. The girl said that she can use and access the telephone in an emergency and called the neighbour because the light bulb had gone out and she was a bit scared.

• She likes helping to care for her brother and wants to be a nursery teacher.

• The three-year-old boy was playing contentedly and spoke freely to the SW about his toys.

• The father and mother are separated but he visits occasionally to support the family.

CASE STUDY

• An 11-year-old girl is left home alone with a 5-year-old boy in a flat on a large housing estate.

• She calls the doctor when the 3-year-old boy is bitten by the family dog.

• The doctor calls an ambulance and makes a referral to children's services.

• Checks within children's services by the social worker (SW) show that there are no previous referrals and the schools have no concerns.

• The hospital doctor tells the SW that the children are well cared for.

• The hospital SW interviews the children. The girl says that she doesn't like being left alone to care for her brother, wants to be out with her friends playing instead and no neighbours were around for her to contact.

• The SW contacts the police child abuse investigation team (CAIT) who have no record of the family. A single-agency approach by children's services is agreed.

Concern about a child left home alone

• Children's services implement child-in-need protocols and the mother is told that, should there be any further incidents, child protection procedures will be actioned.

• The girl is offered a school counselling service to support any further reporting. She tells the SW that her mother has told her that she will not leave her alone again until she is much older.

• SW makes a home visit. In the home there is plenty of food, warmth and it is a child-centred environment.

• The mother says that the dog has never been known to bite a child before.

• The mother is very upset by the incident and acknowledges that she should not have left the children alone.

• Police contacted the RSPCA to arrange collection of the dog which is not a breed covered under the Dangerous Dogs Act 1991.

• Children's services decide that the children should return home and conduct an initial assessment.

• The dog bite is not serious and the hospital discharges the boy with medication.

• The mother provides the father's details and when the SW contacts him he explains that he has the children for holidays as he lives with a new partner some distance away.

• The hospital SW interviews the mother who, when called by the hospital, returned immediately.

• She said she had gone shopping for half a day and thought the children would be fine because the girl can use and access the telephone.

119

CASE STUDY

• A 12-year-old boy and a girl of 2 years are left home alone in a small block of private flats.

• The boy calls 999 from a call box because his mother has not come home and he is anxious that his father might turn up.

• Police refer to children's services and remain with the children until the social worker (SW) arrives.

• The SW reports back to police and it is agreed that, should there be further incidents, there will be a joint investigation and a child protection conference.

• The SW interviews the boy at his home and he tells the SW he finds caring for his sister a chore and is cross with his mother for leaving him in charge.

• The boy also says that his father has a history of drug misuse, sometimes visits unannounced and that there is no one he can call on for help.

• The boy suffers from asthma and uses an inhaler daily.

• The home environment is safe and child-centred. However, after looking in the fridge and cupboards the SW finds there is little food available.

Suspicion of actual or likely significant harm to a child left home alone. S47 enquiry

---

• The school offer the boy one-to-one support from the school counsellor.

• SW checks show that there have been previous referrals to children's services for concerns about neglect and that the school is concerned because the boy often arrives late.

• The health visitor reports that the girl has delayed speech development and the mother often misses appointments.

• The SW holds a strategy discussion with the police child abuse investigation team (CAIT). Following checks the police have no previous information on either parent and an initial single-agency inquiry is agreed.

• The GP sees the mother about her depression and arranges to see the boy about his asthma.

• The SW implements child-in-need protocols and explores any risks posed by the father's contact with the family. The SW interviews the father who agrees to a parenting assessment.

• The SW visits the children the following day.

• The mother returns to the home and tells the SW she doesn't know what the fuss is about as her son is very responsible.

• She says that she had to go out to collect her medication as she gets very depressed. She also had to see a friend who owes her money.

• When asked about the father's visits, the mother says that he is away at the moment and always lets her know when he is coming round.

• The SW tries to contact the father to assess the risk to the children of him visiting and to reassure the children that they are safe.

CASE STUDY

• A 13-year-old girl with a moderate learning disability and a 3-year-old boy who has epilepsy are left home alone.

• The boy requires regular medication.

• They live in a street property.

• The girl runs into the street to call an adult passer-by because the boy is having a seizure. The adult immediately calls an ambulance and the police.

• The police report to children's services that there is little food in the home and no heating on a cold day.

• The children do not have access to a telephone and the girl is vulnerable because she cannot use the public phone.

• A strategy meeting is planned for the next day to plan how to continue the investigation and to consider the need for a paediatric assessment and a child protection conference.

• The boy is to remain in hospital overnight for monitoring.

• The girl returns home to the care of both parents with support from the children's disability team.

• The social worker (SW) makes checks and learns that there have been two previous referrals to children's services because the children were left alone.

• The school staff report that the girl is often left waiting for her mother to collect her and does not always have sufficient food in her lunch box.

• The health visitor reports that the boy is reaching his developmental milestones and the mother takes him for regular hospital check ups.

• Children's services ask the hospital SW to interview the children.

• The girl tells the SW that there is no neighbour available and that her mother had gone to church.

• A strategy discussion takes place with the police child abuse investigation team (CAIT) and a joint investigation is agreed.

S47 investigation of a child left home alone

• The police decide it is not in the children's interests to pursue a prosecution.

• The police and SWs decide that the family need support services and that the boy needs to be provided with a nursery place as a matter of urgency.

• The SW checks with the children's disability team who report concerns about neglect issues and who have known the family for some time.

• The allocated SW agrees to support the father in addressing the basic need for food and warmth in the home.

• The parents are separated and the father visits at weekends. The children tell the SW that they enjoy his visits. The father is not known to the police.

• The father is contacted by the children's disability team SW who meets him at the family address where he agrees to stay during the investigation.

• The home is cold as there is no electricity and there is little food available.

• The father says that he has had concerns about the impact on the children of the mother's religious commitments for some time, although he also sees the church community as supportive.

• The mother responds to a note left by the police and attends the hospital. The police and the SW interview the mother at the hospital.

• The mother tells the interviewers that she had to attend an important church service on the instructions of the pastor.

• She is worried about her little boy and shows both children much affection.

CASE STUDY

• A 15-year old girl is left home alone caring for a 3-year-old boy and a 1-year-old girl.

• The home, a detached property, is in an affluent area.

• The neighbour tells a local councillor that the girl is locked in and never appears to leave the house.

• The councillor reports her concerns to children's services.

• Checks by the social worker (SW) show that there have been no previous referrals.

• The school nurse reported the 15-year-old girl to be sad and withdrawn and that there have been a number of unexplained absences.

• The teacher noted that the girl has limited use of English, that she calls her mother by her first name and that she seems to have a lot of responsibility for the care of her siblings.

• The health visitor said that the 15-year-old girl is a distant family cousin, has been in the household for a year and is often at home when she visits.

• There are no health concerns for the two younger children.

• The police arrange for the parents to be arrested on their return to the UK and to be charged with possible offences relating to cruelty and neglect, false imprisonment and trafficking.

• The child protection doctor conducts a paediatric assessment.

• Children's services recommend that a voluntary organisation with expertise in supporting trafficked children become involved.

• Depending on the outcome of the joint investigation, care proceedings may be commenced.

Immediate action to protect a child left home alone

• The SW contacts the police for a strategy discussion and they agree a joint investigation.

• The police and SW visit the home with an interpreter. They find the children on their own.

• The home is warm and safe.

• The girl says that the adults are away for two weeks on holiday abroad and that an aunty calls in once a week with food. She shows the SW her room where she eats separately from the family.

• The girl has only one contact telephone number which is for the aunt.

• A strategy meeting is planned and following the investigation and a decision will be made about the need for a child protection conference.

• The SW and police are unable to contact the parents.

• The SW applies to court for an Emergency Protection Order (EPO) which is obtained.

• The SW arranges for the three children to be placed in foster care.

• A visually recorded interview with the girl is planned.

• It is suspected that the girl has been trafficked for domestic service and the police make checks with immigration services.

• The police locate the 'aunt' who is not related to the children and who admits that she has been paid to take them food once per week. She provides the police with contact details for the parents but explains that while they are the parents of the younger children they are not the parents of the 15-year-old.

C H A P T E R   S U M M A R Y

Neglect is the cause of about a third of deaths of children from child abuse. The main difficulty for social workers is making decisions about at what stage the neglect of a child has escalated to the point where a protective multi agency response is indicated. This decision is reached only through effective joint working, debating the thresholds of intervention and reaching agreement about when an s47 (CA 1989) should be implemented. The protocol for a core assessment is presented to support a critical approach towards the completion of the required format.

Many types of neglect are discussed in this chapter, both within the family and through wider societal factors. Examples of parental responses are presented to help prepare social workers to challenge and question the explanations provided for harm to children and how social workers might work with families to make judgements about risk. A detailed study of practice, when a child is left at home alone, provides an opportunity to examine a case of neglect in depth.

FURTHER READING

Bridge Child Care Development Service (1995) *Paul: Death from neglect*. London: Islington ACPC. A report of the inquiry into Paul's death.

D'Arcy, M and Gosling, P (1998) *Abuse of trust. Frank Beck and the Leicestershire children's homes scandal*. London: Bowerdean.
As a manager of children's homes, Beck abused hundreds of young people entrusted to his care. This book, written by two local journalists, is based on interviews with victims, survivors, colleagues and friends of Beck.

Frampton, P (2004) *Golly in the cupboard*. Manchester: Tamic.
This is a personal account of a child brought up in care during the 1950s and 1960s.

Howe, D (2005) *Child abuse and neglect: attachment, development and intervention*. London: Palgrave Macmillan
This is an authoritative analysis and application of knowledge about the impact of abuse. It helps make sense of theory and informs understanding and intervention.

Nazer, M and Lewis, D (2004) *Slave. The true story of a girl's lost childhood and her fight for survival*. London: Virago.
This book is Mende Nazer's account of being abducted, trafficked and eventually sold into domestic labour in Khartoum and London and how she escaped slavery.

WEBSITES

www.anationalvoice.org
A National Voice is an organisation run for and by young people who are or have been in care. It supports care leavers and campaigns for changes to the care system.

www.edcm.org.uk
Every Disabled Child Matters is a campaign group to ensure inclusion of disabled children within the Every Child Matters agenda.

www.ecpat.org.uk
End Child Prostitution, Child Pornography and the Trafficking of Children for Sexual Purposes (ECPAT) is a campaigning and children's rights organisation committed to working against the commercial sexual exploitation of children in the UK and internationally.

www.howardleague.org.uk
The Howard League raises awareness about child deaths in prison and chronic neglect of young people and their needs within custodial settings.

www.standup4children.org
The Stop Deporting Children Campaign takes action against the deportation of children to countries where their health, freedom, education and survival are at risk.

www.triangle-services.co.uk
Triangle is an independent organisation working with children and young people, many of whom are disabled. It provides training and consultancy throughout the UK.

Chapter 4
Physical abuse

ACHIEVING A SOCIAL WORK DEGREE

This chapter will help you to meet the following National Occupational Standards (see the Skills for Care website www.skillsforcare.org.uk):

Key Role 1: Prepare for, and work with individuals, families, carers, groups and communities to assess their needs and circumstances.

- Assess needs and options to recommend a course of action.

Key Role 2: Plan, carry out, review and evaluate social work practice, with individuals, families, carers, groups and communities and other professionals.

- Respond to crisis situations.
- Address behaviour which presents a risk to individuals, families, carers, groups and communities.

Key Role 3: Support individuals to represent their needs, views and circumstances.

- Prepare for, and participate in decision-making forums.

Key Role 4: Manage risk to individuals, families, carers, groups, communities, self and colleagues.

Key Role 5: Manage and be accountable, with supervision and support, for your own social work practice within your organisation.

- Manage, present and share records and reports.
- Work within multi-disciplinary and multi-organisational teams, networks and systems.

Key Role 6: Demonstrate professional competence in social work practice.

- Research, analyse, evaluate and use current knowledge of best social work practice.
- Manage complex ethical issues, dilemmas and conflicts.

It will also introduce you to the following academic standards as set out in the social work subject benchmark statements. See

www.qaa.ac.uk/academicinfrastructure/benchmark/honours/socialpolicy.asp#1

5.1.2 The service delivery context

- The significance of legislative and legal frameworks and service delivery standards.

5.1.4 Social work theory

- Research-based concepts and critical explanations from social work theory and other disciplines that contribute to the knowledge base of social work.

5.5 Problem-solving skills

5.5.2 Gathering information.

5.5.3 Analysis and synthesis.

5.5.4 Intervention and evaluation.

5.6 Communication skills

- listen actively to others, engage appropriately with the life experiences of service users, understand accurately their viewpoint and overcome personal prejudices to respond appropriately to a range of complex personal and interpersonal situations;
- follow and develop an argument and evaluate the viewpoints of, and evidence presented by others.

5.7 Skills in working with others
- consult actively with others, including service users, who hold relevant information or expertise;
- act with others to increase social justice by identifying and responding to prejudice, institutional discrimination and structural inequality;
- challenge others when necessary, in ways that are most likely to produce positive outcomes.

7.3 Knowledge and understanding
- an ability to use research and enquiry techniques, to collect, analyse and interpret relevant information;
- a developed capacity for critical evaluation of knowledge and evidence from a range of sources.

Introduction

Initially the child protests, pleads, begs for the adults to stop the terrorising. When the child realises that their objections are not having an impact on reducing the abuse, the child enters a phase of despondency. They shut down their capacities to feel. Sometimes they dissociate by psychologically splitting away from their own bodies. A range of defences are put up to protect the abused child against the devastation of often being reliant on the abuser, simultaneously loving and dreading them. These children, numb in feeling, experience themselves as emotionally frozen, shut-down, but on alert for danger.

(Batmanghelidjh, 2007, p13)

Physical punishment is a counsel of despair – something that is done when we cannot think of anything else to do or when we want to relieve our frustration, not when we want to help a child to learn or develop. If the child will not back down from the confrontation, the parent either has to back off or has to hit harder and harder because he or she has put him or herself in the position of having to win.

(Dawson, 2000, p2)

This chapter focuses on the protection of children from physical abuse. It begins by looking at definitions and moves on to consider the knowledge required to make professional judgements. The complexities of this form of abuse will be examined to support an informed approach to individual children's circumstances. Research into children's views and survivor perspectives provides a basis for sound decision-making. Four case studies provide opportunity for further application of knowledge to practice. The chapter concludes with case examples of physical harm to children involving physical punishment, which will take the reader through an investigative process, escalated through five levels of social work intervention to support in-depth analysis.

Definition of physical abuse

Physical abuse may involve hitting, shaking, throwing, poisoning, burning or scalding, drowning, suffocating or otherwise causing physical harm to a child. Physical harm may also be caused when a parent or carer feigns symptoms of, or deliberately causes ill health to a child whom they are looking after. (Children in whom illness is induced or fabricated by carers with parenting responsibilities.)

(DfES, 2006, 1.30)

The Committee defines 'corporal' or 'physical' punishment as any punishment in which physical force is used and intended to cause some degree of pain or discomfort, however light. In the view of the Committee, corporal punishment is invariably degrading.
(United Nations Committee on the Rights of the Child, 2002)

Learning about physical harm to children

ACTIVITY **4.1**

Think about what the word 'hitting' in the Working together *definition might mean (DfES, 2006,1.30).*

Comment

Of children who die from child abuse, the majority, about 60%, die as a result of physical violence predominantly caused by male perpetrators of physical assault (Reder and Duncan, 1999, p4). The final act that kills is very often a culmination of previous acts of harm. In their study of serious case reviews, Reder, et al. state *the majority of the children had been beaten, bruised and sometimes tortured for a long time prior to their deaths and in some instances their injuries had already led to hospital admissions* (1995, p45). Although the children who die from abuse are the exceptional cases, the lessons learnt from their case histories are relevant to the protection of all children. It is so important for social workers to examine the reasons for delay in recognition and action to protect the children in these cases. For example, the professionals who visited Sukina Hammond accepted the father's explanation of hitting his daughter on the knuckles with a ruler as reasonable discipline rather than as an indicator of physical abuse. After Sukina was unable to spell her own name correctly, her father went on to beat his daughter to death (Bridge Child Care Consultancy, 1991).

Physical abuse may be caused accidentally or deliberately. Medical evidence assists social workers in determining whether or not the physical signs are consistent with explanations given by the child and/or other child and adult witnesses. Some physical signs may in fact be evident through other innocent causes e.g. birth marks such as red strawberry birth marks or the Mongolian blue spot which is a flat blueish mark on the skin of young children of Asian, African origin or of mixed parentage. These are usually recorded at birth. There may be physical abuse without any obvious physical signs of harm, such as when a child has been beaten on the soles of their feet or when bruises are concealed under the hair. Whether or not there is medical evidence of physical harm it is essential that the child's account is taken very seriously. The Secretary General of the United Nations commented on this: *discipline through physical and humiliating punishment, bullying and sexual harassment is frequently perceived as normal particularly when no visible or lasting physical injury results* (United Nations General Assembly, 2006, p10).

Sometimes injuries remain medically unexplained and doubt exists about the origin of unusual markings or conditions. For example, some of Victoria Climbié's injuries were described by paediatricians as looking like belt buckle marks and yet no evidence ever explained the causes of these unusual markings. Despite the uncertainty, these should have been thoroughly investigated as they were in fact indicative of future harm she suffered. Some forms of punishment are unusual, such as making a child kneel or stand in fixed positions for hours or pulling out a child's hair. Cooper, in her account of being a child in care, describes having her mouth washed out with soap for saying *bad words. I choked and retched but she kept ramming it back into my mouth* (Cooper, 2007, p8). Stobart (2006) studied cases of children in particular faith communities who had experienced chilli pepper rubbed into their genitalia, being hit, beaten and burnt when considered possessed by spirits.

Some facts about physical abuse

- In 2007 there were 3,500 children and young people who were the subject of a child protection plan under the category of physical abuse (DCSF, 2007).

- In response to a parliamentary question, Ivan Lewis stated that the number of children up to the age of 14 years who were admitted to hospital as a result of unintentional injury in 2005–6 was 100,194 and in the same year 233 died from unintentional injury (Lewis, 2007).

- In a national UK survey of the childhood experiences of 2,869 young adults aged between 18 and 24 years it was shown that 21% of respondents suffered physical abuse. The respondents reported that 70% of the violence happened at home, most often by the mother (49%) or the father (40%) and more than a fifth had experienced it regularly (Cawson, et al., 2000, pp35–7).

- In 2002 there were 114,000 investigations for animal cruelty and 910 prosecutions, although only extreme cases of severe and deviant acts of cruelty result in prosecutions (RSPCA, cited in Becker and French, 2004, p401).

- Between 2004 and 2005, ChildLine received 12,513 calls from children reporting physical abuse. More than one-third said they were attacked with an implement or that violence had left them wounded. www.childline.org.uk/extra/Casenote_gender-abuse.asp

- Mullender and Morley (1994), in a study relating to domestic violence, found that child victims will not necessarily grow up to be violent or become adult victims themselves. They found that there is no conclusive evidence of a cycle of violence.

- In 90% of incidents involving domestic violence, children are in the same or the next room (Hughes, 1992, pp9–11).

- Rees, in a study of 80 children staying in a safe house, found that physical violence was the most commonly cited reason for running away from home occurring in just under a half of those interviewed (Rees,1993, p20).

- Only 1% of family support services have specialist services for fathers (Henricson, et al., 2001).

- An NSPCC survey showed 86% of adults would be happy to shop in a smack-free shop (NSPCC, 2007).

- A Children's Safety Survey of 2,420 young people aged 9–16 found that 55% reported being physically assaulted and 80% had experienced harassment which they found frightening. The reports were not exclusive to deprived areas and most took place in streets and parks (Deakin, 2006).

CASE STUDY

Sukina

Sukina Hammond died in December 1988 at the age of 5 years. Her father asked Sukina and her sister to spell their names. He then hit Sukina on the hand with a ruler, repeatedly asking her to spell her name. As her father repeated the demand, the attack escalated. She was then hit with a length of plastic tubing and later a kettle flex.

We do not know how long the attack lasted, but at least fifty blows were rained upon her, interspersed with repeated demands that she spelled her name. Sukina, when too weak to stand tried to crawl out of the room to the stairs, asking her father to stop hitting her… Sukina's mother tried to intervene and was herself assaulted, causing injuries to her face.

The attack on Sukina continued until she was barely conscious, at which point she was taken by her parents to the bathroom and placed in a bath of warm water in an attempt to revive her … As she slipped into unconsciousness Sukina told her father she was sorry. Although an ambulance was called, Sukina was already dead on arrival at the hospital.

Sukina's apology to her father meant that she, like so many abused children before her, was coping with the feeling that what happened was her fault.

(*Bridge Child Care Consultancy, 1991, p7*)

Six different agencies were involved with the family and there were many reports by neighbours of ill treatment. Sukina's father attended a martial arts club and it is possible that many beatings were controlled in such as way as to leave no mark. The Inquiry concluded that the professionals needed to discriminate between families under stress, occasional violence and a culture of violence. In order to make such a judgement, separate incidents needed to have been evaluated in the context of the case history. Professionals needed to be open to considering the possibility that some families may use systematic violence.

Disabled children and physical abuse

An estimated 3% of children in the UK have disabilities. Disabled children are nearly four times more likely to be physically abused than non-disabled children (Sullivan and Knutson, 2000a, p1257). The presence of multiple disabilities appears to increase the risk of abuse (DfES, 2006, 11.27). Abuse is underreported because of the relatively powerless position of disabled children.

I can remember being hit at my first home. That was bad because my Dad used to hit me as well. I thought, well one place is as bad as another. He was horrid to my mum as well.

(Laura, quoted in Morris, 1999, p16)

ACTIVITY 4.2

Why do you think disabled children are particularly vulnerable to physical abuse?

Comment

You might have considered the following:

- greater social isolation – particularly in institutional care away from their locality, making it difficult to be heard or observed by protective adults;

- greater dependency on others, at all ages, for personal care, allowing abusers close contact which is not be questioned;

- increased numbers of carers leading to more potential abusers in the child's world;

- a child may be unheard when trying to disclose abuse because of communication difficulties or inability to access support;

- abusers target disabled children thinking that the indicators of physical abuse will be misinterpreted as signs of disability and the abuse will remain hidden;

- they may suffer specific forms of physical abuse such as force-feeding, excessive physical restraint or rough handling.

RESEARCH SUMMARY

Thirty disabled young people living away from home were interviewed and three key factors were identified as making them particularly vulnerable to abuse. They did not have access to a suitable communication system, had no routine access to people who understood their communication needs and had no access to independent facilitators (Morris, 1999, p21).

Sullivan and Knutson (2000b) in an American study found high levels of disabled children among their sample of children who ran away, with maltreatment as the main cause in the majority of cases (cited in Corby, 2006, p190).

The physical abuse of children at different ages

ACTIVITY 4.3

Social workers sometimes think that children are more vulnerable to abuse at particular ages. At what age do you think children are more likely to experience physical abuse?

Comment

All children are at risk even though babies are more vulnerable. CRAE quote the following statistics relating to homicides of 58 children during 2004–5.

They report that 23 were under 1 year old, 17 were between 1 and 4 years old, and 18 between 5 and 15 years old (CRAE, 2006, p29). Babies of substance-misusing parents, such as those who misuse alcohol, may be born with physiological damage such as low birth weight, distinctive facial characteristics, learning difficulties and hyperactivity. Babies born to drug- misusing mothers are likely to be premature and have low birth weights. They may also suffer brain damage and have poor motor co-ordination. The baby may be born with an addiction and suffer withdrawal symptoms during the first weeks of life.

Thinking about types of physical abuse

Physical abuse of children within violent families

Serious case reviews highlight a family history of violence including parental conflict and violent and criminal histories, such as sexual crime, as significant in child deaths from physical harm. Reder and Duncan found that, *a clear history of violent, criminal or other antisocial behaviour from at least one of the caretakers* was evident in a significant number of their sample (1999, p63). Key risk factors are the young age of the child, health problems in the child, young mothers, drug abuse and criminal histories in male carers. Reder and Duncan state that *the abusive behaviour of many of the parents could be understood as a manifestation of severe personal and inter-personal problems* (1999, p62). Bancroft, et al. (2004, p7) emphasise the relationship between parental substance misuse and physical violence. About a third of children living in violent households try to intervene to stop it, thereby risking harm to themselves (Abrahams, 1994). In a study which gave a voice to child victims of domestic violence, children said:

> I tried to help. I tried to guard my Mum so he couldn't hurt her. I didn't talk about it with anyone. I used to run downstairs to see mum was OK. (Errol, 8)

> I make myself be awake so that I can jump up when it happens and get between them … (Lisa, 15)

> I didn't really try to stop the fight. I was too frightened. I used to think 'He'll just beat me up too' so I didn't. (Mona, 8)

> (Mullender, et al., 2003, pp21–3)

There is a high correlation between parental violence and violence to children. A US study of 1,000 women in refuges found that 70% of the women with children said their partners had also been physically violent to the children: The more frequent the violence, the more severe the physical abuse of the children: *the severity of the wife beating is a predictor of the severity of the child abuse* (Bowker, 1988, p65). A study of nearly 2,000 child protection referrals across seven London boroughs found that 27% of cases involved domestic violence (Humphreys and Mullender, 1999, p3). Over a quarter of young adults report violence sometimes takes place between those caring for them. Five per cent of this violence was constant or frequent. Children also make up about two-thirds of the people staying in refuges (Cawson, 2002, p37).

Where conflictual parents have separated and the children remain exposed to violence during contact, Saunders found that between 1994 and 2004, 29 children from 13 families were killed during contact arrangements (Saunders, 2004).

Violence in a household may extend to cruelty towards animals as part of the continuum of abuse within a family. In 1981 Hutton studied 23 families in the UK known for animal cruelty and 82% were known to social services as having children at risk of harm.

> *Mummy shouted at us all the time. She made us leave our dog on its own when we went away. The dog was dead when we came back. I miss him so much.*

(NSPCC, 2002a)

Shaking injuries

One of the most dangerous forms of violence towards children is from shaking injuries. When a baby is shaken the blood vessels may break and bleed as the brain impacts repeatedly against the skull. For those babies who survive they may suffer paralysis or a long-term learning impairment.

RESEARCH SUMMARY

Shaking injuries mainly take place on children between the ages of a few days old and 5 years but the average age of harm is 6–8 months old and is common in 1 in 4,000 children. The mortality rate is as high as 25% (NSPCC, 2001b).

In the London Borough of Newham, 280 parents and schoolchildren were interviewed. The study found that 10% of mothers had shaken their babies and 25% had felt like doing so. Half the parents in the survey were unaware of the dangers of shaking a baby and of those who had shaken a baby, or who felt like it, 90% said it was because the baby cried incessantly. Some 75% felt isolated as parents and other factors such as housing, financial and relationship problems as well as postnatal depression were relevant. The research concluded that most people, if made aware of the risks to babies of shaking, would be less likely to do it (Shepherd, et al., 2000, pp721–35).

Bruising

Most children have bruises on parts of the body that are prominent, such as elbows and knees, but bruising to a pre-crawling or pre-walking baby is unusual. Children may have symmetrical bruising, indicative of gripping or holding a child down. Multiple bruises in clusters may indicate they are caused by knuckles or fingers. Bruising on the inner thighs and buttocks may be indicative of sexual abuse, as may bruising in and around the mouth, although in babies this may indicate forced-feeding. Two simultaneous bruised eyes are rarely accidental. If a child has a disability such as epilepsy and may fall frequently, advice must be sought to clarify whether any patterns of bruising are consistent with the disability or not. It is very difficult to date bruising accurately and sometimes a child may bruise easily due to various medical conditions. A paediatrician will check whether or not this is the case.

Bites

A bite mark may be human or animal, child or adult size. It may be possible to obtain medical measurements in order to assist identification of the perpetrator of the injury. Sometimes, inappropriately, adults bite a child to tell them not to do it to another child or it may be a sadistic act.

Burns and scalds

Medical opinion about burns is usually very helpful to investigating social workers. A child who runs into a cigarette may not have a deep circular burn as would be left from one purposefully inflicted. Sometimes burns may indicate a shape, such as from an iron, hair tongs or an electric fire, and patterns may be matched against the objects described by the child or family. A child may pick up an iron and be burnt but this will leave a different mark from an iron held to the skin. Children will naturally move away quickly from contact with hot liquids and splash marks will occur, but if a child has been dipped or held in hot water or other liquid there may be a clear demarcation line of a burn which would be more indicative of a non-accidental injury. However, an adult may throw a hot drink over a child in anger and this would leave splash marks. Rope and friction burns can be caused deliberately, such as when a child is restrained during sexual or physical abuse. The presence of old scars from burns may indicate a lack of treatment for previous burn injuries.

Fractures and dislocations

> ### RESEARCH SUMMARY
>
> In 28 cases of fractures in children under the age of 5 years, 7 were non-accidental: 5 had been diagnosed and 2 had not. This gives a risk of non-accidental injury of 1 in 4 children in this age group. The research confirmed the greater incidence of fractures in children under 2 years old. The main indicator of abuse in these cases was an inconsistent history (Hoskote et al , 2003).
>
> In an analysis of 17 serious case reviews involving 28 children from 17 families and including 19 children who died, the most common injuries were brain damage, skull fractures, rib fractures, other fractures and poisoning. Ten died before the age of 10 weeks. In every case it was the youngest child or only child in the family that died. Half had previously been treated for suspicious injuries. *We conclude that a great many serious injuries with discrepant explanations, cases both fatal and non fatal, are preventable*. Most had been assessed as children in need and not in need of protection despite parental histories of substance misuse, mental illness and domestic violence (Dale, et al., 2002, p35).

Non-mobile children (e.g. very young or as a result of disability) rarely sustain fractures. It is important for social workers to have some knowledge of child development and to know, for instance, that a baby of 3 months does not roll over and that an infant of 6 months rarely walks or may not be crawling. It is not always the case that a young child with a fracture displays pain or discomfort which may therefore be difficult for an adult to detect.

Poisoning

The most commonly used substances in poisoning children are salt, paracetamol and prescription drugs. When investigated, parents often say that they had not realised the toxicity of the substance and had not considered that the child might suffer harm.

RESEARCH SUMMARY

In one study, 100 mothers were interviewed and all defined salt as a serious poison and had a concept of a safe dosage of paracetamol, but a third did not realise paracetamol could be lethal. The conclusion was that *it is highly unlikely that a mother could administer a harmful dose of salt or paracetamol in the belief that their actions would have no ill effect* (Smith and Meadows, 2000, p16).

Poisoning is more likely to be non-accidental if:

- a substance is repeatedly administered or ingested in large amounts;
- there are other features of physical harm or neglect;
- the child is aged outside 2–4 years;
- a history of self-poisoning is implausible;
- there is a previous history of unusual presentations to hospital.

(Meadows, 1997)

Forced ingestion

This form of abuse is when a child is forced to eat or drink an inedible non-food substance. For example, child sex abusers may force a child to drink alcohol or take muscle- relaxant drugs to make a child compliant in sexual abuse. In her book *Trust no one*, Cooper describes her childhood in a care home where she was forced to take a range of anti-psychotic and sedative drugs (Cooper, 2007). The Laffoy Commission on child abuse in Ireland highlighted the exploitation of children in care for use in drug trials. Numbers of children were vaccinated in trials for rubella, whooping cough, polio and diphtheria (Ring, 2003).

Krugman, et al. (2007) describe cases of young children who have been suffocated through being forced to swallow baby wipes.

Fabricated or induced illness

A supplement to *Working together* (DCSF, 2008a) provides comprehensive guidance on this particular form of physical harm, which may include:

- deliberately inducing symptoms in children by administering medication or other substances by means of obstructing the child's airways or by interfering with the child's body to cause physical signs;
- interfering with treatments by overdosing, not administering them or interfering with medical equipment such as infusion lines;

- claiming the child has symptoms which are unverifiable unless observed directly, such as pain, frequency of passing urine, vomiting or fits – these claims lead to unnecessary investigations and treatments which may cause secondary physical problems;

- exaggerating symptoms, causing professionals to undertake investigations and treatments which may be invasive, are unnecessary and therefore harmful;

- obtaining specialist treatments or equipment for children who do not need them;

- alleging psychological illness in a child.

(DCSF, 2008a, 2.6)

Most children affected are confused about what is happening to them and find it very difficult to speak about it (Neale, et al., 1991). Parents and carers in these cases may have histories of childhood abuse or privation and considerable medical, obstetric or psychiatric histories which may be difficult to verify independently. There may be experience of significant bereavements such as of children in the areas of conception, miscarriage, stillbirths or death, or other losses in their lives that have often taken place within a short timespan (DCSF, 2008a, 2.31). Sometimes the adult's knowledge of medical conditions is so detailed as to indicate a knowledge base in nursing or medicine. The guidance emphasises the importance of considering professionals-only meetings because of the risk of escalating the behaviour and placing the child at increased risk if parents are confronted too soon in the investigation.

The use of covert video surveillance (CVS) must only be used if there is no alternative way of obtaining information which will explain the child's signs and symptoms and the multi-agency strategy discussion meeting considers that its use is justified based on the medical information available (DCSF, 2008a, 6.36). Police are responsible for and accountable for the process. Because of the human rights issues, CVS use must be proportionate to the aim to be achieved – which is the safety of the child.

A parent might invent a symptom in a child in order to protect the child from more extreme forms of child abuse such as sexual exploitation. The action will get the child into hospital for a few days and away from an abuse network.

Bullying as physical violence

A pupil support circular (DfES, 1999) dealt with the unacceptability of and emotional distress and harm caused by bullying in whatever form – be it racial, as a result of a pupil's appearance, related to sexual orientation or for any other reason. *Bullying is when someone picks on someone else because they are different – their race, height, weight, or looks ... [it's about] prejudice and discrimination and when someone gets hurt physically or mentally, or when someone is not respected* (Girl, Year 8). In a sample of 174 children in Year 5 of primary school, 35% reported being kicked, 37% reported being hit on purpose and 44% reported being pushed (Oliver and Candappa, 2003, p51).

Bullying is not currently a criterion for the category of physical abuse of children subject to a child protection plan and does not trigger child protection procedures. However, Sir Ian Blair, the then Metropolitan Police Commissioner, following a series of fatal shootings of teenagers in 2007, said that children at risk of violence from gang members, including children in the families of perpetrators, should gain protection in the same way as children whose parents are violent and abusive. They should be considered under threat and subject to child protection procedures (Laville, 2007). In 18 months between 2007 and mid-2008, 39 young people were shot or stabbed to death in London alone, with the killings related to gangs (Mickel, 2008, p20).

At least 16 children commit suicide every year as a result of bullying. Marr and Field (2001) use the term *bullycide* to describe when children commit suicide rather than face another day of unrelenting bullying. They comment that following the tragedy, parents are likely to find themselves and their dead child vilified and blamed.

Children in custody and use of restraint

No child shall be subjected to torture or other inhuman or degrading treatment or punishment. No child should be deprived of his or her liberty unlawfully or arbitrarily. The arrest, detention or imprisonment of a child shall be in conformity with the law and shall be used only as a measure of last resort and for the shortest possible period of time.

(United Nations, 1989, Article 37)

In 2008 there were 3,037 children in custody in the UK, with 85% per cent held in prison, and 43% sentenced for non-violent crime (Howard League, 2008). The Munby judgement (*R v Sec of State All ER*, 465:2002) gave local authorities a duty of care to young people in prison but an inspector's report stated that it was not possible to be confident that children in prison were safeguarded (CSCI, 2005). Since 1990, there have been 30 deaths of young people, all boys, in prison. Of these, 29 were self-inflicted and one followed restraint by staff (Goldson and Coles, 2005; Howard League, 2008).

The death of children fills us all with a particular horror. First that the children must have been intolerably unhappy and second that responsible adults have failed in their primary duty to keep children safe from harm. In many cases outside prison child suicides come as a surprise but as far as young offender institutions are concerned this manifestly cannot be the case as every child prisoner is known to be at risk of suicide.

(CRAE and NSPCC, 2007)

Thousands of children have also self-harmed in custody. Between 1998 and 2002, 1,659 incidents were recorded of self-injury or attempted suicide. Between November 2005 and October 2006, 3,036 restraints were used in the secure training centres, of which 1,245 were on girls. This means that 41% of all restraints are on girls, who represent only 34% of the secure training centre population (Howard League, 2007).

Much concern has been raised about the use of 'distraction' techniques, which are intended to cause pain and on many occasions have caused harm to children (Carlile, 2006, p38). Lord Carlile said that many of the practices in child custody would be regarded as child abuse in any other setting (CRAE, 2006, p21). The Royal College of Paediatrics and Child Health said that painful restraint methods were unacceptable in their use of pain to bring about compliance (CRAE and NSPCC, 2007, p 22).

The Carlile Inquiry report clarified that restraint should not be used primarily to secure compliance. It should only be used to prevent escape from custody, stop a child hurting themselves or others or damaging property or incitement of another trainee to do certain defined acts. Children gave evidence to the inquiry:

> *The man got my head down and pushed me against the wall. Two people were holding my arms. The man had my head and pushed my nose up and it was bleeding. It makes you feel like you are nothing. People holding you down brings bad memories. It's horrible. Makes you want to head butt them.*

(CRAE and NSPCC, 2007)

In December 2007, the Minister for Children and Minister for Justice announced that in the light of recent deaths of children in custody, two particular forms of restraint used were no longer to be allowed (Lovell, 2008). The Howard League states that the UK government is breaching at least ten articles of the UNCRC (Howard League, 2007):

> *The profligate use of prison for children, the infliction of pain and injury to control children behind closed doors, child deaths in custody, lack of physical exercise and the use of segregation blocks that resemble modern day dungeons are all ways in which the treatment of children in custody amounts to child abuse and in some cases may be criminal.*

Genital integrity – female and male genital mutilation (FGM and MGM)

> *States parties to take all effective and appropriate measures with a view to abolishing traditional practices prejudicial to the health of children.*

(United Nations, 1989, Article 24.3)

Both female genital mutilation and non-therapeutic male genital mutilation (circumcision) are irreversible procedures performed without the child's consent. Sometimes these practices are justified by cultural or religious reasons but social workers need to be aware that these reasons must never stand in the way of the protection of children from harm. MGM is not illegal but FGM has been illegal since 1985 in the UK. Following the Female Genital Mutilation Act 2003 it became illegal to take a child abroad for the procedure. FGM is considered in the UK to be a form of physical abuse of a child and is addressed in child protection guidance (DfES, 2006, 6.11), but non-therapeutic MGM is not formally defined as child abuse. One essential difference between the two is that sometimes male circumcision may be medically required whereas there is never such a reason to justify FGM. However, the British Medical Association is clear that there is no medical basis for non-therapeutic MGM as a routine practice. It can constitute harm when the child acquires an infection as a result of neglect, sustains physical or cosmetic damage, suffers emotional, physical or sexual harm from the way the procedure was carried out, or suffers emotional harm from not having been consulted or having his wishes taken into account. There may be harm through the procedure being conducted incompetently or facilities being inadequate or unhygienic (LSCB, 2007, 5.25). The campaign group NORM-UK (www.norm-uk.org) considers MGM to be abusive because it involves irreversibly removing the foreskin, the child does not and cannot consent and it infringes a child's right to bodily integrity.

137

It is usually performed on babies of about seven days.

Female genital mutilation comprises all procedures that involve partial or total removal of the female external genitalia and/or injury to the female genital organs for cultural or any other non-therapeutic reasons (WHO, 1995, p3). The procedure is mainly carried out by older women with no anaesthetic, using basic tools such as knives and razor blades. The practice is surrounded in secrecy and the girls are often completely unprepared for what happens. It can take up to six women to restrain a child during the procedure. FGM is carried out on girls between the ages of 1 and 16 years but more commonly between age 5 and 10 years. There is concern at the age becoming younger and sometimes girls are cut again before marriage. The harmful emotional, psychological and physical consequences of FGM are well documented (Momoh, 2005).

The majority of cases of FGM are carried out in 28 African countries. In some countries, (e.g. Egypt, Ethiopia, Somalia and Sudan), prevalence rates can be as high as 98%. As a result of migration to Europe, including the UK, the practice of FGM has now spread to the UK. A recent study estimated that at least 24,000 girls under age 15 years have suffered or are at high risk of FGM and about 9,000 at high risk of the most extreme form of the procedure (Dorkenoo, et al., 2007).

The Metropolitan Police have an excellent initiative called Project Azure, to provide a protective response to children in relation to the practice of female genital mutilation. Details are available on the website of Forward, which is the main campaigning group against the practice of FGM (www.forwarduk.org.uk).

Very few children have been spoken to about their experience of FGM. Weil-Curiel tells of 25 separate trials and 90 people being sentenced in France during 1982, as well as two cutters who received prison sentences and the parents suspended sentences. She says *the girls do not accept that they have been cut. They are angry with their parents ... they say the tradition is not ours anymore. We want to be free to make choices* (APPG, 2000, p56). The testimonies of the child victims emphasised their intense suffering, their anger at their parents for handing them over for torture, their shame at having been cut and their distress at not having been protected by society.

In a documentary *The day I will never forget*, Fouzia, a five-year-old child, recites a poem, vividly speaking about the pain and trauma of FGM, to her mother. She tells her mother she will forgive her only if she promises to spare her sister (Longinotto, 2002):

> *In the morning I was dragged and pinned on the ground. I cried until I had no voice. The only thing I said was 'Mum, where are you?' and the only answer I got was 'Quiet, quiet, girl'. The pain I had experienced was one I will never forget for the rest of my life and I would not wish it to happen to my friend or anyone else. That night I had a sleepless night. I could see an old lady with many blades doing it again and again and again. I screamed. My loving parent, is this what I really deserve? I'm asking all of you, is this what I really deserve?*

Adult survivors have also written about their experience of FGM (Nazer and Lewis, 2004; Walker, 1993 and Dirie, 1998).

Every Child matters protocol (DfES, 2003) – an analysis

ACTIVITY 4.4

An initial assessment is completed at the point of first referral to children's services. This form is available through the Every Child Matters website. Social workers have commented that the process is difficult for families and fails to adapt to the specific needs of differing groups of children (Bell, 2008).

Consider how you might complete this form in a case of FGM. The form has sections for health, education, emotional and behavioural development, identity, family and social functioning, social presentation and self-care skills, with space for completion of the child's needs and parenting capacity. Family and environmental factors to be considered are the family history and functioning, wider family, housing, employment, income, social integration and community resources. A case of FGM must be immediately referred to the police child abuse investigation team (CAIT) and a section 47 (CA 1989) strategy meeting with a specialist advisor in FGM must be held. A common or initial assessment must not delay such action to protect the child. However, such assessment would inform a section 47 (CA 1989) investigation. In such cases the family functioning and care of the child is not in question other than for the issue of FGM. Key aspects would be the family history of FGM and beliefs and the influence of the local community in assisting the protection of the child.

Considering the significance of behavioural indicators of physical abuse

Social workers need to recognise specific signs which may indicate physical abuse. Although some indicators will be definitive, most will need evaluation through the child protection processes and multi-agency debate. On their own or grouped together they may be indicative.

- Running away.
- Wary of adults or ducking/hiding when an adult comes near.
- Withstanding examination and painful procedures with little response.
- Not turning to parent for support.
- Child believes she/he is bad and deserving of punishment.
- Constantly trying to please the parent.
- Behaviour extremes, aggressive or withdrawn.
- Afraid to go home.
- Reluctant to undress at school.
- Inappropriately dressed to hide marks.
- Indiscriminately seeks affection.
- Inappropriate maturity.
- Fear of physical contact.

Responding to the child protection needs of physically abused children at an early stage

Physical abuse of children, like all forms of abuse, is damaging. Apart from obvious injuries and even death there is psychological impact, described by De Bellis and Putnam (1994) as causing changes in the neuroendocrine systems that affects arousal, pain thresholds, learning and growth. Physical abuse is also correlated with sexual harm and neglect. There is also the cumulative effect of multiple abuses.

RESEARCH SUMMARY

Interviews were carried out with over 2,000 children age 2–17 years in the USA. They identi-fied that 22% were *poly-victims,* defined as children who had experienced at least four types of violence in the previous year. This definition included sexual violence, physical assault, property victimisation, maltreatment, peer victimisation and witnessing victimisation. Poly-victims were more likely to be black, of low socio-economic status and from single-parent households. Poly-victims had poor mental health outcomes (Finkelhor, et al., 2007).

ACTIVITY *4.5*

What does responding earlier to the protection needs of physically abused children mean?

Comment

There are various ways of understanding the meaning of early intervention.

Responding early can mean:
- working with families before the child is born;
- working with families in the early months of a child's life;
- provision of parenting support programmes;
- a swift professional response to a child needing protection from physical abuse;
- teaching children how to stay safe through school programmes;
- community awareness programmes to support early reporting of physical abuse;
- organisations being responsive to the child's need for safety and hearing the child's voice;
- removal of perpetrators from the world of the child.

Working with families before the child is born

Professionals involved at the beginning of children's lives, such as midwives, GPs, health vis-itors, nursery workers and social workers, need to draw on the knowledge provided by numerous inquiries and research about the children killed or harmed from physical violence.

Antenatal histories are particularly relevant. Failure to attend antenatal care with minimal preparation for the arrival of the baby as well as negative attitudes towards the forthcoming baby and continued misuse of drugs and alcohol throughout the pregnancy were all deemed significant by Reder and Duncan (1999, p64).

Working with families in the early months of a child's life

After the baby was born the absence of post-natal care was also significant, as well as refusal to engage the assistance of health visitors for developmental checks. Reder and Duncan consider that incidents arose out of parental experience of abandonment, neglect or rejection as a child or feeling unloved by parents. Parents may be unable to cope with the dependency of the child, perhaps triggering for them memories of their own difficult childhoods. *We were particularly struck by the number of mothers who inappropriately tried to wean their babies onto solids when only a few weeks old, as though wishing them to be older than they were* (Reder and Duncan, 1999, p64).

Incidents of violence were sometimes triggered by an adult's unrealistic expectation of young child's behaviour, such as defining a child who urinates in the bath or during a nappy change as deliberately wilful. Haskett comments that parents who hold unrealistically high expectations of children's developmental abilities *were likely to view their children as having many behavioural problems and to believe their children misbehaved specifically to annoy them* (Haskett, et al., 2003, p678).

Provision of parenting support programmes

RESEARCH SUMMARY

There has been no public education programme on the right to protection for children from all forms of violence. A MORI poll interviewed 1,077 parents on their attitudes to parenting television programmes. In response to one question about the effectiveness of smacking in helping children understand the difference between right and wrong, only 10% of parents considered smacking to be effective in this respect.

Other responses to children were classified as follows:

spending time with children 67%;

parents themselves setting a good example 67%;

making children feel happy and loved 67%;

rewarding good behaviour 62%;

reasoning with children 48%;

grounding children 27%;

creating a diversion if doing something wrong 18%;

smacking children 10%.

(CRAE, 2006, p28)

Sure Start centres were established in 1997 to provide services to children under four and their families. They were placed in areas of deprivation but they are being converted into the development of children's centres with control shifting from the local community to the local authorities. An emphasis on universal provision has distracted attention and services from deprived communities. Lone parents are often thought to be particularly socially disadvantaged, but Nobes and Smith (2002) in a study of 500 single and two-parent homes found that children in one-parent homes were not a risk group for harsh physical punishment.

A swift professional response to a child needing protection from physical abuse

If a child reports abuse or an adult makes a referral, the child will only gain protection if the professional response is effective and implements local and national child protection guidance. In the case of Aaron Gilbert, who died aged 13 months from head injuries, the serious case review executive summary stated that *the social worker did not initiate an immediate child protection investigation ... the error of judgment could have been identified and the case relabelled as a child protection case* (Swansea LSCB, 2006). Although there was a referral about physical abuse and neglect, the case was defined as one of family support. In a Newcastle case, Baby O, aged 3 months, died of multiple injuries. The executive summary concluded that *analysis of risk was limited across agencies. This could have been avoided if information sharing and planning between all relevant agencies had been consistent throughout, and a comprehensive risk analysis and protection plan drawn up* (Weightman, 2006).

Teaching children how to stay safe through school programmes

Kidscape has developed programmes for schools and children's organisations on how to teach children to be safe. Local police schools involvement officers also teach personal safety including issues of child abuse. While adults are responsible for protecting children, there is no doubt that providing children with the knowledge and skills to recognise abusive behaviour and to know how to report it is essential to furthering their protection.

Community awareness programmes to support early reporting of physical abuse

Barriers to making a referral include:

- fear of exposing the child to further abuse;
- fear of breaking up the family;
- fear of reprisals to oneself or the family;
- fear of presenting evidence in court;
- fear of overreacting to a situation;
- assuming another agency is dealing with the problem;
- the rule of optimism – all will be OK in the child's world;
- assuming one parent will protect;
- believing a child is making the allegation up;
- accepting that abuse is normal within a child's culture/religion;

- being persuaded by a child's retraction;
- allowing a temporary improvement in the situation to distract you from the reality of the cause;
- refusing to believe the unbelievable;
- experiencing the pain of the abuse you have yourself suffered.

The community is a source of protection for children but it can also be the place of violence, including peer violence, violence relating to guns and other weapons, gang violence, physical and sexual violence, abductions and trafficking (United Nations, 2006, p25). How can the resources of a community be mobilised to offer protection to children? The LSCB have a responsibility to keep children safe in their locality. Through awareness, publicity and training programmes, key citizens can become a local network of protective adults for children well informed about the recognition of child abuse and the importance of referral. Both Davies (2004) and Nelson (2002) have developed methodologies for such community awareness strategies that include working with cultural and religious groups working to raise awareness about any practices abusive to children.

Removal of perpetrators from the world of the child

Children will remain unprotected unless abusers are removed from their world or the behaviour of abusers is changed through intervention. The Multi Agency Public Protection Arrangements (MAPPA) in each authority are responsible for managing adults who pose a danger to the community, particularly to children, and the Public Protection Unit police teams implement the risk strategies with other professionals.

The social work response

ACTIVITY 4.6

Deciding to what extent a child is at risk is based on professional judgement and the application of knowledge to individual cases. Here are four cases to which the authors have had to provide a protective social work response. Make a decision about which of the categories of response apply to these cases:

A *The child is not thought to be at any risk of child abuse.*

B *There is concern about physical harm to a child.*

C *There is suspicion of likely or actual significant harm to a child (s47 enquiry, CA 1989).*

D *A section 47 (CA 1989) investigation of child abuse is indicated.*

E *Immediate action to protect. Evidence of actual significant harm and/or criminal offence.*

1. *A baby of 3 months old has a torn frenulum (the frenulum is the bridge of tissue that joins the middle of the inside top lip to the gum).The young, caring parents have been anxious about the baby's lack of weight gain since the health visitor said the baby needed more food intake.*

ACTIVITY *4.6* *continued*

2. *A 6-year-old boy has enuresis (wets the bed). His parents take him to their local church to have the demons cast out of him. The child is beaten as part of a religious deliverance service.*

3. *A teacher hears a girl of 7 years old telling a friend that she is going to be taken abroad during the summer to be stitched up and that her older sister had told her it would hurt a lot.*

4. *A 14-year-old boy in a public school is caned on both hands by a master. His parents are uncritical of this breach of the law, believing it will help to instill obedience in their child.*

In relation to these cases:

- *Think about what criteria you would use in making judgements about physical abuse.*
- *Think about what may influence your selection of these criteria.*
- *How do you differentiate between situations that include risk but do not reach a threshold of actual dangerousness?*
- *At what stage is professional intervention indicated?*
- *What level of intervention is appropriate?*
- *When does physical abuse of a child become a crime?*
- *When is immediate action needed to protect the child from physical abuse?*
- *Are there other children who may be being abused?*

RESEARCH SUMMARY

In a US study of newly-qualified social work responses to the need to report physical harm it was found that the likelihood of reporting was related to personal judgements of the seriousness of the harm to the child. Variables of age, gender, marital status and parenthood were not significant factors affecting reporting. Those incidents most likely to be reported were of imminent harm to a child and to young children whereas incidents of older children experiencing physical punishment were rated as less serious events and were reported less frequently (Ashton, 1999).

Comment

Perhaps you based your decision making on your:

- experience as a child, as a parent or from your observation of and interaction with children;
- professional experience of a particular case;
- cultural or religious perspective of family life;
- knowledge of the law, child protection policy and practice guidance;
- knowledge of lessons learnt from child abuse inquiries and serious case reviews;

- understanding of the concept of physical abuse;

- your knowledge base of the subject from research findings;

- media reporting.

Each of the above cases did require a proactive social work intervention ranging from family support to section 47 enquiries and investigation to legal safeguards. The detailed analysis below will assist your later reflection on your decisions in the above scenarios.

Making judgements when a child is subjected to physical punishment

Hitting people is wrong – and children are people too. Corporal punishment of children breaches their fundamental rights to respect for human dignity and physical integrity. Its legality breaches their right to equal protection under law.

(Global Initiative to End All Corporal Punishment of Children, 2006)

The debate about physical discipline of children commonly centres on whether or not parents and carers should smack their children. *Reasonable chastisement* is not clearly defined in law but it remains a defence at the level of common assault and would be usually deemed unreasonable if the child was hit with an implement or if marks were caused. In 2002 the United Nations Committee on the Rights of the Child recommended that the UK should prohibit corporal punishment in the family, stating that they deeply regretted that the UK persisted in retaining the defence of reasonable chastisement and had taken no significant action towards prohibiting all corporal punishment of children in the family. The Committee distinguished between violence and humiliation as forms of punishment, which it rejected, and discipline of children in the form of necessary guidance and direction which is essential for healthy growth of children. The Committee also differentiated between punitive physical actions against children and physical interventions aimed at protecting children from harm (United Nations, 2002).

The extent of abuse of children in the UK by physical punishment

- 52% of 1-year-olds hit or smacked at least once a week

- 12% of 1-year-olds hit or smacked at least once daily

- 48% of 4-year-olds hit or smacked at least once a week

- 35% of 7-year-olds hit or smacked at least once a week

- 11% of 11-year-olds hit or smacked at least once a week

- 14% of mothers and 15% of fathers used implements such as slippers or wooden spoons

- 90% of parents admitted physical punishment of their children at some time

- 80% had physically punished children within the last year.

(Nobes and Smith, 1997 pp271–281).

The law

States parties shall ensure that no child shall be subjected to torture or other cruel, inhuman or degrading treatment or punishment.

(United Nations, 1989, Article 37)

Government should make sure that children and young people are protected from abuse, neglect and being harmed by the people looking after them.

(United Nations, 1989, Article 19)

In the case of Hopley (*R* v *Hopley 1860*) a schoolmaster beat a child until he died. He had been given the father's permission to chastise the boy. The judge decided that the chastisement was excessive and not reasonable. This was the case that led to the controversial defence of *reasonable chastisement* that still exists.

Corporal punishment was banned in state schools in 1987, a long time after the school strike in 1911 when thousands of children in 60 towns and cities in Britain went on strike for three days to oppose caning in schools. In 1998 parents could no longer beat or cane their children, or instruct someone else to do it for them, thus ending the practice in independent schools. In *A* v *United Kingdom* (1998), A was caned by his stepfather, who was prosecuted but acquitted of actual bodily harm. The European Court of Human Rights held that failure to criminalise such behaviour violated the child's right not to be subjected to inhuman or degrading punishment. In 2003 childminders were no longer allowed to physically punish children in their care (Welstead and Edwards, 2006, p297).

Despite campaigns from over 300 children's organisations, the Children Act 2004, s58 continued to allow the defence of reasonable chastisement in cases of common assault of children.

Sir William Utting, spokesperson for the Children Are Unbeatable Alliance, said:

S58 of the Children Act perpetuates the archaic defence that allows children to be legally hit and hurt. It is unjust and does not satisfy our human rights obligations to children under UN and European agreements. Children are the smallest and most fragile, but s58 denies them the full protection of the law on assault that the rest of us take for granted. Hitting children is wrong and the law should say so, just as it does for bigger and stronger adults. S 58 will create further parental confusion, legal ambiguity, professional uncertainty and policy inconsistency. The only safe and just way forward is to give children the same protection under the law on assault that adults enjoy. Giving children equal protection from assault is a fundamental human rights principle.

(Utting, 2005)

In Scotland it became illegal in 2003 to punish children by shaking, hitting on the head or using a belt, cane, slipper, wooden spoon or other implement. In addition, if a court were looking into the physical punishment which a child had received, it would also consider the child's age, what was done, for what reason and what the circumstances were, the duration and frequency of the punishment, the impact mentally and physically on the child and other issues such as gender and state of health. The Children's Commissioner for Scotland is concerned that Scotland still allows the defence of *justifiable assault* and is campaigning to achieve equal protection for children (Scottish Executive Central Research Unit, 2002).

More than a third of the member states of the Council of Europe now give children equal protection. Sixteen have abolished all corporal punishment: Austria (1989), Bulgaria (2000), Croatia (1999), Cyprus (1994), Denmark (1997), Finland (1983), Germany (2000), Greece (2006), Hungary (2004), Iceland (2003), Latvia (1998), Netherlands (2007), Norway (1987), Romania (2004), Sweden (1979) and Ukraine (2004) (www.childrenare unbeatable.org.uk). Evidence from the experience of these countries shows convincingly that legal reform along with promoting positive discipline strategies reduces reliance on physical punishment and the need for intervention in family life including prosecutions.

The jigsaw of information – working together to protect children

A referral concerning physical abuse may be the result of a child's disclosure, an adult or child observation or allegation, medical findings, photographic evidence or an abuser's admission. On receipt of the referral, the very first consideration must be the need of the child for immediate safety from harm. The document, *What to do if you are worried a child is being abused* (DfES, 2006a) has a series of five flowcharts for action if there are concerns about a child suffering harm. These can lead to confusion in response and the flowchart in Chapter 1 indicates that immediate action to protect must be prioritised.

CASE STUDY

Sukina

Social workers visiting Sukina Hammond accepted her father's account of how he physically punished her as reasonable. The majority of parents found guilty of abuse, when asked how it happened, describe it as ordinary punishment that went too far. It is difficult to distinguish the point where acts of punishment are significant harm. Physical discipline is more likely to escalate when:

- used frequently;

- the punishment is not the result of the child's behaviour but of other reasons such as parents' response to stress;

- there are unrealistic expectations of the child's behaviour;

- parents have limited problem-solving ability and lack knowledge of non-abusive responses to children;

- physical punishment is substituted for non-physical forms which have been seen to fail.

(Lyon, 2000, p48)

ACTIVITY 4.7

How is a judgement made about the child being at immediate risk of harm from physical punishment? Think of some important questions to ask to help inform your enquiries.

Comment

Your questions might have included the following:

- What is the nature of the injuries? Does the child require urgent medical attention?

- What is the child's view of the incident? Are there inconsistent explanations for the injuries or incident from the child and/or parents and/or witnesses?

- What are the adult reasons given for the injuries/incident?

- Is there a history of violence in the family or relating to the alleged perpetrator?

- Is there knowledge about the culture of the family and practices known to be carried out that are harmful to children? What are defined by the family as acceptable methods of teaching children different behaviours?

- Is there material or forensic evidence such as photographs, computer images, mobile phone information, weapons, implements or damage to property which corroborate the child's statement?

There is a distinction between a social worker who hears a disclosure from a child and needs to respond immediately and those conducting a section 47 (CA 1989) investigation who must comply with the Achieving Best Evidence guidance (CJS, 2007). In hearing an initial disclosure a social worker must find out just enough to inform a referral to the children's team. This means asking a few open questions such as: *Tell me more, explain/ describe that further to me* and *how did it happen?* Such questions do not put words in the child's mouth and will not interfere with a subsequent investigation. The social worker should reassure the child that they are taking what they say very seriously rather than say they believe the child at this stage, as whether the statement has validity is a matter for later investigation and possibly a court. They should reassure the child that they are brave to speak about the matter and that they are not in any way at fault. Clarification should be sought of any words or phrases which are difficult to understand with as little interruption to the flow of the child's account as possible. The child should be informed that in order to keep them safe other social workers and the police must be informed and that the disclosure cannot be kept a secret. If the child continues to provide a lengthy account, the social worker should listen, make a careful record and not interrupt.

Recording must be contemporaneous in order to be credible in any civil or criminal proceedings and must include an account of the child's emotional response, any repetition, the exact words used by the child and the context of the disclosure being made.

A children's social worker should be trained jointly with police in the skills of investigative interviewing of children according to the Achieving Best Evidence guidance (CJS, 2007; Davies and Townsend, 2008b). This requires a child to be interviewed by a police officer and social worker, usually in a specialist child-centred interview suite, visually recorded, and conducted according to the phased interview approach. This includes an introductory and rapport stage and supporting the child in providing a free narrative account of what happened, prior to non-leading questioning. The process provides a permanent record of the child's statement which can be presented in court although the child still needs to undergo cross-examination in court. A professional interpreter must be involved in the planning and conduct of the interview if English is not the child's first language and the guidance provides for intermediaries to assist children with particular communication needs.

The child's statements may be analysed using the principles of statement validity analysis, which is a technique used to assess the statements of children which are examined for certain features believed to indicate that the account is truthful. The child's free narrative, without prompting or pressure from the interviewer, is the most evidentially credible statement. The most accurate account by a child is the initial report made spontaneously, which is referred to as the *evidence of early complaint* in criminal proceedings and has high evidential value.

Children's statements are particularly validated if they include sensory perceptions in their account, such as how something smelt, felt to touch or tasted, as this is indicative of an account based on personal experience. Corroborative evidence from witness statements, medical, forensic or photographic sources assist validity when consistent with the child's statements. A child's behaviour may be supportive of the child's account as would their statements if consistently repeated with little alteration. The child's emotional response may support the credibility of the child's statement though children rarely respond stereotypically. A lack of emotion may indicate a history of repeated abuse and subsequent trauma. During an investigative interview a child may provide detail through drawing or make spontaneous gestures while describing an abusive incident. It is not advisable for interviewers to ask a child to point to a part of the body as this may involve the child replicating the abusive incident.

Children need to understand what abusive behaviour is and be able to identify potentially unsafe situations. A useful example is a website to assist children to keep safe online, **www.thinkuknow.co.uk/5_7/hectorsworld/**. With clear channels for reporting abuse, and a knowledge of how to use these, children can more easily speak about their feelings and access help at an early stage.

It is not easy for social workers to set aside time for direct work with children. Abused children in particular require sustained and regular contact with social workers to build up trust and find a way to talk about their distress. Such work does not fit easily into target-driven professional practice and rigid timescales have no place in the conduct of this skilled and complex aspect of social work.

In order to provide children with opportunities to tell about abuse, toys, drawing materials and resource books are essential. The *Anti-colouring book* (Striker and Kimmel, 2004) enables the social worker to enter into the child's world by facilitating the child's view without prejudging or imposing professional responses. Children can express their worst nightmare, how they visualise their future or their feelings about friends and family. An excellent resource to assess the child's feelings about *Yes* and *No* touches, particularly when there is high suspicion of harm with no forensic evidence or disclosure from the child, is *My Book, My Body* (Peake and Rouf, 1989). This book does not introduce concepts of abuse or contaminate the evidence of the child. The Turning Point training pack (NSPCC, 1997b) and *Creative therapy: Activities with children and adolescents* (Hobday and Ollier, 1998) both provide many useful basic tools for work with children, such as how to create a wall of hope or build a first-aid kit of resources to assist healing. Storytelling allows children to gain healing without any professional interpretation. Nancy Davis provides stories for children addressing a wide range of circumstances. She believes that it is within the power of a child to tell the truth and to keep telling the truth to adults who are powerful and can protect them (Davis, 1999). The child absorbs the message contained within the story and relates this to their unique situation. For instance, a story for children who have not disclosed trauma, *The burned tree,* is available from www.therapeutic-stories.com/stories/burnedtree.pdf. A tree which has been struck by lightning receives assistance from a beaver to remove the burnt branches and to be nurtured and achieve regrowth.

The child's view

In an ITV programme *I smack and I'm proud,* four families were portrayed who believed in smacking their children. The programme showed children being hit repeatedly including with implements. The NSPCC issued a statement saying that, we *believe it was wrong to film the children in this way, and wrong to transmit the programme* (NSPCC, 2006b). There were only 36 complaints about this programme. If it had shown men being proud to hit their wives, perhaps the public might have shown more of a negative reaction. The children were clear about how negatively they experienced the abuse. One stated:

> *You feel you want to hurt the person so bad but you realise you can't because it's your Mum. If it was anyone else, just a random person or your brother or sister I'd punch them back or hurt them. So you clench your fist and wish you could do something but you can't.*

(ITV, 2006)

ACTIVITY **4.8**

Consider what the public response might have been had this programme portrayed a:

- *man belting a woman;*
- *man punching a man;*
- *woman slapping a woman;*
- *carer hitting an older person;*
- *jockey whipping a horse;*
- *prisoner being tortured;*
- *pet being hit with a stick.*

RESEARCH SUMMARY

Evidence from four key studies across the UK based upon the views of over 1,500 children between the ages of 4 and 15 years about physical punishment provide us with ten key messages.

Smacking is hitting – a hard or very hard hit:
When someone hits you very hard.
They call it a smack, instead of a hit.

Smacking hurts physically and emotionally:
It hurts and it's painful inside.
It's like hell, I feel scared and cry.
It's sore, very sore.
Sad – feel that mummy and daddy don't love me.

Smacking is wrong:
Sitting down and talking to them and asking them why they did what they did and explaining why it was wrong and why they shouldn't do it.
They are big, the child is small it's not fair.
They could hurt them and make them think hitting is right.
It hurts and you could break a bone or something.

Smacking upsets children and sometimes makes them want to smack someone else:
Sad, hurt, feel ill, it stings, inside it hurts, upset, angry.
Grumpy, cross, afraid, feel bad or naughty, feel embarrassed, ashamed.

Adults regret smacking:
They are a bit sorry but don't want to say.
They feel upset, bad.

Adults hit children because of how the adult is feeling and not because of what the child does:
They just keep doing what they do.
They turn beetroot when they are mad

Parents and other grown-ups, aunts, uncles, grandparents, nannies and babysitters most often smack children:
Male relatives were more likely to smack.

Children often get smacked indoors; particularly the bedroom was the most common place followed by when out shopping. They were hit on their bottom, arm or head:
Somewhere no one can see – they know that it's bad.
Somewhere on their own – and nobody's watching.

Children don't hit adults because they are scared they will get hit again:
No-one should smack anyone.
Because grown-ups are bigger and they slap you back even harder.

Half said they wouldn't smack their children when they were adults:
We know what it feels like.
Because it's mean and it hurts the child and they'll just learn to smack.

(Crowley and Vulliamy, 2000; Cutting, 2001; Horgan, 2002; Willow and Hyder, 2004)

Is the carer proactively protective?

ACTIVITY *4.9*

Do you think parents and carers have the right to decide how to discipline their children within a definition of reasonable chastisement? In the following cases think about what a child might perceive as reasonable.

- *A father who had recently come to the UK caused serious whip marks on his 14-year-old son after he caught him stealing. When interviewed he said that he loved his son dearly and did it to prevent him being killed, which is what happened in his country of origin if a child stole.*

- *A father hit his son of 12 years with a spade, causing a deep wound on his leg. The father was the sole carer. The son was out every night with a network of older men who were sexually exploiting him. The father had felt powerless to protect his child and had lost his temper.*

- *A father cut his child's hair, causing cuts to her scalp to curtail her behaviour as she was taking drugs. He said this was a cultural norm for his family.*

Comment

These cases illustrate that the motivation for physical violence towards a child may be protective. Such action is still unreasonable and requires challenge and the implementation of child protection procedures. Sometimes a child will request that no action is taken because they love their parent and understand the reason for the violence. They may blame themselves for, in some way, precipitating the harm. However, a child can never be responsible for child abuse. While understanding parental motivation is important to an investigation, it can never excuse the abusive action and adults must provide the child with protection in spite of the child's own wishes. The best interests of the child are always paramount and may override the wishes and feelings of the child – although these are always taken into account. In some cultures cutting a female child's hair is a way of shaming them. This behaviour is unacceptable and is child abuse.

ACTIVITY *4.10*

How might you refer to a child being hit as a form of discipline? Think about euphemisms used commonly, such as:

- *six of the best;*
- *a good hiding;*
- *a loving tap;*
- *a good spanking;*
- *a licking.*

Comment

It is important to understand the reasons for parental behaviour that is physically harmful to children. A parent may be themselves frightened of physical harm from another member of the household and may minimise or be in denial about what has happened to the child. When first confronted with evidence or suspicion about a child's injury it is not unusual for parents to respond as if in shock or disbelief and to be unhelpful to the social worker making enquiries.

It takes time to build trust between the social worker and the parent to gain a full understanding of what happened. It is very important for the child to know that they have the support of a non-abusive carer. Professionals will have to make judgements about whether the carer is also a protector of the child, and if the parent is the abusive carer whether or not that behaviour is likely to be repeated, and assess the risk of future harm.

Research conducted of parents' views on disciplining children adds to professional understanding and reflects the children's comments from the previous research summary.

RESEARCH SUMMARY

The Scottish Executive Central Research Unit (2002) interviewed 600 parents and examined their views of disciplining children. They concluded that smacking remained deeply embedded in Scottish parenting culture, with 8 out of 10 children between the ages of 3 and 5 having been smacked within the last year and 1 in 5 within the last week. Yet only a few parents seriously supported the need to smack. Many acknowledged the risks for children and accepted that there were other more appropriate ways of parenting and yet still reserved the right to smack when they chose. The findings included that:

- only 3% of incidents were reported as taking place in a public place such as a supermarket and the majority of incidents were within a private space;

- in one-third of incidents smacking was used to signal danger but even for young children it was most commonly used as a punishment for persistent or challenging behaviour;

- smacking was mainly associated with parents feeling powerless and stressed and was typically a highly emotional event leaving parents feeling guilty or upset when at the *end of their tether* rather than a deliberate, calculated imposition of adult power;

- although it was not the case, more than half the parents believed that hitting children was illegal and this knowledge did not alter their behaviour.

Evaluating the safeguards in place for the child who has been physically punished

---

ACTIVITY *4.11*

A child tells you that they are physically punished. Your manager directs that the case is defined as child in need (s17, CA 1989) and recommends that the parents attend a parenting programme including anger management. You might:

- *follow your manager's instructions, carry out a common or initial assessment and arrange the parenting programme while feeling unsure about the child's safety and being afraid that you might be making a mistake;*

- *analyse the case, informed by knowledge of research and inquiry reports, and wish to convene a section 47 (CA 1989) strategy meeting, because in your judgement, you consider the child to be at risk of significant harm and requiring multi-agency child protection procedures.*

Child abuse inquiries provide us with a list of 'if only' reflections.

If only ...

> *the child had been heard;*
>
> *the adults concerned about the child had been heard;*
>
> *signs had been recognised;*
>
> *someone had called children's services or the police;*
>
> *the fax had been followed up;*
>
> *the workers had had proper supervision and safe working conditions;*
>
> *a suspicion had been checked out;*
>
> *someone had blown the whistle;*
>
> *budgets hadn't been cut and services not restructured;*
>
> *quality training, supervision and management had been in place.*

How would you make sure you were not left with these 'if only's' and were empowered to intervene to protect the child?

Comment
Social workers as effective voices for abused children

Investigating child abuse requires social workers to be courageous in practice. It is also important to know how to fully represent the child's voice. The professional child abuse accommodation syndrome may lead to a social worker being met with disbelief and denial, mirroring the probable adult response to the child. They may find themselves unheard, unsupported or even prohibited from acting to protect the child. If children's voices are to be heard, then professional voices must also be heard when they are carrying the message for the child. Powerful adults abuse children and networks of perpetrators extend to the highest levels of society. It can be difficult and even frightening to carry the message forward to protect children. It may require individuals, organisations or processes to be challenged in order to break the secrecy and silence that perpetuates abuse (Cairns, 2006).

Speaking out on behalf of abused children is supported by legislation and statutory guidance. *Working together* states: *clear procedures and support systems should be in place for dealing with expressions of concern by staff and carers about other staff or carers. There should be a guarantee that procedures can be invoked in ways which do not prejudice the whistleblower's own position and prospects* (DfES, 2006, 11.6). Also the Public Interest Disclosure Act 1998 provides statutory protection to workers who speak out against corruption and malpractice at work and who experience victimisation and dismissal. The law states that a disclosure must be reasonable – a concept open to interpretation. It is expected that a professional will first raise the issues through the usual channels provided by management such as informing a team manager, child protection manager or a member of the local safeguarding children board (LSCB).

There have been many social workers, police officers, doctors and other professionals who have suffered public vilification for speaking out about child abuse. Alison Taylor spent 15 years disclosing the abuse of children in children's homes and was dismissed from her post as residential worker (Taylor, in Hunt, 1999, pp41–64). In two recent cases of whistle-blowing six social workers in Wakefield who were sacked for raising issues concerning child sexual abuse gained a settlement from the council (Waugh, 2007) and Simon Bellwood, a social worker in Jersey, raised issues concerning children as young as 11 years old being kept in solitary confinement (Ahmed, 2007).

In order to proactively protect children, social workers need to work within safe working environments:

> *At a general level, every professional requires a 'secure setting' in order to undertake the demanding work of child protection ... Many factors contribute to a secure setting, including adequate training, regular supervision and support, clear procedural guidelines, adequate funding and staffing, low staff turnover, an optimal caseload, continuity in management, a stable organisational structure, good secretarial back up, requisite facilities and so on. All these elements combine to provide the mechanical means for effective communication and also a context within which the workers feel valued, respected and supported ... professionals operating from a position of chronic stress are excessively prone to commit errors of judgement and action, even becoming dangerous professionals.*
>
> (Reder and Duncan, 1993, p69)

In their analysis of serious case reviews, Reder and Duncan discovered that in one-third of the inquiries the key worker was unqualified or recently qualified and most did not receive supervision (1993, p7). In the judgement of the Care Standards Tribunal concerning Lisa Arthurworrey, social worker for Victoria Climbié, the judge upheld that child protection work is a complex and specialist task and said that:

the office environment was chaotic, the reference tool totally inadequate and the mistakes made by Ms Arthurworrey in dealing with Victoria's case must be considered within that context as well as her inexperience, lack of training and lack of any effective supervision. Ms Arthurworrey was inexperienced, untrained in child protection, had a high workload, poor supervision and worked to flawed policies.

(Pearl, 2005)

This was equally emphasised in the Care Standards Tribunal decision which, eight years after the death of Victoria Climbié, overturned the General Social Care Council's (GSCC) decision not to register Arthurworrey as a social worker (Oliver, 2008).

There is no statutory requirement for qualified children's social workers to receive regular supervision but it is recognised as good practice to provide at least one hour of uninter-rupted supervision every fortnight with an experienced manager. Student social workers are expected by the GSCC to receive at least 90 minutes of supervision on a weekly basis. Managers should also encourage peer supervision and multi-agency forums. Very unfortu-nately there is also no requirement for children's social workers to receive advanced-level child protection training which should consist of joint investigation and investigative inter-view training held jointly with the police (Davies and Townsend, 2008a).

For further information on safe practice in child protection, Munro (2005) provides a systems-based analysis of professional responsibilities. The British Association of Social Workers (BASW) provides a legal representation and advice service to their members.

Investigating allegations about physical harm to a child – deciding the threshold for intervention

ACTIVITY **4.12**

The following case studies are designed to aid a questioning approach to the process of protecting children. They usually progress from referral to investigation and action to pro-tect. When reading the case studies structure your thinking and questioning around the points listed in Chapter 1, but do not be limited by this list, continue to add your own questions and to consider the implications of these in each case.

• A 9-year-old boy tells a school welfare assistant that his mother hit him.

• The welfare assistant refers to the named teacher, who makes a referral to children's services. The school have no prior concerns.

• There are no concerns about other children in the family. Professionals agree to implement child-in-need protocols to support the family.

• The social worker (SW) liaises with the police child abuse investigation team (CAIT).

• Police and SW checks show no history of physical violence in the family and a single-agency SW response is agreed.

Child alleged being hit by parent and not thought to be at risk of abuse

• The medical examination by the general practitioner showed a red mark to the back of the boy's leg which was said to be consistent with light hand pressure.

• SW checks with health services show that the boy has been diagnosed with attention deficit hyperactivity disorder (ADHD).

• When interviewed on his own, the child tells the SW that he was upset because he had never been hit before and he confirmed he had been climbing the ladder.

• The father had previously told the head teacher that it is difficult to keep the child safe. Both parents had asked for help in managing the child's behaviour.

• The mother tells the SW that she did hit her son's leg when trying to stop him falling off a ladder while they were decorating his bedroom.

• The school staff have high regard for the parents and comment on their good relationship with their son. The boy does have some one-to-one support in school because of his diagnosis.

CASE STUDY

• A 15-year-old girl tells her teacher that she was slapped on the face by her mother.

• She says that she and her mother usually get on well but recently there have been a lot of arguments.

Concern about a child who has alleged being hit by a parent

• The girl is unusually reluctant to go home from school and tells the teacher she has a boyfriend who her mother does not like and this makes the girl feel angry.

• The teacher notes there are no visible marks but makes a referral to children's services who contact the police child abuse investigation team (CAIT).

• A strategy discussion confirms that there are no prior police concerns.

• A single agency social work response is agreed.

• The social worker (SW) interviews the girl at school.

• The girl speaks positively about her family and her boyfriend of a year who is the same age as her. They plan to stay together but she says her mother is upset because she thinks she is too young and he is not of the same religion as her famiy.

• She says she was hit because she refused to remain at home to help with the children and that she has not been hit before.

• The girl attends school regularly and achieves well. She accesses school nurse health advice sessions.

• The health visitor reports no concerns about the younger children.

• The SW interviews the mother who admits to slapping her daughter who she thinks she is becoming beyond parental control

The parents are separated. The mother cares for three younger children and the father lives nearby and is supportive of the mother.

• The father has a good relationship with his daughter but tells the SW that he is also worried about his daughter's relationship with her boyfriend who is of a different religious faith from the family. He says that the mother is finding it hard to cope.

• The professional strategy is to implement child-in-need protocols. Both parents are offered advice on parenting skills and the daughter is referred to the school counsellor.

CASE STUDY

• A 3-year-old boy, when playing in the home corner at nursery, says *this is what Mummy does* and hits a doll repeatedly.

• The nursery school staff have no concerns about the boy's development but are worried as the child is hitting other children.

• The nursery worker tells the named teacher, who makes a referral to children's services.

• A telephone strategy discussion with the police child abuse investigation team (CAIT) leads to an agreement of a single-agency social work response.

• A referral is made by the SW to the child and adolescent mental health service (CAMHS) for a playtherapist to see the boy and make recommendations to the nursery staff and parents about how to respond to the child's needs.

• Child-in-need protocols are implemented. Both parents agree to attend classes to develop their parenting skills and to learn to respond to the child positively and non-punitively.

Suspicion of actual or likely significant harm to a child alleging being hit by a parent. S47 enquiry

• The children's services checks show prior health visitor concern about unexplained bruising on the boy's arm when he was 18 months old. An investigation at the time showed no child protection issues.

• A further record showed a referral for a nursery place as the mother was finding it difficult to cope.

• During the interview the mother tells the SW that she believes physical punishment, such as a tap on the hand, benefits the child.

• Checks with the GP show no health concerns but the mother has been seen in the surgery waiting room smacking the boy on his bottom.

• The parents tell the SW that they define a smack as using the flat of the hand which does not leave any marks and only smacks on the child's arm or bottom are acceptable.

• The father tells the SW that the mother smacks the child when the child is naughty and touches the TV remote control.

• The father says that he does not agree with physical punishment because he did not experience it as a child.

• On a home visit the social worker (SW) notes a close and relaxed relationship between the boy and his parents. The SW sees the child on his own in the living room and notices that he plays with toy characters making them fight each other and that he is a bit anxious about his toys being tidied up.

159

CASE STUDY

• A 16-year-old tells the teacher he was hit by his mother after intervening in a parental fight.

• There are no visible injuries. He shows the teacher various old injuries on his torso and arms.

• He says that he wants to remain at home to protect his mother.

• The named safeguarding teacher reports to children's services who liaise with police child abuse investigation team (CAIT).

• The police and social worker (SW) agree to hold a strategy meeting and agree a joint investigation.

• A child protection conference is planned and will discuss issues of contact between tthe young person and his father.
• The mother agrees to seek an injunction to exclude the father from the household.
• Her capacity to protect her son and herself is the subject of a risk assessment.
• The police are to consider the possibility of prosecution of the father.
• The young person is introduced to a mentor to support his recreational interests.

• The named safeguarding teacher tells children's services that the young person is noted to be hungry at school, poorly dressed and lacks concentration during lessons.

• The GP reports concern about the young person's suicidal thoughts and makes a referral to a specialist adolescent counselling service.

S47 investigation of a child alleging being hit by a parent

• The police checks show evidence of the father having been found drunk in charge of his son when he was younger and several calls to the address for domestic disputes.

• The police report that the parents have said that the young person has gone missing twice. It was found that he had gone to stay with a friend overnight on both occasions.

• The RSPCA report to children's services an incident of cruelty to the cat by the father. The father received a warning from the police.

• The housing officer reports to children's services that neighbours complain of noise and arguments throughout the night.

• The father tells the police and the SW that the mother does hit her son. The mother says that the father hits his son.
• There are inconsistent parental accounts and a varied history of the incident.
• The father agrees to leave the household during the investigation.
• Children's services help to find him alternative accommodation.

• The young person agrees to a paediatric examination.
• There is evidence of old bruising on his back and two scars on his arm.

• During a visually recorded interview the young person tells the police and SW interviewers of a history of assault by his parents and of ongoing parental conflict.
• The young person describes how he was hit by his mother because he came in between both parents who were fighting.
• He was very distressed about his father hitting his mother.

CASE STUDY

• A 12-year-old girl tells her paternal aunt that her father hit her with a wire coat hanger across the back and that it *hurts a lot.*

• She has a 6 month-old sister.

• Both children are subject to a child protection plan under the category of physical abuse.

• The aunt calls children's services and wishes to remain anonymous. The social worker (SW) liaises with the police child abuse investigation team (CAIT) and they hold a strategy discussion.

• A joint investigation is agreed.

• Both children are placed with foster carers pending assessment of the paternal aunt and of the mother's capacity to protect.

• The child protection review conference is brought forward.

• Police charge the father with actual bodily harm (ABH).

• SW checks show that the health visitor is concerned about the 6-month-old baby who was noted, when seen a week ago, to be unsettled and miserable. Otherwise there have been no concerns.

• After a medical examination, to which the child consented, the paediatrician confirms that the injuries are consistent with the young person's account.

• The paediatrician also confirms that there is no current evidence of injury towards the baby.

Immediate action to protect a child/children from physical abuse

• The police checks show that the father has a conviction for grievous bodily harm (GBH) which occurred during an incident at a football match. The mother has two convictions for assaults on neighbours.

• There have been numerous previous referrals to children's services for a range of issues.

• On arrest, the father does not comment. The mother, on interview by the police and SW, says she does not know what happened as she wasn't in at the time.

• Both parents agree to both children being accommodated under section 20 (CA 989) and agree to supervised contact arrangements.

• The SW and police interview the girl on her own at the child's home and she says she wants to live with her aunt.

• She provides a full account of the incident. She is frightened and worried her father might hit her again and she is also concerned for the safety of the baby as she says her mother can't stop her dad's violence.

• She shows them the coat hanger which is kept as evidence by the police.

• A visually recorded interview is arranged.

• The SW is frightened of the parents and learns of threats to previous SWs.

• The SW discusses the implications of this with the SW manager in supervision..

• The school nurse informs the named safeguarding doctor of the girl's frequent visits to her office with sickness and stomach pains and that sometimes she wets herself.

• The named teacher reports continued concerns about the girl being withdrawn and not wanting to participate in physical education activities.

Now return to the four cases in Activity 4.6 and try constructing some diagrams for these cases. What factors might make these children more or less safe?

C H A P T E R   S U M M A R Y

A wide range of different types of physical harm to children is presented in this chapter and the controversial subject of physical punishment provides the basis for an in-depth debate on the subject from a children's rights perspective. The need to respond early to protect a child from harm is explored, particularly with reference to action to protect children from perpetrators. Prevention is explored as an integral aspect of protection rather than an alternative to it. The use of the initial assessment protocol is critically examined and the importance of implementing immediate action to protect a child at risk of significant harm and to investigate as section 47 (CA 1989) is emphasised. This chapter provides information to social workers about how to respond to a child who discloses abuse to them and how to be heard themselves as the voice for the abused child.

FURTHER READING

Bridge Child Care Consultancy (1991) *Report on the death of Sukina*. London: The Bridge.
This report evaluates the learning from the death of Sukina Hammond and shows where there are gaps in identifying risk of significant harm.

Children's Rights Alliance for England (2007) *State of children's rights in England*. London: CRAE.
This annual report shows key developments, both positive and negative, in children's rights in the UK.

Lyon, C (2000) *Loving smack or lawful assault? A contradiction in human rights and law*. London: Institute for Public Policy Research.
This book examines the inconsistencies in the law in relation to physical punishment and analyses the evidence about physical punishment of children.

Mullender, A, Burton, S, Hague, G, Imam, U, Kelly, L, Malos, E and Regan, L (2003) *Stop hitting mum. Children talk about domestic violence*. East Molesey: Young Voice.
This book gives a voice to children who have witnessed and experienced intimate partner violence.

Oliver, S, Judge (2008) *LA v General Social Care Council* 2 June 2008.
www.carestandardstribunal.gov.uk/Public/View.aspx?ID=890.
The judgement in the successful appeal against a decision by the GSCC to exclude Lisa Arthurworrey from the professional social work register.

Pearl, D, Judge (2005) Care Standards Tribunal, *Lisa Arthurworrey v The Secretary of State* (2004) 355.PC.
The judgement in the case of Lisa Arthurworrey, who successfully appealed against her name being placed on the Protection of Children Act list.

Williams-Garcia, R (2004) *No laughter here*. New York: Harper Collins.
A story for children about the practice of female genital mutilation.

Willow, C and Hyder, T (2004) *It hurts you inside. Young children talk about smacking*. London: CRAE and Save the Children.
This is a report of research into the views of children. The aim was to ensure children would be part of a public debate about physical punishment in the family.

WEBSITES

www.basw.co.uk
British Association of Social Workers (BASW) represents social work and social workers in the UK and provides access to a legal advice and representation.

www.childrenareunbeatable.org.uk
This is a coalition of organisations opposed to physical punishment of children.

www.womensaid.org.uk
Women's Aid Foundation works to end domestic violence against women and children.

www.forwarduk.co.uk
Forward campaigns against the practice of female genital cutting.

www.norm-uk.org
NORM UK campaigns against and provides information about male circumcision.

www.napac.org.uk
National Association of People Abused in Childhood (NAPAC) is a charity providing information and support to adult survivors of child abuse.

www.therapeutic-stories.com
Nancy Davis is psychologist who specialises in working with survivors of all ages who have experienced trauma. The website provides healing stories and other therapeutic resources to respond to the trauma related to child abuse.

Conclusion

Children will know if you can hear or not hear.
(Nelson, 2008, p25)

Silent words

I crouched in the corner

Curled up as small as can be.

One part hoping that you

Wouldn't notice me

The other half hoping that you'd

Hear the words I'd spoken

Without uttering a word.

(Nelson, 2008, p21)

The most important message of this book is for social workers to listen to children's voices. They are included in every topic where researchers have recorded children's views about abuse. In Nelson's research, the children say that nothing matters more than some-body noticing and somebody caring what happens to them. *She didn't judge me, she understood the kinds of ways I would feel without me telling her ... and gave me space even when my behaviour must have seemed weird and didn't make sense – even to me.* Social work students often say they might not be suitable for the work because they are too sensitive, feel too much and become over-involved. Yet abused children are saying that they want social workers, first and foremost, to care about them. The point where a social worker ceases to emotionally connect with a child's situation is the time for them to access support as they are probably burnt out and could place children at risk through not hearing the child's account.

Children want to speak to professionals who understand about abuse. Social workers need to be confident to place their feelings in a context of analysis based on knowledge of the subject of child abuse. A comprehensive knowledge base is presented throughout this book to support analysis and to challenge dogmatism. Children want professionals who are not *rigidly wedded to a narrow understanding of procedures.* They also want staff *who stick with them over time* (Nelson, 2008, pp31–7). Yet, in many authorities, an initial referral is soon passed on to a long-term team and if the child becomes looked after there is yet another transfer. Children who disclose abuse might have three or more social workers within the same number of weeks. High staff turnover also results in a lack of continuity, which adds to the abuse children have already experienced, reduces the social worker's involvement with children and results in social work becoming mechanistic and dissatisfying. To offer abused children the service they tell us they want is a difficult task for social workers working in a conveyor-belt system focused on performance targets which relate more to resource limitation than to the needs of abused young people. Social workers need to be creative and persistent in making existing systems work for the benefit of children.

Children especially want to speak about the abuse in settings where they are free to respond away from the abuser – preferably neutral settings away from their home and school where confidentiality is respected as far as is consistent with the child's safety. However, social workers cannot be effective without resources. Children say they want staffed drop-in facilities without appointments. Some such settings are available through the voluntary sector but most statutory services are difficult for children and young people to access and may not be child-centred. It is important to think about how children become informed about services which are known to be safe with rigorous child protection policy and practice in place.

Young survivors want it recognised that the impact of child abuse can be severe and long lasting.

> *Even after they are safe, many young survivors blame themselves sometimes right through adulthood. They still struggle with mixed feelings of shame, lack of self worth, guilt and confusion. At times this means mood swings, self harm, difficult or withdrawn behaviour, fearfulness and underachievement can continue for some time after children have been protected from further abuse.*

Yet children are now increasingly criminalised and pathologised. *You felt lost and scared. People look at you like you're a problem* (Nelson, 2008, p35). The Every Child Matters (DfES, 2003) emphasis on children achieving outcomes in order to be good citizens focuses services and interventions mainly towards children defined as potential threats to society. In this political context, it becomes a complex, demanding task for social workers to reach out to children as victims of abuse.

The importance of social workers working closely with law enforcement agencies to target child abusers and seek justice for abused children has been emphasised in this book as no child will find safety unless the abuser is either removed from their world or the abuser's behaviour is challenged and changed. Proactive protectors must also be identified and actively engaged in supporting the child. Responding to the needs of children for protection will not be met by the narrow use of prescriptive assessment processes but only through joint investigation with police and other agencies in compliance with section 47 (CA 1989) and the protocols in *Working together* (DfES, 2006). For children to survive abuse takes vast courage and determination and being heard by even one social worker can and does make all the difference. *The adults praised were honest, thoughtful, empathetic, kind and imaginative in trying to make difficult and humiliating situations easier for children* (Nelson, 2008, p38). It is each social worker's responsibility to do whatever they can to make current systems in children's services work in children's best interests, to know how to seek the support they need to do this and to be fully informed and confident about how to proactively protect children.

References

A National Voice (2006) *Brothers and Sisters: siblings matter to children in care*. Manchester: ANV. www.anationalvoice.org/docs/bro_n_sis.pdf

Abbott D, Morris, J and Ward, L (2001) *The best place to be? Policy, practice and the experiences of residential school placements for disabled children*. York: Joseph Rowntree Foundation/York Publishing Services.

Abrahams, C (1994) *Hidden victims: Children and domestic violence*. London: NCH.

Adcock, M and White, R (eds) (1998) *Significant harm: Its management and outcome*. London: Significant Publications.

Adonis, Lord (2008) Response to parliamentary question, 20 March 2008. London: Hansard.

Ahmed, M (2007) UK social worker blows whistle on Jersey.

www.communitycare.co.uk/Articles/2007/09/07/105628/exclusive-uk-social-worker-blows-the-whistle-on-jersey.html

Ainsworth, M and Bell, S (1970). Attachment, exploration, and separation: Illustrated by the behavior of one-year-olds in a strange situation. *Child Development*, 41, 49–67.

Aldridge, J and Becker, S (2003) *Children caring for parents with mental illness*. Bristol: Policy Press.

All Party Parliamentary Group on Population Development and Reproductive Health (2000) *Female Genital Mutilation – Hearings Report*. London: APPG.

Allen, V (2004) *Home alone arson death*. 30 June.
www.mirror.co.uk/news/topstories/tm_method=full&objectid=14378614&siteid=94762-name_page.html

Ammerman, RT, Van Hasselt, VB, Hersen, M, McGonigle, JJ and Lubetsky, MJ (1989) Abuse and neglect in psychiatrically hospitalized multihandicapped children. *Child Abuse and Neglect*, 13, 335–43.

Association of Chief Police Officers (ACPO) (1998) *Child prostitution: A Report on the ACPO guidelines and the pilot studies in Wolverhampton and Nottinghamshire*. ACPO.

Ashton, V (1999) Worker judgments of seriousness about and reporting of suspected child maltreatment. *Child Abuse and Neglect*, 23 (6), 539–-48.

Bancroft, A, Wilson, S, Cunningham-Burley, S, Backett-Milbern, K and Masters, H (2004) *Parental drug and alcohol misuse*. York: Joseph Rowntree Foundation.

Barker, J and Hodes, D (2007) *The child in mind*. Abingdon: Routledge.

Barnardo's (2002) *Bitter legacy. The emotional effects of domestic violence on children*. London: Barnardo's.

Barrett, D (ed.) (1997) *Child prostitution in Britain – Dilemmas and practical responses*. London: The Children's Society.

Barter, C (1999) *Protecting children from racism and racial abuse: A research review*. London: NSPCC. Policy Practice Research Series.

Batmanghelidjh, C (2006) *Shattered lives. Children who live with courage and dignity*. London: Jessica Kingsley.

Batmanghelidjh, C (2007) *Where angels need to tread*. Birmingham: *Professional Social Work*. July.

Batty, D (2006) Q & A the sex offenders register. *Guardian,* 18 January.
http://education.guardian.co.uk/schools/story/0,,1689261,00.html

Batty, D (2008) Jersey police enter new secret chamber in children's home abuse inquiry. *Guardian,* 10 March. www.guardian.co.uk/uk/2008/mar/10/ukcrime.childprotection

Becker, F and French, L (2004) Making the links: Child abuse, animal cruelty and domestic violence. *Child Abuse Review*, 13, 399–414.

Beckett, C (2007) *Child protection: An introduction*. London: Sage.

Beddoe, C (2007) *Missing out. A Study of children trafficked in the North West, North East and West Midlands*. London. ECPAT.

Bee, H (1992) *The developing child*. New York: HarperCollins.

Bell, C, Conroy, S and Gibbons, J (1995) *Operating the child protection system*. London: HMSO.

Bell, M (2008) Research finds disquiet with ICS. *Community Care*, 5 June 2008. www.communitycare.co.uk/Articles/2008/06/05/108421/analysis-of-the-integrated-childrens-system-pilots.html

Bentovim, A and Bentovim, M (1996) The effect on children and their families. In Bibby, P (1996) *Organised abuse*. Bury St Edmunds: Arena.

Bernard, C (1999) Child sexual abuse and the black disabled child. *Disability and Society*, 14 (3), 1 June, 325–39 (15).

Bibby, P (ed.) (1996) *Organised abuse. The current debate*. Bury St Edmunds: Arena.

Biehal, N, Mitchell, F and Wade, J (2003) *Lost from view: Missing persons in the UK*. Bristol: Policy Press.

Blake, N, QC (2006) *The Deepcut Review report*. London: TSO.

Bokhari, F (2008) Removing barriers, protecting children in tourist destinations. *ChildRight*, May. Colchester: Children's Legal Centre.

Bonomi, B (2006) *Report on Yarls Wood calls for complete overhaul of child detention*. London. Institute of Race Relations, 10 August. www.irr.org.uk/2006/august/ak000006.html.

Booth, T and Booth, W (1993) Parents with learning difficulties: lessons for practitioners. *British Journal of Social Work*, 23, 459–90.

Border and Immigration Agency (2008) *A Code of Practice for Keeping Children Safe from Harm*. London: Home Office.

Bowker, L (1988) On the relationship between wife beating and child abuse. In Yllo, K and Bograd, M (eds) *Feminist perspectives on wife abuse*. Thousand Oaks, CA: Sage.

Bowlby, J (1969) *Attachment and loss, Vol. 1. Attachment*. New York: Basic Books.

Brady, B and Owen, J (2008) Our children are missing. Most vulnerable children are targeted. *Independent,* 8 August. www.independent.co.uk/news/uk/home-news/our-children-are-missing-most-vulnerable-youngsters-are-targeted-793496.html

Brandon, M, Belderson, P, Warren, C, Howe, D, Gardner, R, Dodsworth, J and Black, J (2008) *Analysing child deaths and serious injury through abuse and neglect: What can we learn? A biennial analysis of serious case reviews 2003–5*. London: DCSF.

Brannan, C, Jones, JR and Murch, JD (1993) *Castle Hill Report: Practice guide*. Shropshire County Council.

Bray, M (1997) *Poppies on the rubbish heap. Sexually abused children. The Child's Voice*. London: Jessica Kingsley.

Bridge Child Care Consultancy (1991) *Report on the death of Sukina*. London: The Bridge.

Bridge Child Care Development Service (1995) *Paul: Death from neglect*. London: Islington ACPC.

Bridge Child Care Development Service (1999) *Neglect and developmental delay: Part 8 Case Review. Overview report re case 1/99 in Caerphilly*. London: The Bridge.

Briscoe, C (2006) *Ugly. The true story of a loveless childhood*. London: Hodder & Stoughton.

BBC (2000) *Suicide wish of gay bullying victims*. BBC on line, Tuesday, 18 July http://news.bbc.co.uk/1/hi/education/838032.stm

BBC News (2005) Deportation terrorises children. 1 September. http://news.bbc.co.uk/1/hi/scotland/4203670.stm

BBC (2006a) *Saving Becky. Real story documentary*. 29 August.

BBC (2006b) *Mother allowed baby son's murder*. http://news.bbc.co.uk/1/hi/wales/south_west/5410682.stm

BBC (2007a) *Gay bullying in schools 'common'*. 26 June. http://news.bbc.co.uk/1/hi/education/6239098.stm

BBC (2007b) *Man jailed for child sex attacks*. http://news.bbc.co.uk/2/hi/uk_news/england/lincolnshire/4939076.stm

BBC (2007c) *Paedophiles who were ordinary people*. http://news.bbc.co.uk/go/pr/fr/-/1/hi/england/6929408.stm

BBC (2007d) *Toddler fight family spared jail*. 20 April. http://news.bbc.co.uk?go/pr/fr/-/1/hi/england/devon/6574907.stm

BBC News (2008) *Home alone mother's jail warning*. 14 February. news.bbc.co.uk/1/hi/wales/7245389.stm - 39k -

Brody, S (2007) Hackney slammed over mother who killed her children. *Community Care,* 3 August. www.communitycare.co.uk/Articles/Article.aspx?liArticle!D+1

Brooks, D (2006) *Steve and me: My friendship with Stephen Lawrence and the search for justice*. London: Brooks Books.

Bunting, L (2005) *Females who sexually offend against children: Responses of the child protection and criminal justice system*. London: NSPCC.

Burke, J, Chandy, J, Dannerbeck, A and Wilson Watt, J (1998) The parental environment cluster model of child neglect: an integrative conceptual model. *Child Welfare*, 77, 389–405.

Burton, D, Nesmith, A and Badten, L (1997) Clinicians' views on sexually aggressive children and their families. *Child Abuse and Neglect*, 21,157–70.

Butler-Sloss, Lord Justice E (1988) *Report of the inquiry into child abuse in Cleveland 1987*. Cmnd 412. London: HMSO.

Cairns, K (2002) *Attachment, trauma and resilience: Therapeutic caring for children*. London: British Association For Adoption And Fostering.

Cairns, K (2006) Surviving paedophilia – *Traumatic stress after organised and network child sexual abuse*. Gloucester: Akamas.

Calder, M (1997) *Juveniles and children who sexually abuse: Frameworks for assessment*. Lyme Regis: Russell House.

Calder, M (2008a) *Complete guide to sexual abuse assessments*. Lyme Regis: Russell House.

Calder, M (2008b) *Contemporary risk assessment in safeguarding children*. Lyme Regis: Russell House.

Calder, M and Hackett, S (eds) (2003) *Assessment in child care*. Lyme Regis: Russell House.

Campbell, B (1988) *Unofficial secrets. Child sexual abuse. The Cleveland case*. London: Virago.

Carlile, Lord (2006) *An independent inquiry by Lord Carlile of Berriew QC into physical restraint, solitary confinement and forcible strip searching of children in prisons, secure training centres and local authority secure children's homes*. London: Howard League.

Cawson, P (2002) *Child maltreatment in the family*. London: NSPCC.

Cawson, P, Wattam, C, Brooker, S and Kelly, G (2000) *Child maltreatment in the United Kingdom: A study of the prevalence of child abuse and neglect*. London: NSPCC.

Chamberlain, A, Rauh, J, Passer, A, McGrath, M and Burket, R (1984) Issues in fertility control for mentally retarded female adolescents I: Sexual activity, sexual abuse, and contraception. *Pediatrics*, 73, 445–50.

Chand, A (2008) Every child matters? Critical review of child welfare reforms in the context of minority ethnic children and families. *Child Abuse Review*, 17, 6–22.

Child Exploitation and Online Protection Centre (CEOP) (2007) *A scoping project on child trafficking in the UK*. London: CEOP.

ChildLine (2007) *Calls to ChildLine about sexual abuse*. London: ChildLine. www.childline.org.uk/casenotes.asp

Children's Rights Alliance for England (CRAE) (2006) *State of children's rights in England.* London: CRAE.

Children's Rights Alliance for England (2007) *State of children's rights in England.* London: CRAE.

Children's Rights Alliance for England and NSPCC (2007) *Joint briefing to MPs. Change in law on physical restraint on children in secure training centres.* SI 2007.1709 www.nspcc.org.uk/Inform/Policy AndPublicAffairs/Westminster/nspcc_crae_commonsbriefing_si1709_gf47410.pdf

Christopherson, R (1983) Public perspectives of child abuse and the need for intervention. *Child Abuse and Neglect,* 7, 435–43, in Garrett (2001).

Cleaver, H, Unell, I and Aldgate, A (1999) *Children's needs – parenting capacity: The impact of parental mental illness, problem alcohol and drug use, and domestic violence on children's development.* London: The Stationery Office.

Clyde, Lord (1992) *Report of the inquiry into the removal of children from Orkney in February 1991, HOC195.* London: HMSO.

Colton, M, Vanstone, M and Walby, C (2002) Victimisation, care and justice. Reflections on the experiences of victims/survivors involved in large scale historical investigations of child sexual abuse in residential institutions, *British Journal of Social Work,* 32, 541–51.

Community Care (2007) *ASBOs given routinely to young people with mental health issues.* www.communitycare. co.uk/Articles/2007/02/26/103563/new-report-claims-asbos-routinely-given-to-young-people-with-mental-health.html

Cooke, P and Standen, P (2002) Abuse and disabled children, hidden needs? *Child Abuse Review,* 11, pp1–18.

Cooper, T (2007) *Trust no-one.* London: Orion.

Corby, B (2006) *Child abuse – towards a knowledge base.* Buckingham: Open University Press.

Coy, M (2005) Leaving care, loathing self. *Community Care,* 3–9 February, 38–9.

Creighton, S and Russell, N (1995) *Voices from childhood.* London: NSPCC.

Criminal Justice System (CJS) (2007) *Achieving best evidence in criminal proceedings: Guidance on interviewing victims and witnesses and using special measures.* London: CJS.

Cross, M (1998) *Proud child, safer child: A handbook for parents and carers of disabled children.* London: Women's Press.

Cross, M (2001) Bringing disabled children into the fold. *Child Abuse Review,* 10,148–9.

Crowley, A and Vulliamy, C (2000) *Listen up! Children talk about smacking.* Cardiff: Save the Children.

CSCI (2005) *Safeguarding children; The second Joint Chief Inspector's Report.* Newcastle: CSCI.

Cutting, E (2001) *It doesn't sort anything. A report on the views of children and young people about the use of physical punishment.* Edinburgh: Save the Children.

Dale, P, Green, R and Fellows, R (2002) Babies in danger. *Community Care,* 7–13 March.

Daniel, B (1998) A picture of powerlessness: An exploration of neglect and ways in which social workers and parents can be empowered towards efficacy. *International Journal of Child and Family Welfare,* 3, 269–85.

D'Arcy, M and Gosling, P (1998) *Abuse of trust. Frank Beck and the Leicestershire children's homes scandal.* London: Bowerdean.

Davies, L (2004) The difference between child abuse and child protection could be you: Creating a community network of protective adults. *Child Abuse Review,* 13, 426–32.

Davies, L (2006) *Protecting Children.* Gloucester: Akamas.

Davies, L (2007) Responding to the protection needs of traumatized and sexually abused children. In Hosin, A (ed.) *Responses to traumatized children.* Basingstoke: Palgrave.

Davies, L (2008a) *In the shadow of a tragedy.* www.guardian.co.uk/society/2008/jan/28/climbie.childprotection

Davies L (2008b) Reclaiming the language of child protection. In Calder, M (ed.) *Contempoary risk assessment in safeguarding children*. Lyme Regis: Russell House.

Davies, L and Townsend, D (2008a) *Working together*. Joint investigation in child protection. Lyme Regis: Russell House.

Davies, L and Townsend, D (2008b) *Working together, training together. Achieving best evidence.* Lyme Regis: Russell House.

Davies, N (1998) *Dark heart. The shocking truth about hidden Britain*. London: Vintage.

Davis, N (1999) *Once upon a time. Therapeutic stories to heal abused children*. Charleston, SC: Bibliobazaar.

Dawar, A (2008) Yarlswood detainees suffering emotional damage, report says. *The Guardian* 22nd August. www.guardian.co.uk/uk/2008/aug/22/immigration.childprotection

Dawson, H (2000) *Hansard debates for 25 January 2000 (pt 8 p2).*

Deakin, J (2006) Dangerous people, dangerous places: The nature and location of young people's victimization and fear. *Children and Society*, 20, 376–90.

De Bellis, M and Putnam, F (1994) The psychobiology of child maltreatment. *Child and Adolescent Psychiatric Clinics of North America*, 3, 663–78.

Department for Children, Schools and Families (DCSF) (2007) *National statistics. Referrals, assessments and child protection and young people who are the subject of a child protection plan or are on child protection registers, England, ending 31 March 2007*. http://dcsf.gov.uk/rsgateway/DB/SFR/s000742/index.shtml

Department for Children, Schools and Families (2008a) *Safeguarding children in whom illness is fabricated or induced*. London: DCSF.

Department for Children, Schools and Families (2008b) Response to a parliamentary question on care place-ments. *Hansard* WA56. 20 March.

Department for Children, Schools and Families (2008c) *Leaflet for children and young people on the Common Assessment Framework*. www.everychildmatters.gov.uk/resources-and-practice/TP00004).

Department for Education and Employment (2000) *Sex and relationship education guidance*. Nottingham: DFEE.

Department for Education and Skills (1999) *Social inclusion, Pupil support. Circular 10/99*. London: DfES.

Department for Education and Skills (2003) *Every Child Matters*. London: DfES.

Department for Education and Skills (2005) *Early impacts of sure start local programmes on children and families*. London: National Evaluation of Sure Start team. London: DfES.

Department for Education and Skills (2006) *Working together to safeguard children: A guide for inter-agency working to safeguard and promote the welfare of children*. London: TSO.

Department for Education and Skills (2006a) *What to do if you are worried a child is being abused*. London: DfES.

Department of Health (1995) *Messages from research*. London: HMSO.

Department of Health (2000a) *Framework for the assessment of children in need and their families*. London: TSO.

Department of Health (2000b) *Working together to safeguard children involved in prostitution*. London: Department of Health.

Department of Health (2001) *National plan for safeguarding children from commercial sexual exploitation*. London: HMSO.

Department of Health (2002) *Safeguarding children. A joint chief inspector's report on arrangements to safeguard children*. London: HMSO.

Dhanda, P (2007) *Response to parliamentary question by Annette Brooks M.P.* 5 February 2007. London: Hansard.

Dickens, J (2007) Child neglect and the law: Catapults, thresholds and delay. *Child Abuse Review*, 16, 77–92.

Dirie, W (2001) *Desert flower.* London: Virago.

Dobson, R (2003) The Long Goodbye. *Independent,* 22 September.

Dorkenoo, E, Morison, L and Macfarlane, A (2007) *A statistical study to estimate the prevalence of female genital mutilation in England and Wales.* London: Forward.

Dover, S, Leahy, A and Foreman, D (1994) Parental psychiatric disorder: Clinical prevalence and effects on default from treatment. *Child Care, Health and Development*, 20, 137–43.

Douglas, A (2006) Legacy of separation. *Community Care*, 7 September 2006, pp 36–7.

Downey, R (2002) Victims of wonderland. *Community Care*, 7–13 March.

Doyle, C (1997) Emotional abuse of children. Issues for intervention. *Child Abuse Review*, 6, 330–42.

Doyle, C (2003) A framework for assessing emotional abuse. In Calder, M and Hackett, S (eds) (2003) *Assessment in child care*. Lyme Regis: Russell House.

Elliott, M, Brown, K and Kilcoyne, J (1995) Child sexual abuse prevention: What offenders tell us. *Child Abuse and Neglect*, 19 (5), 579–94.

Falkov, A (1995) *Study of Working together Part 8 Reports. Fatal child abuse and parental psychiatric disorder. An analysis of 100 case reviews.* London: Department of Health.

Falkov, A (ed.) (1998) *Crossing bridges. Training resources for working with mentally ill parents and their children.* Brighton: Pavilion Publishing.

Farmer, E and Owen, M, cited in Tomison, A (1995) Spotlight on child neglect. *Issues in Child Abuse Prevention*, 4, Winter.

Fergusson, D and Mullen, P (1999) *Childhood sexual abuse: An evidence based perspective.*
London: Sage.

Fever, F (1994) *Who Cares? Memories of a childhood in Barnardo's.* London: Warner.

Finkelhor, D, Ormrod, R and Turner, H (2007) Poly-victimisation: A neglected component in child victimisation. *Child Abuse and Neglect*, 31, 7–26.

Ford, H (2006) *Women who sexually abuse*. Chichester: Wiley.

Foreign and Commonwealth Office (2004) *Young people and vulnerable adults facing forced marriage. Practice guidance for social workers.* London: Foreign and Commonwealth Office.

Forrester, D and Harwin, J (2006) Parental substance misuse and child care social work. *Child and Family Social Work*, 11 (4), 325–35.

Frampton, P (2004) *The golly in the cupboard.* Manchester: Tamic Publications.

Fyfe, M (2007) *Survivors' stories.* Hitchin: 11th Commandment Publishing.

Gallagher, B (1998) *Grappling with smoke.* London: NSPCC.

Garrett, PM (2001) Interrogating 'Home Alone': the critical deconstruction of media representations in social work education. *Social Work Education*, 20 (6).

Garrett, P (2006) Protecting children in a globalised world, 'Race' and 'Place' in the Laming report on the death of Victoria Climbié. *Journal of Social Work*, 6(3), 315–36.

Gaudin, J (1993) *Child neglect: A guide for intervention*. Washington, DC: US Department of Health and Human Services.

Gelles, RJ (1999) Policy issues in child neglect. In Dubowitz, H (ed.) *Neglected children. Research, practice, and policy*. Thousand Oaks, CA: Sage.

171

Gerhardt, S (2004) *Why love matters: How affection shapes a baby's brain*. Abingdon: Brunner-Routledge.

Gibbons, J, Conroy, S and Bell, C (1995) *Operating the child protection system*. London: HMSO.

Glaser, D and Prior, V (1997) Is the term child protection applicable to emotional abuse? *Child Abuse Review*, 6, 315–29.

Glaser, D and Prior, V (2002) Predicting emotional abuse and neglect. In Browne, K, Hanks, H, Stratton, P and Hamilton, C (eds) *Early prediction and prevention of child abuse – a handbook*. Chichester: Wiley.

Global Initiative to End All Corporal Punishment of Children (2006) *Ending legalised violence against children. A contribution to the UN Secretary General's Study on Violence against Children*. www.endcorporalpunishment.org

Goldson, J (2006) *Hello, I'm a voice, let me talk. Child-inclusive mediation in family separation. Innovative practice report*. Wellington, New Zealand: Families Commission.

Goldson, B and Coles, D (2005) *In the care of the state: Child deaths in penal custody in England and Wales*. London: Inquest.

Gordon, D, Parker, R and Loughran, F, with Heslop, P (2000) *Disabled children in Britain: A re-analysis of the OPCS disability surveys*. London: The Stationery Office.

Gorin, S (2004) *Understanding what children say about living with domestic violence, parental substance misuse or parental mental health problems*. www.jrf.org.uk/knowledge/findings/socialpolicy/514.asp

Greater London Authority (GLA) (2003) *Young people, big issues*. London: GLA. www.mayor.london.gov.uk/gla/publications/crime_policing/young_people_big_issues.pdf

Green, R (2002) *Mentally ill parents and children's welfare*. www.nspcc.org.uk/Inform/research/Briefings/mentallyillparent

Grubin, D (1998) *Sex offending against children: Understanding the risk*. Police Research Series Paper 99.

Guardian (2003) He threatened to rape me. 9 October. www.guardian.co.uk/uk/2003/oct/09/politics.children

Guardian (2007) Couple found guilty over toddler abuse death. 3 August. www.guardian.co.uk/uk/2007/aug/03/ukcrime1/print

Hames, M (2000) *The dirty squad*. London: Little Brown.

Hamilton, C (2007) Would you leave your child alone? http://women.timesonline.co.uk/tol/life_and_style/women/families/articles

Harbert, W (2005) *Bent twigs*. London: Blackie.

Harris, J and Grace, S (1999) *A question of evidence? Investigating and prosecuting rape in the 1990s*. London: Home Office Research Study 196.

Hart, S and Brassard, M (1991) Psychological maltreatment: progress achieved. *Development and Psychopathology*, 3, 61–70.

Haskett, M, Scott, S, Grant, R, Ward, C and Robinson, C (2003) Child-related cognitions and affective functioning of physically abusive and comparison parents. *Child Abuse and Neglect*, 27, 663–86.

Hawton, K, Rodham, K and Evans, E (2006) *By their own young hand. Deliberate self harm and suicidal ideas in adolescents*. London: Jessica Kingsley.

Henricson, C, Katz, I, Mesie, J, Sandison, M and Tunstill, J (2001) *National mapping of family services in England and Wales – A consultation document*. London: National Family and Parenting Institute.

HM Government (2007) *Safeguarding children from abuse linked to a belief in spirit possession*. London: TSO.

HM Chief Inspector of Prisons for England and Wales (2006) *Annual report*. London: TSO.

Hewitt, S (1998) *Small voices: Assessing allegations of sexual abuse in preschool children*. Thousand Oaks, CA: Sage.

Hildyard, K and Wolfe, D (2002) Child neglect: Developmental issues and concerns. *Child Abuse and Neglect*, 26, 679–95.

Hobday, A and Ollier, K (1998) *Creative therapy: Activities with children and adolescents*. Oxford: Wiley-Blackwell.

Home Office and Department of Health (2002) *Complex child abuse investigation – Inter agency issues*. London: Home Office.

Home Office (2004) *Paying the price. A consultation paper on prostitution*. London: Home Office.

Home Office (2006) *A coordinated prostitution strategy and summary of responses to Paying the Price*. London: Home Office.

Home Office (2007) *Keeping children safe from sex offenders. How sex offenders are managed*. London: Home Office.

Home Office (2008) *Crime reduction toolkit – Trafficking*. www.crimereduction.homeoffice.gov.uk/toolkits/tp00.htm

Hood, R, Shute, S, Feilzer, M and Wilcox, A (2002) *Reconviction rates of serious sex offenders and assessments of their risk*. Findings No.164. London: HMSO.

Horgan, G (2002) *It's a hit not a 'smack'. A booklet about what children think about being hit or smacked by adults*. Belfast: Save the Children.

Hoskote, A, Martin, K, Hormbrey, P and Burns, E (2003) Fractures in infants: One in four is non accidental. *Child Abuse Review*, 12, 384–91.

House of Lords (1985) *Gillick v West Norfolk and Wisbech Area Health Authority* (1985).

Howard League (2007) *Press release. UK government flouting United Nations Convention on the Rights of the Child*. 21st June.

Howard League (2008) *Growing up, shut up*. www.howardleague.org/fileadmin/howard_league/user/pdf/press_2008/Growing_Up__Shut_Up_2_July_2008.pdf

Howe, D (2005) *Child abuse and neglect: Attachment, development and intervention*. Basingstoke: Palgrave Macmillan.

Hughes, H (1992) Impact of spouse abuse on children of battered Women. *Violence Update*, August 1, 9–11.

Humphreys, C (2000) *Social work, domestic violence and child protection*. Bristol: Policy Press.

Humphreys, C and Mullender, A (1999) *Children and domestic violence: A research overview of the impact on children*. Dartington: Research in Practice.

Humphreys, M (1996) *Empty cradles*. London: Corgi.

Hunt, G (1998) *Whistleblowing in the social services*. London: Hodder Arnold.

Hutton, J (1981) *Animal abuse as a diagnostic approach in social work*. London: RSPCA.

Ibbetson, K (1995) *Neglect: Learning the lessons of a UK inquiry. The social service perspective*. London: Islington ACPC.

ITV (2006) *I smack and I'm proud*. 21 September.

Iwaniec, D (1995) *The emotionally abused and neglected child. Identification, assessment and intervention*. Chichester: Wiley.

Iwaniec, D, Sneddon, H and Allen, S (2003) The outcomes of a longitudinal study of non-organic failure to thrive. *Child Abuse Review*, 12, 216–26.

Jenkins, R (2007) Tennis coach Claire Lyte told she faces prison for lesbian sex with people age 13. www.timesonline.co.uk/tol/news/uk/crime/article2691122.ece?p

Johnson, T (1989) Female child perpetrators: Children who molest other children. *Child Abuse and Neglect*, 13, 571–85.

Kane, J (1998) *Sold for sex*. Bury St Edmunds: Arena.

Kelly, Sir Christopher (2004) *Serious case review 'Ian Huntley'*. North Lincolnshire: North Lincolnshire Area Child Protection Committee.

Kennedy, M (1989) The abuse of deaf children. *Child Abuse Review*, 3, 3–7.

Kennedy, M (1996) Sexual abuse and disabled children. In Morris, J (ed.) *Encounters with strangers: Feminism and disability*. London: Women's Press, pp116–34.

Kennedy, M and Kelly, L (eds) (1992) Abuse and children with disabilities.

Child Abuse Review, 1 (3) (special edition).

Kent, A and Waller, G (1998) The impact of childhood emotional abuse: An extension of the child abuse and trauma scale. *Child Abuse and Neglect*, 22 (5), 393–9.

Kerrigan Lebloch, E and King, S (2006) Child sexual exploitation: A partnership response and model intervention. *Child Abuse Review*, 15, 362–72.

Khanum, N (2008) *Forced marriage, family cohesion and community engagement. National learning through a case study in Luton.* Luton: Equality and Diversity.

Korbin, J and Spilsbury, J (1999) Cultural competence and child neglect. In Dubowitz, H (ed.) *Neglected children research and policy*. Thousand Oaks, CA: Sage.

Krugman, SD, Lantz, E, Sinal, S, De Jong, AR and Coffman, K (2007) Forced suffocation of infants with baby wipes. A previously undescribed form of child abuse. *Child Abuse and Neglect*, 31 (6) 615–21.

Laming, H (2003) *The Victoria Climbié inquiry report*. London: TSO.

Laville, S (2007) Met chief: put gang siblings on protection register. *Guardian,* 3 May.

Lewis, I (2007) *Response to a parliamentary question from Tim Loughton MP.* www.publications.parliament.uk/pa/cm200607/cmhansrd/cm070726/text/70726w0024.htm#column_1333W

London Safeguarding Children Board (LSCB) (2006) *Safeguarding trafficked and exploited children.* London: Association of London Government.

London Safeguarding Children Board (LSCB) (2007) *London child protection procedures*. London: Association of London Government.

Longinotto, K (2002) *The day I will never forget*. Available from: Women Make MoviesFilm and Video Department. www.wmm.com

Lovell, C (2008) *Deliberate infliction of pain violates children's rights in STC's.* www.communitycare.co.uk/Articles/2008/03/07/107528/jchr-abolish-use-of-distraction-techniques-on-children-in-custody.html

Lyon, C (2000) *Loving smack or lawful assault? A contradiction in human rights and law*. London: Institute for Public Policy Research.

Marchant, R (1991) Myths and facts about sexual abuse and children with disabilities. *Child Abuse Review*, 2, 22–4.

Marr, N and Field, T (2001) *Bullycide. Death at playtime. An expose of child suicide caused by bullying*. Oxford: Success Unlimited.

Martin, L (2005) *Ruined lives of islanders in child sex fiasco*. Guardian, 11 December. www.guardian.co.uk/society/2005/dec/11/childrensservices.childprotection

Mason, M (2000) *Incurably human*. London: Working Press.

Mason-John, V (2005) *Borrowed body*. London: Serpents Tail Books.

Masson, H and Erooga, M (1999) Children and young people who sexually abuse others: Incidence, characteristics, causation. In Erooga, M and Masson, H (eds) *Children and young people who sexually abuse others: Challenges and responses*. Abingdon: Routledge.

McCarthy, M (1996) Sexual experiences and sexual abuse of women with learning disabilities. In Hester, M, Kelly, L and Radford, J (eds) *Women, violence and male power.* Buckingham: Open University Press, 119–29.

McSherry, D (2004) Which came first, the chicken or the egg? Examining the relationship between child neglect and poverty. *British Journal of Social Work*, 34(5), 727–33.

McSherry, D (2007) Understanding and addressing the 'neglect of neglect.' Why are we making a mole hill out of a mountain? *Child Abuse and Neglect*, 31(6), 607–14.

Meadows, S (1997) ABC of child abuse. 3rd edition. London: British Medical Journal Publishing.

Meghji, S (2007) Children's homes left in limbo. *Children and Young People Now*, 3–9 October 2007.

Melrose, M, Barrett, D and Brodie, I (1999) *One way street. Retrospectives on childhood prostitution.* London: The Children's Society.

'Michael and Fernando' (2007) The problem with social workers. *Community Care*, 13 September, 20–1.

Mickel, A (2008) Gang bustaz. *Community Care*, 8 May 2008.

Ministry of Justice (2008) *The public law outline.* London: Ministry of Justice.

Momoh, C (Ed) (2005) *Female Genital Mutilation.* Oxford: Radcliffe Publishing.

Morris, J (1993) Feminism and disability. *Feminist Review*, 43, 57–70.

Morris, J (1999) Disabled children, child protection systems and the Children Act 1989. *Child Abuse Review*, 8, 91–108.

Morrison, T (1998) Partnership, collaboration and change under The Children Act. In Adcock, M and White, R (eds) Significant Harm: its management and outcome. London: Significant Publications.

Mullender, A and Morley, R (1994) *Children living with domestic violence: Putting men's abuse of women on the child care agenda.* London: Whiting and Birch.

Mullender, A, Burton, S, Hague, G, Imam, U, Kelly, L, Malos, E and Regan, L (2003) *Stop hitting mum. Children talk about domestic violence.* East Molesey: Young Voice.

Munro, E (2002) *Effective child protection.* London: Sage.

Munro, E (2005) A systems approach to investigating child abuse deaths. *British Journal of Social Work*, June 2005, 35 (4), 531–46.

Munro, E and Calder, M (2005) Where has child protection gone? *The Political Quarterly*, 76 (3), 439–45.

Narain, J (2007) Sex pervert may have abused up to 135 girls at anorexia clinic. *Daily Mail*, 14 August. www.dailymail.co.uk/pages/text/print.html?in_article_id=4752.

National Children's Home (NCH) (2007) Research shows children's emotions key to life chances. Press release. www.nch.org.uk/information/index.php?i=77&r=651

National Criminal Intelligence Service (2003) *UK threat assessment: The threat from serious and organised crime.* London: NCIS.

NSPCC (1993) *Home alone.* www.nspcc.org.uk/HelpAndAdvice/Publications/Leaflets/Homealone_pdf_wdf36243.pdf

NSPCC (1997a) *Childhood matters. National Commission of Inquiry into the Prevention of Child Abuse.* London, NSPCC.

NSPCC (1997b) *Turning points. A resource pack for communicating with children.* NSPCC.

NSPCC (2001a) *Out of sight. Report of child abuse deaths 1973–2000.* London: NSPCC.

NSPCC (2001b) *Fragile – handle with care.* London: NSPCC.

NSPCC (2002) *Equal protection for children.* London: NSPCC. www.nspcc.org.uk/inform/publications/downloads/equalprotectionforchildren_pdf_gf25285.pdf

NSPCC (2002a) *Understanding the links. Child abuse, animal abuse and domestic violence.* London: NSPCC.

NSPCC (2003) *It doesn't happen to disabled children. Child protection and disabled children. Report of the National Working Group on Child Protection and Disability.* London: NSPCC.

NSPCC (2006a) *Emotional abuse survey and debate.* http://society.guardian.co.uk/emotional abuse/page/0,,1975352,00.html

NSPCC (2006b) *NSPCC statement on ITV's I smack and I'm proud programme.* www.nspcc.org.uk/whatwedo/ mediacentre/pressreleases/21_september_2006_nspccstatementonitvi_ismackandimproud_wdn38979.html

NSPCC (2007) *NSPCC looks to work with retailers to create smack free shopping.* www.nspcc.org.uk/whatwedo/mediacentre/pressreleases/2007_10_april_nspcc_looks_to_work_with

NSPCC (2008) *I can't tell people what is happening at home. Domestic abuse within South Asian communities. Executive Summary.* London: NSPCC.

Nazer, M and Lewis, D (2004) *Slave. The true story of a girl's lost childhood and her fight for survival.* London: Virago.

Neale, B, Bools, C and Meadow, R (1991) Problems in the assessment and management of Munchausen's syndrome by proxy abuse. *Children and Society,* 5 (4), 324–33.

Nelson, S (2001) *Beyond trauma. Mental health care needs of women who survived childhood sexual abuse.* Edinburgh: Health in Mind (EAMH).

Nelson, S (2002) Physical symptoms in sexually abused women: Somatisation or undetected injury? *Child Abuse Review,* 11 (1), 51–64.

Nelson, S (2004) *Neighbourhood mapping for children's safety.* Edinburgh: Womanzone.

Nelson, S (ed.) (2008) *See us – hear us. Schools working with sexually abused young people.* Dundee: Violence is Preventable.

Nelson, S and Baldwin, N (2002) Comprehensive neighbourhood mapping: Developing a powerful tool for child protection. *Child Abuse Review,* 11, 214–29.

Nobes, G and Smith, M (1997) Physical punishment of children in two-parent families. *Clinical Child Psychology and Psychiatry,* 2, 271–81

Nobes, G and Smith, M (2002) Family structure and physical punishment of children. *Journal of Family Issues,* 23 (3), 349–73.

New Philanthropy Capital (2007) *Not seen and not heard. Child abuse – a guide for donors and funders.* London: NPC.

Office of the Deputy Prime Minister (ODPM) (2006) *Statistical release: Statutory homelessness, 4th quarter 2005, England.* www.odpm.gov.uk

O'Hagan, K (2006) *Identifying emotional and psychological abuse, a guide for childcare professionals.* Buckingham: Open University Press.

Oliver, C and Candappa, M (2003) *Tackling bullying: Listening to the views of children and young people.* RR400 Thomas Coram Research Unit. London: DfES.

Oliver, S, Judge (2008) *LA* v *General Social Care Council* 2 June. http://www.carestandardstri-bunal.gov.uk/Public/View.aspx?ID=890

Parton, N (2005) *Safeguarding childhood.* Basingstoke: Palgrave Macmillan.

Paul, A and Cawson, P (2002) Safeguarding disabled children in residential settings. *Child Abuse Review,* 11, 262–81.

Peake, A (1996) Help for children and their families. In Bibby, P (ed.) *Organised abuse.* Bury St Edmunds: Arena.

Peake, A (1997) *Strong mothers: A resource for mothers and children who have been sexually assaulted.* Lyme Regis: Russell House.

Peake, A and Rouf, K (1989) *My Book, My Body*. London: Children's Society.

Pearl, D, Judge (2005) Care Standards Tribunal, *Lisa Arthurworrey v The Secretary of State* (2004) 355.PC

Reder, P and Duncan, S (1999) *Lost innocents. A follow up study of fatal child abuse*. Abingdon: Routledge.

Reder, P and Duncan, S (2002) Predicting fatal child abuse and neglect. In Browne, K, Hanks, H, Stratton, P and Hamilton, C (eds) (2002) *Early prediction and prevention of child abuse – A handbook*. Chichester: Wiley.

Reder, P and Duncan S (2004) Making the most of the Victoria Climbié inquiry report. *Child Abuse Review*, 13, 95–114.

Reder, P, Duncan, S and Gray, M (1993) *Beyond blame. Child abuse tragedies revisited. A summary of 35 Inquiries since 1973*. Abingdon: Routledge.

Rees, G (1993) *Hidden truths: Young people's experience of running away*. London: Children's Society.

Rees, G and Lee, J (2005) *Still running. Children on the streets in the UK*. London: Children's Society.

Renold, E, Creighton, SJ, with Atkinson, C and Carr, J (2003) *Images of abuse: A review of the evidence on child pornography*. London: NSPCC.

Richards, J (2007) Sex offenders can use social sites, say police. *Times*, 25 July. http://technology.timesonline.co.uk/tol/news/tech_and_web/the_web/a.

Ring, E (2003) *State investigation into vaccine trials under threat*. Cork, *Irish Examiner*, 2 August.

Robinson, M (1999) *Inter-professional perceptions of neglect*. Cardiff: Family Studies Research Centre.

RSPCA (2003) *News – A violent and brutal year*. 22 May www.rspca.org.uk

Rushton, A and Dance, C (2005) Negative parental treatment of the singled out child. *Clinical Child Psychology and Psychiatry*, 10(3), 413–28.

Safe on the Streets Research Team (2005) *Still running: Children on the streets in the UK*. London. Children's Society.

Salter, D, McMillan, D, Richards, M, Talbot, T, Hodges, J, Bentovim, A, Hastings, R, Stevenson, J and Skuse, D (2003) Development of sexually abusive behaviour in sexually victimised males: a longitudinal study. *The Lancet*, 361 (9356), 471–6.

Saradjian, J (1997) *Women who sexually abuse children*. Chichester: Wiley.

Saunders, H (2004) *29 child homicides*. London: Women's Aid.

Scott, C (2007) *Crying out to be heard*. http://women.timesonline.co.uk/tol/life_and_style/women/families/article2181920.ece

Scott, S and Harper, Z (2006) Meeting the needs of sexually exploited young people: The challenge of conducting policy relevant research. *Child Abuse Review*,15, 313–25.

Scottish Executive Central Research Unit (2002) *Disciplining children. Research with parents in Scotland*. Edinburgh: Scottish Executive.

Sereny, G (1999) *Cries unheard. The story of Mary Bell*. London. Macmillan.

Shepherd, J and Sampson, A (2000) Don't shake the baby: Towards a preventive strategy. *British Journal of Social Work*, 30, 721–35.

Sheppherd, M (2003) The significance of past abuse to current intervention strategies with depressed mothers in child and family care. *British Journal of Social Work*, 33, 769–86.

Sheridan, M (1992) *From birth to five years. Children's developmental progress*. Abingdon: Routledge.

Smith, R (2007) Brains and misbehaviour. *Children and Young People Now*, 31 October–6 November, 20–1

Smith, D and Meadows, S (2000) Maternal understanding of the toxicity of substances used in non accidental poisoning. *Child Abuse Review*, 9, 257–63.

Sobsey, D (1994) *Violence and abuse in the lives of people with disabilities*. Maryland: Paul Brooks.

Social Work Inspection Agency (SWIA) (2005) *An inspection into the care and protection of children in Eilean Siar.* Edinburgh: Scottish Executive.

Somerset, C (2001) *What the professionals know: The trafficking of children into and through the UK for sexual purposes*. London: ECPAT UK.

Spandler, H (1996) *Who's hurting who? Young people, self harm and suicide*. Manchester: 42nd Street.

Spindler, P and Fairhurst, D (2005) Are the police failing victims of child sexual abuse? BBC Radio 4, *Women's Hour*, 2 November.

Squires, J and Busuttil, A (1995). Child fatalities in Scottish house fires 1980–1990. A case of child neglect? *Child Abuse and Neglect*, 19 (7), 865–73.

Sroufe, A (1996) *Emotional development: The organization of emotional life in the early years*. New York: Cambridge University Press.

Staffordshire (1991) *The Pindown experience and the protection of children. The report of the Staffordshire child care inquiry 199*. Stafford: Staffordshire County Council.

Stanley, N, Penhale, B, Riordan, D, Barbour, R and Holden, S (2003) *Child protection and mental health services. Inter-professional responses to the needs of mothers*. Bristol: Policy Press.

Stanley, N, Manthorpe, J and Penhale, B (1999) *Institutional abuse*. Abingdon: Routledge.

Stevenson, O (1998) *Neglected children: issues and dilemmas*. Oxford: Blackwell.

Stobart, E (2006) *Child abuse linked to accusations of 'possession and witchcraft'*. Research Report 750. London: DfES.

Stone, B (1998) Child neglect: practitioners' perspectives. *Child Abuse Review*, 7, 87–96.

Striker, S and Kimmel, E (1979) *The anti-colouring book*. London. Scholastic Press.

Stuart, M and Baines, C (2004) *Safeguards for vulnerable children: three studies on abusers, disabled children and children in prison. Progress on safeguards for children living away from home. A review of actions since the People Like Us Review*. York: Joseph Rowntree Foundation.

Sullivan, P and Knutson, J (2000a) Maltreatment and disabilities. A population based epidemiological study. *Child Abuse and Neglect*, 24 (10), 1257–73.

Sullivan, P and Knutson, J (2000b) The prevalence of disabilities and maltreatment among runaway children. *Child Abuse and Neglect*, 23, 1275–88.

Sullivan, PM, Vernon, M and Scanlon, JM (1987) Sexual abuse of deaf youth. *American Annals of the Deaf*, 3, 256 –62.

Summit, R (1983) The child sexual abuse accommodation. syndrome. *Child Abuse and Neglect*, 7, 177–93.

Sunday Herald (2003) *Slipping through the net*. 19 January. http://xuk.biz/UKLR/Landslide/library/44/Sunday%20Herald.htm

Svedin, C and Bach, K (1996) *Children who don't speak out about being children being used in child pornography*. Sweden: Radda Barnen.

Swann, S and Balding, V (2002) *Safeguarding children involved in prostitution. Guidance review*. London: Department of Health.

Swansea LSCB (2006) *Executive summary, Aaron Gilbert*. Swansea: Swansea LSCB.

Tanner, K and Turney, D (2003) What do we know about child neglect? A critical review of the literature and its application to social work practice. *Child and Family Social Work*, 8 (1), 25–34.

Taylor, A (1998) Hostages to fortune; the abuse of children in care. In Hunt, G (1998) *Whistleblowing in the social services*. London: Hodder Arnold.

Taylor, M (2005) Schools accused of abandoning thousands of gay children to classroom bullies. *Guardian,* 9 May. www.guardian.co.uk/uk/2005/may/09/bullying.children

Taylor-Browne, J (2002) *More than one chance! Young people involved in prostitution speak out*. London: NCH.

Taylor-Browne, J, et al. (2002) *Voicing our views*. Ecpat. www.ecpat.org.uk/voicing%20our%20views.pdf

Tomison, A (1995) Spotlight on child neglect. *Issues in Child Abuse Prevention*, 4, Winter.

Townsend, M (2008) *Babies the new target. Met warns as paedophile threat spirals*. www.guardian.co.uk/society/2008/aug/24/childprotection

Tunnard, J (2002) *Parental drug misuse – A review of impact and intervention studies*. Dartington: Research in Practice.

Tunnard, J (2004) *Parental mental health problems: Key messages from research, policy and practice*. Dartington: Research in Practice.

Turning Point (2005) *Bottling it up report*. London: Turning Point. www.turning-point.co.uk/ Campaigns+and+Policy/Bottling+it+Up/bottling+it+up+campaign.htm

United Nations (1989) *Convention on the Rights of the Child* (UNCRC). Geneva: United Nations.

United Nations Committee on the Rights of the Child (2002) www.endcorporalpunishment.org/ pages/frame.html

United Nations General Assembly (2006) *Rights of the Child: Report of the independent expert for the United Nations study on violence against children 23 August 2006*. available online: www.unama-afg.org/docs/_ UN-docs/_human%20rights/Violence%20Against%20Children%20Report%20-%20English.pdf

Utting, W (1997) *People like us. The report of the review of the safeguards for children living away from home*. London: Department of Health.

Utting, W (2005) *Progress on safeguards for children living away from home*. York: Joseph Rowntree Trust.

Valios, N (2003) Why schools are so reluctant to challenge homophobia among pupils. *Community Care*, 13 August, 32–3.

Vevers, S (2008) Alerting professionals to signs of emotional abuse. *Community Care*, 31 January, 16–17. www.communitycare.co.uk/Articles/Article.aspx?liArticleID=107100&PrinterFriendly=true

Vizard, E (2006) Sexually abusive behaviour by children and adolescents. *Child and Adolescent Mental Health*, 11 (1), 2–8.

Walker, A (1993) *Possessing the secret of joy*. London: Vintage.

Ward, J and Patel, N (2006) Broadening the discussion on sexual exploitation: ethnicity, sexual exploitation and young people. *Child Abuse Review*, 15, 341–50.

Waterhouse, Sir R and the Tribunal of Inquiry into the abuse of children in care in the former county council areas of Gwynedd and Clwyd since 1974 (2000) *Lost in Care*. London: TSO.

Waugh, R (2007) Sacked whistleblowers win £1 million payout from council. www.yorkshirepost.co.uk/news? articleid=3107592

Weightman, C (2006) *Serious case review executive summary, Baby O*. Newcastle: Newcastle LSCB.

Welbourne, A, Lipschitz, S, Selvin, H and Green, R (1983) A comparison of the sexual learning experiences of visually impaired and sighted women. *Journal of Visual Impairment and Blindness*, June, 256–9.

Welstead, M and Edwards, S (2006) *Family law*. Buckingham: OUP.

West, AM (1995) *Out of the shadows*. London: Simon & Schuster.

Wilding, J and Thoburn, J (1995) Family support plans for neglected and emotionally maltreated children. *Child Abuse Review*, 6, 343–56.

Williams-Garcia, R (2004) *No laugther here*. New York: HarperCollins.

Willow, C and Hyder, T (2004) *It hurts you inside. Young children talk about smacking*. London: CRAE and Save the Children.

Wolmar, C (2000) *Forgotten children: The secret abuse scandal in children's homes*. London: Vision.

World Health Organisation (1995) *Female genital mutilation: Report of a WHO technical working group*. Geneva: World Health Organisation, 3.

Wyre, R (1996) The mind of the paedophile. In Bibby, P (1996) *Organised abuse*. Bury St Edmunds: Arena, pp87–105.

Young Minds (2000) *Minority voices*. www.youngminds.org.uk/minorityvoices/

Index